Stalag Wisconsin

Inside WW II prisoner-of-war camps

BY BETTY COWLEY

Badger Books Inc.
Oregon, Wis.

Contents

Introduction

Teaching history to very skeptical high school students for thirty-five years forced me to be prepared to prove anything that sounded the least unlikely. One of those facts the students disbelieved was that Altoona, the community in which I taught, housed 175 German POW's in 1945. To make matters worse, neither of the two local histories of the community mentioned their presence. Even Thompson's chronicle *History of Wisconsin* disappointed me by suggesting that perhaps only several hundred POW's would ever be employed in the state.* Shocked at the lack of information readily available from our local libraries, Fort McCoy, and the Wisconsin State Historical Society, I began my research. When I retired, I had time to seriously research the subject and quickly decided to expand my search to discover information about the other camps as well. Initially I intended a short, very factual report on the camps in Wisconsin. When the National Archives informed me that all the records of the branch camps had been destroyed in the 1950's, my research direction had to change. Subsequently, I combed the 1944 and 1945 newspapers around the state looking for information. I found such news coverage very limited and heavily censored, especially in 1944. Furthermore, several camps had existed in very small rural communities without a local paper. So, I searched community records and histories, locating several oral histories recalling the camps and personal encounters with POW's. These fascinating stories compelled me to include them. One compelling recollection came from Stuart Olson about Camp Milltown:

Grabbed and carried up the ladder to the top of the stack of pea silage by a tall husky German prisoner, six year old Stuart Olson was terrified. He struggled to get free. For what seemed like forever to the boy, the POW squatted down, holding Stuart tight

---

* Thompson, Wm. F. *The History of Wisconsin, Continuity and Change, 1940-1965.* Madison, WI: State Historical Society of Wisconsin, 1988, p. 92.

Author Betty Cowley, center, interviews PW's Kurt Pech-mann, left, and George Hall at the Hartford Ballroom on July 17, 1998.

as he rubbed his head. Eventually the prisoner started to cry. A conversation in German took place between this POW and others still on the ground. One prisoner spoke enough English to make Stuart and his horrified older friends, Lowell and Dale Fradeen, understand the situation. Stuart reminded the POW of his own little boy left behind several years ago, and the man just could not resist hugging this small child.

I set about finding additional stories for each camp. The result of my three year effort is this book, *STALAG WISCONSIN: Inside WW II prisoner of war camps*. *STALAG WISCONSIN* explains why our government held POW's in Wisconsin, where they were located, how they were treated, and the immediate and long term consequences of that treatment. The book dispels the typical stereotypes of POW camps. The variety of personal recollections included within the individual Branch Camps section also reminds the reader of what life was like around the state during the war years. These stories review the wide diversity of Wisconsin's agricultural and industrial economy at that time.

In 1945 Wisconsin actually housed about 20,000 captured enemy soldiers, true prisoners of war. This facet of Wisconsin history still remains very illusive more than a half century after the end of World War II. With the POW's tucked away in rural communities and on two military bases, most of the state's residents were unaware of their existence. Many revelations about WW II have since surfaced, but little has been mentioned about *STALAG WISCONSIN*. As the years passed, the military records of the thirty-eight POW branch camps around the state were destroyed. Many individuals having first hand experience with the camps and POW's interned in the camps pass away even as this author researches and writes.

Camp McCoy housed large numbers of POW's. The secured military base of Camp McCoy held 3,500 Japanese, Koreans, Formoseans and other Asian nationalities. Because authorities never allowed them to work outside that base, interaction between them and the general population was almost nonexistent. Therefore, the story of these Asian POW's became intertwined with that of Camp McCoy, and I have included it there as well as throughout the POW Camp Life and Resistance and Escape sections of the book. Camp McCoy also housed about 5,000 German POW's while another 13,000 under the command of Fort Sheridan, Illinois, were scattered in the branch camps. This book focuses on the German prisoners distributed around Wisconsin. These German prisoners often worked side by side with local residents. The Branch Camp section of this book tells their story.

The reaction from most of the people I made contact with was positive and helpful. In fact, after fifty years have elapsed, many individuals admitted to activities that at the time would have bordered on illegal and/or treasonable. Any fraternization with the enemy, certainly giving aid and comfort to them, might have been punishable. The reader must remember that most of this type of fraternization occurred during 1945. By then the war with Germany was over, having ended May 8, 1945. Although most POW's stayed in America until 1946, there was no longer a war in progress. These prisoners bided their time, awaiting their trip home and repatriation. In interviews with over three hundred individuals, few expressed any personal fear for their lives at the hands of this enemy among us. The Camp Oakfield recollections include a clear example of the lack of fear of the enemy as told by Maynard Chadwick:

"The first men I ever saw wearing shorts" were the PW's in the canning factory at Oakfield, said Maynard Chadwick Jr. His father reported the lax attitude of the guards while working on the Better Farms Inc. sugar beet harvest. One day the weather turned cold with a light covering of snow on the ground. The southern born MP's found the temperatures very uncomfortable. They would take every opportunity to ride in the trucks with the sugar beets to the railroad siding, often leaving the prisoners unguarded in the fields. One guard who had left his gun at the far end of the row sent one of the POW's back to get it.

What negative reactions I have encountered have been from families who lost men in the war or from men who had seen heavy combat against the Japanese or German army. A few had actually been held as POW's of the Germans. Their attitude about the entire German Nazi Army remains harsh and bitter.

The reader should also remember the two different worlds Americans lived in at the time. In the world of the combat soldier, terror and death lurked everywhere. To survive, everyone had to be considered hostile. In the world of the Wisconsin home front, such personal dangers were very generalized, remote and dubious. Until Vietnam, the media kept the true horrors of war from the general public, and the soldiers returning from earlier wars generally remained silent, attempting to repress their horrendous memories. So, while the combat soldier learned to fear and hate all Japanese and Germans, the civilians on the home front saw only the smiling faces of disarmed German soldiers far removed from any combat zone.

Finally, we must recognize that in the mid-1940's, approximately one third of the state's population had German ancestry. Many were immigrants themselves or first generation Americans who still spoke German as their primary language. As a result, many of our state residents had family members fighting on both sides of each European battle. Some of the German POW's held in Wisconsin were actually related by blood to our own citizens. Within the Branch Camp section of the book several such relationships are unveiled. For example, in the Camp Sheboygan recollections Robert Lawrenz provided a detailed account of such an encounter, when his astonished father answered the door of his Sheboygan home and found his brother standing there in a PW uniform.

Among our German speaking population, many had earlier immigrated here to avoid the Kaiser's military conscriptions. They quickly recognized that most of the soldiers in Hitler's army were not philosophical Nazis but just draftees caught up in the times. With such strong German ties, many citizens sympathized with the prisoners but not with Germany's role in the war.

This book records a unique part of the home front war experience as personally recalled by that generation. It recognizes their dedication to hard work, their compassion and their generosity. This account tells of children trying to be children during the war years and of people coping as best they could under the circumstances of war shortages, rationing and fears about family members fighting in foreign lands. To that generation I dedicate this book. Without the more than three hundred individuals who graciously shared their experiences with me, this book could never have been written. Finally, special thanks goes to those individuals and organizations sharing their precious and few photos and artifacts of this unique segment of our history.

Why POW's in Wisconsin?

To answer why POW's were in Wisconsin, we first need to understand why our military brought POW's to America from overseas battlefields. By spring of 1942, the war in Europe was already in it's third year. With the December 7, 1941, attack on Pearl Harbor, America entered the war with a vengeance. The U.S. war propaganda machine went immediately to work, playing to America's anger and frustration. This propaganda effort was successful in turning some of that anger not only into the determination to win but also into hate and racism. England stood alone in Europe against Hitler and was bulging at the seams with German prisoners of war. Rumor spread that Hitler planned on air dropping weapons to the several hundred thousand German troops held as prisoners in England, precluding the necessity of an invasion. So as plans advanced for the allied joint attack on North Africa, the U.S. reluctantly agreed to take custody of all prisoners captured by Great Britain after November, 1942.[1]

To imprison these captives overseas would require tying up thousands of troops and supply ships. All the necessities of life — housing, food, water, medical units and supplies — would have to be transported to Europe, perhaps North Africa. Guarding them would require major installations and troops enough not only to prevent escapes but also to defend against nearby enemy armies attempting to overrun the prison camps to free their comrades. The military made the decision to transport the POW's stateside on returning empty liberty ships. They would be housed at preexisting military bases. This decision drastically reduced the logistical nightmare of supplying and guarding these captives overseas. Only later did plans for the utilization of POW labor developed. As a result, our severe labor shortages diminished and through their work, the POW's paid for their own keep. The personal experiences of the individual prisoners as they experienced the American landscape, its people and its culture have lasted a lifetime, changing

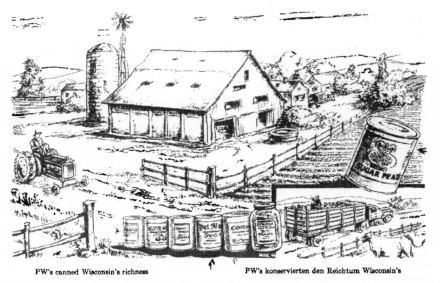

PW's canned Wisconsin's richness   PW's konservierten den Reichtum Wisconsin's

"PW's canned Wisconsin's richness," illustration by PW W. Hoernchen, 1946. Photo courtesy of Willi Rau, permission U.S. Army, Fort McCoy.

many attitudes forever.

The incoming wave of prisoners arriving on our shores swelled to over 5,000 Japanese, 371,000 Germans, 51,000 Italians as well as assorted Koreans, Russians and other nationalities.[2] In fact, by the late spring of 1944, the army already found itself handling more German and Italian prisoners than there had been American soldiers in the entire prewar U.S. Army.[3] As the war progressed, so did the number of captured enemy combatants interned. Ultimately the U.S. military designated 156 sites throughout the U.S. as "base camps." By the end of the war, only four states never housed POW's at any time during the war. In September 1942, the military selected the abandoned CCC (Civilian Conservation Corps.) camp at Camp McCoy in Monroe County as one of the first locations to house these prisoners for the duration of the war. With McCoy designated as one of the first "base camps," Wisconsin quickly became home to thousands of captured enemy soldiers. The state continued to house POW's into June 1946.

After several changes, the U.S. War Department finally assigned the supervision of these war prisoners to the Provost Marshall General who report directly to the Chief of Staff, Army Service Forces. With typical military flair there were continual changes in opinions and then orders about objectives of and limitations/requirements for the housing, treatment and utilization of the "PW's" as these prisoners were now called.

The local reaction to this invasion of enemy troops greatly concerned many government officials. The Army worried that local populations might panic, fearing escaping prisoners. Civilians might take revenge and retaliate against these captured enemy soldiers if word spread that hundreds, then thousands of them, safely and comfortably slept in our midst. The Branch Camps section of this book notes that in the end, local residents had very mixed reactions to their presence. In a few areas the local communities protested so vehemently that the military found alternate locations for their planned camps. In other places, the local community seemed to go out of the way to make the prisoners' stay as comfortable as possible. The reaction of most communities fell somewhere in the middle, usually personal and based upon individual experiences before and during the war. An unexpected but real problem also surfaced as visitors of German descent seeking information about relatives back in Europe regularly inundated many camps.

With Camp McCoy a base camp, and Fort Sheridan, Camp Ellis, and Camp Custer nearby, Wisconsin gained a unique opportunity to utilize these prisoners to fill severe labor shortages. PW's became especially useful in the seasonal employment of our agricultural industry. Patriotism brought on by the war as well as a much less skeptical attitude of the media of the day encouraged cooperation with the U.S. government in keeping a very low profile of this enemy among us. Therefore, little was reported or printed about the PW work camps appearing across the state. Furthermore, the military located most of these "branch" camps in rural settings which helped to keep knowledge of and direct contact with the PW's to a minimum. In fact most Americans were unaware of their presence. Yet, at the peak, Wisconsin housed nearly 3,500 Japanese,[4] 5,000 Germans,[5] and nearly 500 Koreans[6] at Camp McCoy. In addition to those staggering numbers, Fort Sheridan also placed nearly 13,000 more PW's seasonally or year round in the 38 "branch" camps scattered across Wisconsin during the war.[7]

The work of PW's at these seasonal branch camps filled the labor shortages brought on by our men being called into the military and others who moved to take the better paying industrial jobs in the cities. As the war dragged on, the deferment system tightened and the labor shortages grew worse. Since the Geneva Convention rules on the treatment of PW's allowed prisoners to be put to work, our military quickly responded with the "branch" camps system and set them up primarily in agricultural areas where seasonal workers were impossible to hire. In many areas of the state the PW's literally saved the crops. Because of the agricultural employment needs of Wisconsin, the state housed over three times as many PW's as neighboring Minnesota.

The results of this effort became tremendously successful. The PW's filled vital labor shortages, working primarily in agriculture, lumber and some industry. In Wisconsin they were contracted to the canning companies to help harvest and process crops that would have gone to waste, to bale hemp, and to work in nurseries, tanneries, dairies, and some industrial factories. Even as the war in Europe ended, local farmers and factories pleaded with the government to keep the prisoners for the entire 1945 harvest season. The work of PW's also relieved many American military personnel for other war jobs as the prisoners filled clerical, maintenance, kitchen, laundry, construction and road building jobs at the base and branch camps and other military installations. Between March 1943 and June 1946, the labor of the PW's nationwide earned over $360 million for the U.S. Treasury. In Wisconsin, alone, it is estimated the PW's realized $3.3 million for the government.[8]

Camp McCoy

An officer called out "*Auchtung!! Auchtung!!*," each morning as the sun rose over Wisconsin during WW II. As the rising sun hit west central Wisconsin other calls to order also rang out in Japanese, Polish and Korean. Early in the war Allied armies agreed to take care of their own captives. Then in 1942 America agreed to help England by housing its future captives. As a result, the incoming wave of over 450,000 prisoners started arriving on our shores.[1] In fact, by the late spring of 1944, the Army already found itself handling more German and Italian prisoners than there had been American soldiers in the entire prewar U.S. Army.[2] The military quickly selected an abandoned CCC (Civilian Conservation Corps) camp at Camp McCoy in Monroe County as one of the first of 130 sites throughout the U.S. to house these prisoners of war.

Even before the military agreements with England, Camp McCoy housed enemy aliens (civilians) interred for the duration of the war. The first enemy aliens arriving in early 1942 included 106 Germans, 5 Italians and 181 Japanese.[3] Ensign Kazua Sakamaki, the commander of a midget submarine captured at Pearl Harbor on December 8, 1941, arrived with the Japanese civilian contingent, with whom he was allowed to mingle freely.[4] With this March 9, 1942, arrival of Sakamaki, America's first prisoner of war, McCoy became the primary holding camp for all Japanese prisoners of war brought stateside.[5]

Train crewmen first reported the Japanese sailor captured at Pearl Harbor among the 200 to 300 members of an enemy force aboard the Northwestern Railroad train arriving at Camp McCoy. Shortly thereafter a statement by General Cummings released a report that labeled most of these internees as alien civilians, whose court hearings had been completed and who had been ordered by the Federal Government to be permanently interred for the protection of the U.S. Authorities relocated these Japanese and other civilian aliens before the first wave of Japanese military prisoners arrived.[6] Until late January 1945, McCoy was the only permanent location for Japanese prisoners. By then the numbers of Japanese prisoners overwhelmed McCoy authorities, and the military transformed Camp Clarinda, Iowa, from German housing to Japanese housing. Camp Clarinda then took the overflow of Japanese prisoners. Rising discontent and turmoil among Japanese troops at McCoy forced the removal of some officers to Camp Kennedy, Texas.

Shorty after agreements between the U.S. and Britain were approved, the British began to transfer some of their prisoners to American custody.[7] As a result, the numbers of internees at Camp McCoy quickly grew as many of Rommel's elite Afrika Korps were captured and brought to Wisconsin. Over the next three years thousands of prisoners swelled Wisconsin's PW roster at McCoy and other branch camps. At its peak, McCoy's PW population numbered 3,500 Japanese,[8] 5,000 Germans,[9] nearly 500 Koreans,[10] as well as several Formoseans and other nationalities. Finally in early fall of 1945, the long process of repatriation began and the movement of these men reversed. The Army destroyed the camp compounds as sites became vacant. But not until June of 1946 did the last of the PW's leave McCoy.[11]

Camp McCoy tower and fence. Photo courtesy of U.S. Army, Fort McCoy.

When first selected as a PW base camp, the Old Camp McCoy had thirty to thirty-five buildings consisting of kitchens, bath (shower) houses, mess halls and barracks within a 20-acre enclosure. The Japanese prisoners later built a bath for their own use as their customs included bathing rituals. Preparations for the arrival of it's first foreign guests included the building of a double wall of eight foot cyclone-type fences thirty feet apart. Barbed wire bent inward topped the inner fence. McCoy officials consistently denied rumors that either fence had been electrified.[12] Equipped with powerful spotlights six guard towers rose around the perimeter with another tower in the center of the compound. By burying the fences about five and a half feet deep, authorities hoped to prevent tunneling underneath. Because of the sandy nature of the soil, experts determined that any deeper tunneling would cave in. With these precautions officials became confident there would be no escaping this PW camp.[13]

But DuWayne Scott of Fort Atkinson, WI recalled that like any other base, McCoy sometimes had trouble with it's own soldiers. The area immediately outside the PW compound was restricted for quite a few feet. One night an officer had too much to drink at the Officer's Club and walked into the area. Though challenged, he continued to stumble on. Finally, the guard in the tower shot right in front of his feet, and guards on the ground immediately took him into custody. On a dark stormy night another guard attempted suicide in one of the towers. He stabbed himself in the chest five times with a knife. After the fifth blow, the knife stuck in his chest as the tip had penetrated his heart. After emergency care at the Camp McCoy Station Hospital the military transported him to a general hospital as quickly as possible. While reports suggest he did survive, that guard never returned to McCoy.[14]

As a final security measure, McCoy authorities kept a kennel of guard dogs. This Canine Corps along with the handlers regularly patrolled the perimeter of the PW compound. Dogs also became a common part of the security when large PW work patrols went to clear brush or build roads some distance from camp. These dogs provided a tremendous psychological asset to the camp security. Prison entertainment often included demonstrations of the skills and abilities of these dogs which struck terror in the hearts of the prisoners and encouraged compliance with camp rules.[15]

But Robert Gard, a Camp McCoy guard, remembered one unconvinced PW. After watching a display of the dogs working, that German PW remarked; "I'm not afraid of those dogs!" A trainer immediately ordered his dog after that PW who climbed the first tree available. With the dog stationed at the foot of the tree, the prisoner remained hanging in his tenuous position until lunch time, when the trainer finally called the dog off. Bob also recalled that while the other dogs could be called off an attack and immediately taken into the group of prisoners to be petted as he walked by, one

Airedale was never friendly. Even when traveling in a truck, this Airedale sat next to the window, never between the driver and his handler as the other dogs did.[16]

During prisoners' internment the military daily transported some of the Germans to and from nearby farms and canning factories or transferred them to branch camps for the harvest. But most Germans and all the Japanese and other nationalities remained within

Dog trainer demonstration at Camp Mc-Coy, April 1944. Photo courtesy of Robert Gard.

the confines of Camp McCoy. The PW's completed much of the general construction and maintenance at McCoy. Prisoners built barracks and roads, cleared bombing and artillery ranges, assisted in the motor pool, ran the laundry facilities and incinerators, did routine KP, cleaning, and maintenance for the entire base. Their labor released GI's for more serious military duty.

"By November 1945 some of the German PW's at McCoy had the run of the place," recalled Arthur Hotvedt, stationed at Camp McCoy from 1945 to 1946. Assigned to fire the coal furnaces in all the barracks, the prisoners drove around from building to building unguarded. When the fire went out in our barracks, the PW assigned to our building became very concerned fearing he might be in trouble. They were not shy about using our latrines either. While sharing our latrine, I asked one PW how he was captured. He indicated by hand gestures that his plane had been shot down. Then the German said, "Wait till next time!"[17]

George Mueller recalled the regular interaction between the

John Wasieleski, former Camp McCoy MP and personal guard of Ensign Sakamaki, December 1997.

PW's and U.S. military personnel on the base at the refuse incinerator. The PW's operated the incinerator even as GI's unloaded refuse from all over the base. Located outside the PW compound, the incinerator sat on the north and west of the highway near the large motor pool.[18]

Because of the mix of prisoners in the camp, McCoy had several unique problems. While a fence separated the Japanese and German barracks, each evening became potentially explosive as all prisoners shared the same canteen, barbershop, and PX facilities. The Germans and Japanese both believed in their own racial superiority and openly ridiculed each other. Perhaps they also remembered being enemies during WW I. Commander Lieutenant Colonel H. I. Rogers told *COLLIER'S* Magazine, "but for each race, the other is nonexistent. They never look at each other even in furtive curiosity. They hate each other."[19] An even more acrimonious and deeply rooted relationship existed between the Koreans and their Japanese invaders.

Within the Japanese camp additional and very serious problems developed. The rivalry between the army and navy personnel quickly surfaced. As Japanese naval defeats mounted, the number of naval prisoners grew and greatly outnumbered those from the army. The warrior class despised the naval personnel, blaming them for Japan's continuing defeats in the Pacific. Furthermore, captured naval officers outranked army officers and therefore claimed authority in that compound.[20]

Conflict between the Nazis and anti-Nazis within the German section of the camp continued, even after the altercation that injured several and sent other Nazi-types to a court-martial and Leavenworth Penitentiary.[21]

Yet another group, the Polish soldiers in the Nazi army, had a different outlook. Two Free French captains spent several weeks at McCoy recruiting Poles to go to Canada with them and join a Polish army unit. Although over fifty men did volunteer for this assignment, most refused. Hating the Russians as much as the

Germans, most Polish soldiers didn't see the advantage of again joining the fight.[22]

During the war years the Old Camp McCoy continued to expand to house the rapidly growing number of prisoners. At the same time, adjacent to it, the military built a New Camp McCoy as a major military training center. This new base housed as many as 70,000 American troops at its peak in summer of 1943. For a short time a special group of Japanese trained at the New Camp McCoy. Included among the 1942 trainees was the U.S. 100th Infantry Battalion, a 1,400 man unit of Japanese-Americans from Hawaii. They were stationed at McCoy for six months of training, and the Army took all measures to absolutely segregate these "Hawaiians" from the Japanese PW's. After their training the 100th Battalion joined the famous 442nd (all Japanese) Infantry Division.[23]

As the war ended, repatriation of the PW's at McCoy slowly started with the Japanese. All of the Japanese PW's evacuated Camp McCoy in October, 1945. Transported by rail to California they harvested the fruits and vegetables there before returning to Japan.[24] Many German prisoners continued working across the state until the 1945 harvest and canning season ended. On June 14, 1946, Captain Daniel F. Brewer, PW camp commander, finally reported the departure of the last 403 German prisoners from Camp McCoy. They boarded a train and headed to Fort Custer, Michigan, on their way back to Europe.[25] Camp McCoy's tenure as a PW camp had ended.

Work and contract labor

Following the 1929 Geneva Convention relating to the treat ment of prisoners of war and subsequent Red Cross Accords, prisoners of war could be used as labor if the following stipulations were followed: Officers could not be forced to work; the work must not be directly related to the war effort; the work must not be dangerous to the safety and well-being of the prisoners; and the work must not be demeaning. Further, the workers must be paid for their labor.[1]

Our government quickly saw the advantage in putting the PW's into the work force as quickly as possible. While not required to work, many officers volunteered for the work brigades. Initially prisoners started working around their camps doing as much of the work as possible. Therefore, within the branch camps as well as at McCoy, they became the cooks and did other KP duty, served in the local motor pools, and worked on other camp maintenance. The military also utilized the talents of skilled prisoners whenever possible, putting some to work as medical technicians, interpreters, barbers, carpenters, welders, and mechanics. The PW's generally erected the buildings and tent cities that housed them in the branch camps and dismantled them as they left.

Most of the non-Japanese prisoners generally cooperated and some even eagerly looked forward to work details. Much of the routine camp work assignments such as KP and cleaning latrines needed a minimal number of guards. The PW's also completed much clearing of brush, cutting trees, and building roads outside the PW compound but within Camp McCoy perimeters. These work details generally numbered 104 prisoners and 4 guards, 2 with dogs.[2]

With the camp work completed, the military then distributed these captives around the nation and state to fill severe labor shortages especially in agriculture. In this capacity, their efforts helped to provide essential foodstuffs to our military and allies as well as to those on the home front. Keeping only a small minority to do contract work for the government, private companies contracted for the labor of most prisoners. The individuals and companies that hired the prisoners paid those wages to the military. The military then compensated the men in scrip. The efforts of the PW's earned money for the U.S. Treasury, thus saving taxpayers millions of dollars.

In some situations the military began paying on incentive programs including piecework and team task assignments. By implementation of such plans the military attempted to increase productivity and prevent laggards from collecting undeserved pay. Although these plans proved generally successful, many individual contractors also found various ways to provide incentives of their own, though sometimes these went beyond the rules.

The prisoners received eighty cents per day for their labor. (Prisoners also received a 10 cents per day gratuity, for personal needs.) Thus the prisoners earned about nineteen dollars a month while pay of American enlisted men at that time started at twenty-one dollars a month.[3] Distributing this pay in camp scrip instead of cash prevented a prisoner from accumulating money useful in any escape attempt.[4] The scrip was negotiable only at camp canteens for tobacco, reading materials, candy, toiletries, stationery, other sundries, and sometimes even a limited amount of beer or sake.

The military also allowed each prisoner to establish and deposit into an individual savings account. Such savings would be redeemable upon repatriation. As a result, many prisoners left for home at the end of the war with about a hundred dollars in their pockets. George Hall, the oldest PW held at Hartford, left with $132 while his comrade, Kurt Pechmann, had $91 in his pocket on his return voyage.[5] This hard currency had an unplanned but important and constructive impact on the economies of war ravaged Europe.

With the wartime shortage of labor, the demand for PW labor grew as news of its availability spread. However, the War Department had to first overcome strong union opposition as well as local concerns for safety. To lessen the resistance from the unions, the government quickly made two decisions. First, the government would charge civilian employers the prevailing wage for whatever work the prisoners did. (Door County orchards might pay prisoners forty cents per hour while canning factories generally paid around fifty-five cents per hour, and a farmer might pay by the pound of beans picked.) The PW's could not work more than twelve hours per day, must receive regular breaks, and must return to camp when their work shift ended.[6] Second, prospective employers had to show that they had made every effort to hire civilian employees before applying for PW's labor.[7]

Employers channeled all requests for PW labor through the local War Manpower Commission officials, who certified the need for workers. These officials generally worked with local canning and farm associations and agricultural extension agents. The military kept its bargain, quickly shipping PW's to other regions if enough help became available in a local area. Usually the military could not provide as many prisoners as the factories and farms requested. These rules eliminated the possibility of cheap prisoner labor undermining or competing with the civilian work force.

The military responded to local safety concerns and fears with a show of force, as they made guards and guns very visible. They released tough policy statements to the press and surrounded the camps with fencing of one sort or another and guard stations or towers. However, reflecting the attitude of local commanders, the true nature of the security was irregular, to say the least, and grew progressively weaker as the war with Germany ended. Sometimes an armed guard rode along or in a follow-up vehicle as the work crews went to their stations, while at other locations no guard or weapon accompanied them. Around Wisconsin evidence of these differences in security abounded. At the Hipke Canning Factory in New Holstein, guards with sub-machine guns watched the prisoners in the building.[8] At other factories, seldom did guards show up and then with only a carbine in hand or a sidearm. A guard at the Dairyland Cooperative in Hartford regularly set his rifle down and took a little nap, the friendly PW's prepared to wake and warn him if an officer arrived.[9] Yet in the Milltown area, an armed guard walked the rows of corn as PW's picked the harvest.[10]

Eventually the military formally adopted the policy of "calculated risk" and nationally eased established rules to slowly put the prisoners to work off base.[11] This ultimately led to many individual farmers hiring a few PW's as day labor without any guards or guns or security at all. By 1945, ninety-five out of every one hundred prisoners of war who could be employed worked for private employers or at various military establishments.[12]

In Wisconsin, most of the work the captives performed involved agriculture. Like migrant labor, the PW's moved from harvest to harvest, crop to crop. These prisoners pitched peas, worked the viners, detasseled and husked corn, and picked beans, berries, tomatoes, and potatoes. They raked hemp and hay and shocked the oats. Carrying machetes and other specialty knives designed for specific crops, they harvested cabbage, beets, rutabagas and sugar beets. From bending over to harvest ground crops they also extended their reach as they picked cherries and apples in our orchards. While some waded in the cranberry marshes, others worked in state forest nurseries, and a small detail cut pulp wood. Additional tasks assigned these PW's included making cans for canned milk and working in dairies producing canned and powdered milk and ice cream. They also filled labor shortages across the state in hemp mills, tanneries, and even on a huge fox farm.

To distribute the prisoners to areas where labor shortages existed, the military established a total of thirty-eight temporary or "branch camps" around Wisconsin during 1944 and 1945. Some communities hosted PW's in local branch camps only one year, others housed them both years. While most camps operated an average of only three months a season, Camp Rockfield, Camp Billy Mitchell Field and Camp Hartford each held prisoners up to eighteen months straight. While the military established most of these branch camps at local fairgrounds or in tent cities adjacent

PW's board a military truck headed to work sites. The last seat on each side was reserved for guards, one with a dog. Photo courtesy of Robert Gard.

to the major canning company in the area, a few were installed in rather unique locations. The abandoned Insane Asylum at Sheboygan housed 450 PW's,[13] the Swartz Ballroom at Hartford billeted up to 600 Germans,[14] 250 Germans checked into the Lake Keesus Hotel and Resort for the season,[15] the remodeled Curling Rink at Galesville accommodated 500 prisoners,[16] and the County Courthouse at Bayfield quartered 125 Germans.[17]

A few PW's simply marched to nearby factories. But generally, civilian drivers hired by the military or canning factory contracting their labor transported the prisoners by truck or bus to and from the assigned work sites. The drivers followed prepared routes, dropped the prisoners off early in the morning at the canning factories or farms, and picked them up again in the evening. At some factory locations prisoners worked all shifts, and the drivers just exchanged one group for the other. Some small farmers actually drove to the camps to pick up the few prisoners they hired for the day and returned them in the evening.

Initially, the military provided each prisoner a meal and the employer provided the water. Determined by the work situation and proximity to the base camp, lunch might be a simple sack lunch carried by the prisoner or a more elaborate soup or stew brought to the work site from the camp kitchen. Sometimes authorities called on local restaurants to provide meals.

Bus driver Burnell Spuhler recalled getting into some trouble when he arranged to feed PW's who worked at Hartford's Libby, McNeil, Libby Canning Company. Before meal time, he regularly purchased boxes of hamburgers or other sandwiches and big kettles of coffee in town at Hetzel's Bar for lunch. He picked up soup and vegetables for the dinner shift from Sammy the Greek's restaurant. Spuhler's trouble came when a couple of American military officers reported his usual routine. It seemed he customarily took two PW's with him to help haul the quantities of food.[18]

At Juneau, Janesville, Lake Geneva, Fort Atkinson, Whitewater and Elkhorn their guards literally took the PW work crews to nearby cafes for lunch.[19] Yet, the military denied the Garden City Pickle factory further use of PW's because it also took its few prisoners to a nearby cafe. The factory attempted to defend itself noting the military required the company to feed the PW's, and that it had no cooking facilities on the grounds.[20]

Except for the PW painted across their clothing, little distinguished the prisoners from other hired help with whom they sometimes mingled. While rules against fraternizing clearly existed, many work situations offered much opportunity for interaction and conversation. Many locations had civilians and PW's working side by side. Language barriers were a significant problem in some work sites, but in most locations civilian supervisors and many employees often spoke German well or at least well enough to communicate with the prisoners. Many farmers needed only one or two additional hired hands, yet others hired larger crews for major jobs. On the farms, the German prisoners often found the farmer to be of German heritage and fluent in the language. Many farm families invited the prisoners into their homes to be fed with the family and any other hired help.

As a girl of about seventeen, Allene (Hatz) Richgruber, became very disgruntled when the German PW hired by her father could not drive the tractor. As a result, she had to trade jobs with him. While she disked the fields the prisoner mowed the lawn. But the PW only took a couple of swipes with the mower and watched, fascinated, as the young American girl drove that tractor. Allene had to mow the lawn the following day as well, and her father never hired another PW.[21]

Canning factories around the state filled their labor shortages with prisoners, often one hundred or more on a shift. At the Clyman Canning Company at Hartford, co-workers sometimes referred to the PW's as "*landsmann*" or countrymen. Against military regulations, the civilian workers sometimes offered prisoners treats and even allowed them to take precious sugar or fresh milk back to camp.[22] At Hipke Canning Factory in New Holstein some of the local employees shared their lunches with the PW's.

"Not liking Chicago too well," George Lorenz remembered, "I was allowed to stay the summer with my grandparents, Bill and Ida Euler in West Salem. PW's from Camp McCoy were trucked in daily to work in the local canning factory and the skating rink that the canning company used as a storage area for the canned goods. Several times, my grandmother made fudge or popcorn for me to take down to the prisoners. Many other neighbors of German extraction also went with goodies or just to visit with the prisoners."[23]

Several Germans fell in love with the local female co-workers and corresponded with them after being repatriated. Some sexual liaisons eventually surfaced as well.

Other factories kept the prisoners entirely segregated from

civilian employees. But even there, sometimes circumstances dictated otherwise and forced interaction. In Eau Claire, a civilian employee was called upon to communicate with and translate for a prisoner who had become entangled in the canning machinery. The local employee helped to calm the young man as he awaited rescue and medical attention.[24]

Legal or not, some employers also had unique "incentives" to increase the work of the PW's. The McKay Nursery outside Madison provided a hearty breakfast each day before the hard work of digging out and wrapping tree root balls began.[25] The Libby, McNeil, Libby plant of Hartford provided a piecework incentive by punching a PW's ticket for each kettle of beets sliced. The completed ticket earned a package of cigarettes.[26]

The work situation for the Japanese and other Asian PW's differed greatly as McCoy prohibited them from performing any contract work in the civilian community. The authorities there reflected contemporary American attitudes, and their anti-Japanese sentiment became obvious in a McCoy press announcement that stated, "The Japanese, with their reputation for trickiness and sneakiness are apt to make a greater attempt to disturb our home front security than the Germans ever did." The military warned residents of nearby Sparta to be on alert and immediately report any suspicious activity.[27] Because of these attitudes, the Japanese prisoners remained securely behind the fences of Camp McCoy where they completed regular camp work detail assignments. At night some Japanese prisoners went to the training section of the base for laundry detail where they did the laundry of the entire base and hospital in nearby Tomah and perhaps more laundry shipped in from as far away as Madison's Truax Field. The other primary job assigned to the Japanese prisoners involved clearing out roads and new target areas within the base compound.

At Camp McCoy, the Japanese prisoners proved themselves reluctant workers. The army personnel refused to take orders from the higher ranking naval officers. Many in both branches of service believed any work they performed assisted the American war effort and was therefore treasonous. It took the imposition of "administrative pressure," the "no work, no eat" rule combined with reduced privileges to gain compliance of these recalcitrant captives.[28] Also more sullen, depressed and destructive than prisoners of other nationalities, the Japanese carried out considerable sabotage of equipment and facilities during the performance of their assigned tasks. But in the end, the Japanese prisoners worked their way home. To fill an acute labor shortage, the California officials requested the work of prisoners. So the first week in October 1945, the 3,500 Japanese prisoners left Camp McCoy for a work stop in California.[29] There, joined by prisoners from Camp Clarinda, Iowa, they harvested the California crops before being returned to Japan.[30]

For many of the German PW's, Wisconsin became just a stop along the road. Like the migrant workers, they may have come from the fields and orchards of Nebraska or Texas to our farms and factories. After completing the harvest in Wisconsin, most PW's moved on. Some went to Upper Michigan or Minnesota to work in the logging industry for the winter, others went West to dig potatoes, many again returned to southern agriculture. Most did not leave America until 1946.

Camp life

The Office of the Provost Marshall General issued general orders regarding the confinement, treatment, and utilization of the PW's. But living conditions within the camps varied from camp to camp and even from commander to commander within an individual camp. At Camp McCoy and the branch camps, the prisoners generally did the cooking and kitchen clean up, housekeeping, laundry, yard work and as much of the maintenance as possible.

Initially, the food served to the PW's was identical to that of the GI's guarding them. But in 1943, Prisoner of War Circular No. 1 allowed the serving of more ethnic foods.[1] The only limitation in this order from the Provost Marshall required that the cost of such food not exceed the cost of the original rations and that food not be wasted. Not only did this procedure keep the prisoners amiable, but it often proved cheaper to feed the prisoners their ethnic food rather than the regular soldiers' menu. Whatever the menu, the talents of the prisoners cooking determined the results, including palatability of the meals.

Soon, the Japanese diet at McCoy included rice, sukiyaki, dried fish and pickles, while the Germans found pork, pigs knuckles, and wurst on their plates.[2] Some of this Japanese food came from captured non-perishable supplies returned to the states on empty supply ships. From these confiscated supplies, single serving size bottles of sake occasionally were issued or sold to the Japanese prisoners, just as German PW's received their beer.[3] When given the choice, many guards preferred to eat the German prisoner food over that of the regular army mess or meals at home.[4]

Civilians sometimes expressed outrage when they heard of the type of foods provided to the prisoners during this time of national shortages and rationing. Most of what they heard was erroneous rumor. The prisoners never ate better than their guards, and usually their diet consisted of lower quality foods. Our military followed the Geneva Convention rules, which required that prisoners be fed and housed equal to the host's military. To that end, the mess sergeants always kept track of the calories within the rations of

On April 20, 1944, the Camp McCoy stage was ready for the PW celebration of Hitler's 55th birthday. The picture of Hitler, center stage, was painted by a PW. Photo courtesy of Robert Gard.

all menus. Through its adherence to the international conventions and our treatment of enemy soldiers, the American government hoped to encourage good treatment of Americans held in captivity. A noticeable deterioration in quality and reduction in the quantity of food rations took place in 1945 once American soldiers had been liberated from captivity in Germany.[5] International Red Cross personnel, usually from Switzerland, regularly inspected the camps throughout the state and nation, reporting their findings to the world and homelands of the prisoners. Occasionally, German military personnel also participated in inspection tours of U.S. camps housing German soldiers.[6]

Holidays, especially Christmas, were celebrated with traditional foods when possible. Such meals seemed like feasts to many of the prisoners.[7] The Red Cross distributed traditional German gifts. In 1943 the German government transferred 1,440,000 francs to the Swiss embassy for Christmas gifts from the Fuhrer to the PW's in the U.S.[8] PW's also celebrated their own cultural holidays such as the Asian new year or even Hitler's birthday.[9]

The military made every effort to make church services regularly available to the prisoners. Even Buddhist celebrations were held at a shrine built by the Japanese at Camp McCoy.[10] Then reverend, later monsignor, Stephan Andrel from the La Crosse Diocese was the Chaplain at Camp McCoy. Andrel found a relative from Austria among the prisoners.

Branch camps generally had their own chapel, in which military chaplains or area ministry held regular services. These clergy generally made themselves available for private consultations as well. At some branch camp locations, local congregations were altruistic enough to allow guard details to march or truck those PW's wishing to attend services to and from nearby churches each Sunday.

The internees looked forward to mail call and Red Cross package distributions. The military limited outgoing mail to a postcard one week and a short letter the next. While severely censoring all prisoner correspondence, the military dispatched outgoing and distributed incoming PW mail weekly. Because of deteriorating circumstances overseas, outgoing mail often didn't reach the addressees for weeks and sometimes months. With the displacement of so many families in Europe, the old addresses were often no longer useful. Because of the chaos of the war, the incoming mail became even more irregular.

Distributed as they became available, Red Cross packages received by the PW's usually contained German candies, cigarettes, cigars, shirts, and reading material. Some prisoners became disheartened when they received treats like canned bacon sent from their families because these PW's knew the tremendous sacrifices their families made to send this unneeded food to them. Ravaged by the hardships of war around them, families would not believe letters from their captive sons telling of being well treated and better fed than those left behind in Germany.[11]

Scrip earned by working could be redeemed at the camp canteen for razors, toiletries, stationery, socks, haircuts, hair nets, sometimes soda, sweet treats, and a limited quantity of tobacco and beer. However, at some small temporary work camps, no canteen existed.

Camp Hartford and Camp Markesan allowed local photographers to enter and take group and individual pictures of the PW's. To justify allowing civilians into the camps, the commanders suggested that these photos would be useful to authorities in case of escape. However, individual photos and fingerprints of each PW had been gathered at the processing points upon their arrival in this country. Individual prisoners actually purchased the pictures as souvenirs.[12]

The military provided both medical and dental care to the PW's.

Camp McCoy contained a station hospital as well as a separate dispensary for the Old Camp. When MP John Wasieleski experienced an appendicitis attack, he was rushed to the dispensary. Transferred to the New Camp the following morning, he received an appendectomy from Lieutenant Kim, an American doctor of Korean ancestry. As the camp medical officer, he provided health care to the PW's and MP's alike. Later, German American Captain Schwartz replaced Kim.[13] While recuperating from his surgery, Wasieleski discovered several Japanese officers billeted at the hospital. A sergeant in the Registrars Office of the Camp McCoy station hospital, DuWayne Scott, described the setting as follows.

"Within the station hospital there were three fenced in wards for the PW's and one for GI prisoners (American soldiers in trouble with the law) who needed medical attention. Behind, but separate from the PW wards, was an area in which Sakamaki and other Japanese officers were kept. In one ward was a Korean prisoner whose entire body except for the soles of his feet had been severely burned with napalm. He was kept enclosed in some yellow "raincoat material" and was still alive when the Asian prisoners were sent to San Francisco on their way home."[14]

In the branch camps the military generally contracted a local doctor to visit two to three times a week to monitor injuries and illnesses of the PW's. In serious emergencies camp officials trans-

Church services for PW's at Camp McCoy, April 1944. Photo courtesy of Robert Gard.

Camp McCoy PW mail room, April 1944. Photo courtesy of Robert Gard.

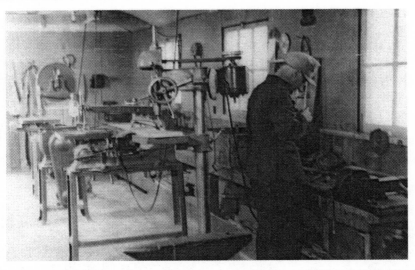

Camp McCoy woodworking shop available to PW's, April 1944. Photo courtesy of Robert Gard.

ported prisoners to a local hospital until their condition stabilized enough to be safely moved to a secured hospital at Camp McCoy, Truax Air Base, or Camp Billy Mitchell Field.

While the military took responsibility for the general maintenance of the prisoners' existence, religious or humanitarian organizations, usually the YMCA, supplied the daily amenities of life. The War Prisoners Aid of the YMCA provided stationery, musical instruments, books, sports equipment, phonograph records, hobby materials and religious items of all sorts. Dr. Howard Hong, representative of the YMCA, cited the need for incense sticks for the Buddhist worship at Camp McCoy.[15] Through the efforts of Hong and his counterparts recreation was available in many forms. Prisoners worked off excess energy with calisthenics, volleyball, fist ball or football (soccer) during their free time. In some camps the prisoners held intramural soccer matches. A few branch camps also provided an opportunity to swim.

Mary Lee recalled her husband solving a peculiar problem for the PW's under his command in Camp Janesville. Many of the PW's wore their hair long which became a problem when hanging in their eyes during soccer. On his next trip into Rockford, Captain Hugh Lee, commander of Camp Janesville (1944), bought a box of hair nets which he sold at cost in the limited canteen. They were a fast selling item.[16]

PW's usually had access to general reading materials, often in native languages. By the end of the war, Camp McCoy could boast a collection of 600 books in Japanese.[17] Even more readily available around the state, German language books regularly traded among the camps. Also made available to the PW's, American newspapers and picture magazines served as propaganda tools to inform the prisoners of what American democracy and capitalism produced.

Many prisoners took advantage of the opportunities for correspondence courses available to them. Over 40 percent of the Japanese PW's enrolled in various courses, including full time high school classes. During their stay many Germans earned college credits, some from the University of Wisconsin in Madison. No record exists of Japanese earning university credits.[18]

Camp McCoy also provided a full woodworking shop to the prisoners. Some camps provided arts and crafts materials. PW's always seemed to have decks of cards. Still other prisoners drew, painted or carved a wide variety of items, usually presenting them as gifts to a favorite guard, foreman or farmer.

In the larger and permanent camps, regularly shown movies became a source of entertainment. Just as in the downtown theater, news reels usually accompanied the main feature. Initially, most

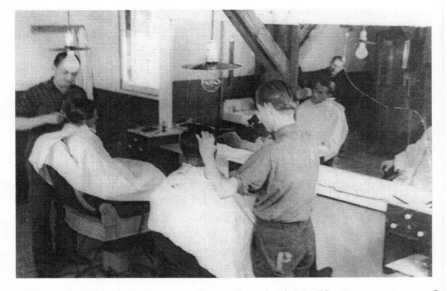

Camp McCoy PW barbershop, April 1944. Photo courtesy of Robert Gard.

prisoners believed all war news stories to be nothing but propaganda, but by 1945 most stoically accepted as true the scenes of the destruction of Europe and their homelands in Germany. Held at Hartford, one prisoner from Dresden, having received word of his family being killed and having seen the destruction of his city in the newsreels, did not want to return to Germany. Many of Hollywood's most popular movies had war themes meant to boost American morale. Often racist and offensive, the movies angered the PW's who would sometimes boo, hiss or walk out. Many a camp commander selected the musicals for the enjoyment of his captives. Of course, most of these musicals starred such beauties as Rita Hayworth, Lana Turner and Ginger Rogers, popular attractions to these female starved men. In some camps, designated prisoners volunteered to preview the movie and translate it for the others. Planned pauses in the movie for translations/explanations were commonly established.[19]

MP John Wasieleski recalled a game he occasionally played with a group of PW's he accompanied to the theater in the New Camp. "I also remember a little fun I would sometimes have. When I would march up to 500 Germans at one time to the camp theater, I would have them goose-step. That was always quite a sight!"[20]

Most camps had their own singing choruses or quartets. Some camps with sufficient talent also organized bands and/or orchestras to occupy the internees. The Camp Hartford band occasionally left the camp to entertain local civilians elsewhere. Again, the local YMCA generally provided the instruments on loan to the camps.

Most commanders opened their camps one day a month for family visits. Because of the large numbers of German immigrants and families with German ancestry in the state and country, apparently many prisoners received visitors from all over the U.S.[21] One young lady from Chicago regularly drove to Camp McCoy. Her brother, drafted as he visited the homeland, was now a PW there.[22] A Hartford PW, Adolf Jesse, had an uncle in nearby Ripon. Regularly, his uncle picked him up and took him home for the visitation day. He could not, however, convince the camp command to allow nephew Adolf to work for him as a butcher in his meat shop.[23] Not all relationships among family members were so cordial. An uncle in Antigo refused any contact with his nephew being held as a PW at that local camp.[24]

Camp commanders determined by order or by encouragement a wide variety of activities within their jurisdictions. Some even allowed the PW's to keep an assortment of pets in their camps. Robert Gard recalls several pets he witnessed while stationed at Camp McCoy:

"One Japanese PW kept birds. He would trap them, keep them in cages for a time and let them go. But they often returned to him. Another prisoner kept two orphaned fawns, which regularly followed him around the yard. There were several dogs, none of which answered a call in English. It seemed they understood only Japanese or German."[25]

Captured enemy soldiers held in camps throughout Wisconsin as well as the nation received treatment better than required by the Geneva Conventions and Red Cross Accords. Provided nourishing food, appropriate clothing, shelter, medical attention, religious opportunities, a variety of recreational activities, and work to occupy their time, most PW's thrived. While some camp commanders maintained very strict discipline, no incidents of abuse of the PW's in Wisconsin were reported. The prisoners returned to Europe and Asia healthy in body, and most healthy in spirit as well.

Resistance and escapes

At each point of entry, the military usually identified and segregated Hitler's SS men as they checked their papers and looked for telltale tattoos. Nevertheless, across the country, Nazi supporters often emerged and sometimes took control of a camp. While the U.S. propaganda machine equated all German soldiers with Nazis, military intelligence estimated only 10 to 15 percent of the enlisted men to be hard-core Nazis.[1] In fact the military knew that the Third Reich regularly drafted anti-Nazis and other resisters and quickly dispatched them to combat zones. As a result, substantial differences of attitudes and opinions existed among the German PW's. As various incidents occurred around the nation between the Nazi and anti-Nazi factions, the military attempted to remove this Nazi influence but never eliminated the problem entirely. By the end of the war, U.S. military courts-martial sentenced to death and hanged fourteen German PW's found guilty of murders within the PW camps.[2] Many others convicted of lesser crimes completed their prison sentences before being repatriated.

At Camp McCoy prisoners staged a near riot as a diversion while pro-Nazis beat several of their anti-Nazis comrades. Though perpetrators were court-martialed and sent to the military penitentiary at Fort Leavenworth, those victims that testified feared for their families back home.[3] In Wisconsin's branch camps, their comrades generally disciplined troublemakers among the prisoners, and the military separated a few others as quickly as identified.

Korean soldiers who were captured among the Japanese units, regularly volunteered to join the ranks of the U.S. Army.[4] Though the U.S. military always rejected them, it believed these soldiers sincere in their request to join the fight against the Japanese who had conquered their country, then drafted them. As captives the Koreans resigned themselves to their imprisonment and became cooperative and willing workers. However, trouble often erupted between the antagonists so the military attempted to segregate them from their hated enemy, the Japanese prisoners.

In Wisconsin, the major incident among the German PW's was

the 1943 fight between the Nazi and anti-Nazi factions at Camp McCoy. German PW's within the state also staged a couple of work stoppages at branch camps and a few individual prisoners made attempts at sabotage and escape. But recognizing themselves as well fed, well treated and not being shot at, most German prisoners accepted their circumstance.

In contrast, the Japanese never accepted their situation. While some resistance and escape attempts occurred among all groups of prisoners, the military found the Japanese the most difficult to manage. Trouble frequently erupted within their ranks.

Resistance by prisoners came in several forms: suicide, aggression, passive resistance, and sabotage. Each type of action eventually occurred somewhere within the Wisconsin camps.

Bushido philosophy, the Japanese military code of honor, did not permit surrender. Therefore Japanese prisoners believed themselves to be failures and expected rejection and probably even execution upon their return to Japan at the end of the war. As a result of these beliefs, the Japanese prisoners had very poor morale and several went insane.[5] Since suicide was the honorable resolution of most personal failures in Japan, it became an issue for the PW's and their American guards. Suicide attempts by Japanese prisoners quickly became a special problem, and authorities often placed suicide watches on despondent prisoners. At least twenty-three successful suicide attempts occurred en route to the U.S. from New Caledonia.[6] In the early months of his internment at Camp McCoy, Ensign Kazua Sakamaki, the nation's first and most famous prisoner, attempted suicide on several occasions. In November, 1944, guards found a Japanese prisoner hanging in his Camp McCoy barracks during mess. Unable to revive him, the Army medical officers pronounced him dead, and listed the cause as suicide.[7] Guard Harold Hoffman reported five other suicides at McCoy but noted many more occurred on the return voyage to Japan at the end of the war.[8]

Aggression might appear as personal attacks on guards and officials. Though the military officially recorded few instances, guard John Wasieleski reported witnessing a prisoner spitting on Colonel Rogers, Camp McCoy commander. Another guard bayoneted the prisoner and Rogers quickly reprimanded the guard for action not acceptable under the Geneva Agreements.[9] The contemptuous prisoner suffered only a minor wound.

Authorities recognized the collecting and building of weapons with the intention to kill captors as another form of aggression. The Japanese proved the most resourceful at this activity. On at least one occasion, the Japanese actually built a bomb but never detonated it.[10] Japanese work details also found three undetonated artillery shells on the McCoy firing range and somehow smuggled them into their barracks. Chief Petty Officer Ichiro Yamashita kept one of those bazooka shells as a souvenir for about six weeks. On October 16, 1944 , as Yamashita walked through his barracks calling for volunteers for a camp wrestling match, he banged the rocket shell on the edges of the metal bunks he passed. The shell exploded, killing Yamashita and sending five others to the hospital. After a thorough search of the compound and the discovery of the other rockets, the authorities determined the other two shells true duds.[11]

Following military policy, an MP and a uniformed Japanese prisoner, who acted as a witness, accompanied the body of Yamashita to Milwaukee for cremation. The ashes returned with the men to McCoy and remained in storage until the war ended when the remains returned to Japan with the repatriates.[12] *

During spot searches of some branch camps, guards found a variety of weapons collected by German PW's as well. The wire cutters, hammers, knives, hand saws, and sharpened screwdrivers had usually been stolen from farmer employers. But there is no report of anyone ever injured by these items.

Refusing to cooperate in daily tasks or work detail indicated passive resistance. If an undetected SS officer joined other German prisoners, he usually stirred up trouble and resistance. It quickly became observable to the guards that something had changed. They immediately initiated procedures to identify the agitator. Once they identified him, authorities removed the SS man or other troublemaker. The German barracks usually returned to a lifestyle of resignation, peaceful coexistence and cooperation.

While not the only work stoppage among the PW's, the largest took place among the Japanese at Camp McCoy. On May 9, 1944, they went on "strike" and refused the call to mess and to work the following day. Camp commander Colonel Rogers declared a

---

*While in Milwaukee, the MP and Japanese witness ate at a local cafe. Several days later a *Milwaukee Journal* letter to the editor reported the complaint of a black GI who had been refused service at that same cafe which willingly fed enemy prisoners.[13]

"riot" existed and removed all officers to a special ward of the compound infirmary. To preclude prisoners from holding grudges against their regular guards, he called in an infantry unit for special action the following morning. With the guard dogs on their heels and bayonets at the ready, the infantry forced the prisoners to march at the double to their work station five miles away where they worked without breaks. The PW's returned to camp at noon at the double as well. The prisoners became exhausted. About a dozen stragglers received minor bayonet wounds, and a few became so overcome they had to be picked up by a truck ordered along for the purpose.[14]

The military had in place three options to deal with insubordination. These included the "no work, no eat" policy, the withholding of pay, and solitary confinement. The "no work, no eat" policy called for a restricted diet of not less than eighteen ounces of bread a day and all the water the prisoner desired. This policy was occasionally used at other trouble sites as will be mentioned in branch camp reports. Both the work pay and the monthly gratuitous allowance could also be withheld.[15] In the case of this Japanese riot, the camp command imposed both of these punishments. But they considered the primary factor in breaking the strike the removal of the officers. Without leadership of their officers, the Japanese prisoners capitulated the following day and resumed their work assignments. Later a Red Cross representative, Señor Gonzales, investigated and approved the actions taken by the Camp McCoy authorities.[16]

The cultural background and military training of the Japanese soldiers gave them a unique outlook on their situation. First of all, on the whole they tended to believe in and were more emotionally involved in the success of the war than their counterparts from Europe. They worshiped their emperor and accepted his call to duty. Unlike American University educated Kazua Sakamaki, one of their ranking officers, most Japanese soldiers had no knowledge of the Geneva Conventions. They did not understand or believe their rights and responsibilities as prisoners even when explained to them. They believed any work treasonous to their homeland and throughout their internment resisted work and sought escape, which included suicide for many.

The Geneva Conventions recognized it a duty of each PW to attempt escape and dictated a limited punishment for any such attempt. The Convention permitted punishments of up to thirty days at hard labor and thirty days on bread and water or both. The commanding officer of the camp where the escape occurred determined the specific punishment. But if the prisoner was caught in the act of escape, the Convention also recognized authorities had the right to shoot the escapee on sight.

For Japanese prisoners, escape was not only an expected behavior of all military captives but also sometimes attempted in hopes of getting shot and therefore heroically dying for the motherland.

In 1943, nine-year-old Edward Kostuch, on his way to Saint Stanislaus Grade School in Winona, Minnesota, encountered several escapees. "Coming out of the alley onto East Zumbro Street, I noticed three men across the street. They wore brown jackets with a PW on the back of their jackets. One of them looked at me and said something to the others. Suddenly one jumped over the fence at Frank Ramczyk's house and the other two ran up the alley going west. When I got to school, I told the nun what I had seen. Then at noontime over the radio came news that three prisoners had escaped from a Camp McCoy PW truck and authorities were looking for them. When I got back to school after lunch the nun and the principal called me aside and asked me about this incident I had reported earlier. The principal asked what color clothing they wore. I told her brown with letters PW on the back. She said you must mean khaki color. I didn't know what that was, but it is a brown. They knew that I had actually seen the escaped prisoners when I told them they were short and appeared oriental. (Actually they were Japanese.) I heard later in the day that the three had been recaptured by authorities around 4:00 p.m. and returned to Camp McCoy."[17]

Since McCoy housed all Japanese prisoners and never contracted them out around the state, their escapes had to be made from that secured position. As a result, few successful attempts actually took place and all fourteen escapees were quickly recaptured.

In mid-June, 1944, Kazuyuki Maeda walked away from his work project sometime between 1:30 p.m. and 4:30 p.m. However, authorities located him about 5:30 p.m. the same afternoon near the post hospital about five miles from the PW compound. Maeda explained he wanted to aid the U.S Army without the other Japanese in camp knowing about it.[18]

Next, Terumasa Kibata attempted to flee. On July 3, 1944, he walked away from his work detail ten miles north of the camp, slipping into the forest. He intended to catch a train and get away.

An extensive search by both military, F.B.I., and civilian agencies immediately followed. Two Army planes flew in for air surveillance. However, Kibata had no idea where he was or how to survive in his situation and turned himself in to Camp McCoy authorities the following day.[19]

Takeo Nakamura, Hajime Hashimoto, and Kokei Tanaka had the best organized plan of escape. Nakamura had stolen both a Texaco road map and a topographical map of the camp, a pair of bolt cutters, and extra food, planning to lead his group to the Mississippi River and down to the Gulf of Mexico. On May 21, 1945, Nakumura used the stolen bolt cutters to slip through the fences, but the barking dogs frightened him and he didn't wait for his companions. They followed behind some time later. Because of a prior ankle injury, escapee Hashimoto found the rough terrain too difficult to travel, so he and Tanaka stayed on the roads. La Crosse County patrol officers Chief Ivan Wright and Jerome Breske arrested Hashimoto and Tanaka on June 1. When located traveling along county road "B" outside of West Salem, the escapees still wore their PW garb. Authorities found in the their possession a home made dagger, an improvised hatchet, another small dagger, a fish line and rope.[20] As planned, Nakamura followed the railroad tracks to the Mississippi River, and then stole a rowboat and headed downstream. When Nakamura failed to return the wave of fisherman Lloyd Hartman, the civilian got suspicious and sailed closer to discover an Asian. He returned to shore and picked up two companions and weapons. The three picked the escapee up on the river bank, returned to Prairie du Chien and turned him over to Sheriff Ulysses Day.[21] The sheriff found the escapee hungry and exhausted, having survived on turtles and tree bark during his eight days on the run.[22]

In early July, two more Japanese managed to leave the confines of McCoy. Hiraswawa Mitsuhei escaped during the night of July 3 and Masao Kitamura made his getaway the following night. Both left under cover of heavy rainfall and darkness. Driven by hunger, Mitsuhei stopped at the Paul Zuehlke farmhouse near Norwalk. He rubbed his belly to show he was hungry. Startled and frightened, Mrs. Zuehlke gave him a couple of slices of bread and then notified the sheriff. Highway officer Hans Biegel arrived and searched the woods for about an hour before finding the man. When apprehended without resistance, Mitsuhei possessed a sock full of shelled corn and a few green apples.[23] Although reported near Cashton and elsewhere, Kitamura eluded recapture until July 17 when a worker spotted him in the La Crosse rail yards, hiding in a Chicago & North Western railroad car full of crushed rock.[24]

At almost the time of Kitamura's apprehension, Mitsuo Yamamoto escaped. However, he was stopped shortly after leaving the McCoy Compound. In mid-July, two more escapees turned themselves in shortly after their escape. Found only 100 yards from the compound, Toshio Yano said he was about to give himself up after escaping the day before.[25] Three more escapees barely made it outside the fences before being quickly arrested. On interrogation this trio claimed they feared other prisoners whom they hoped to avoid.

The last Japanese to escapee from Camp McCoy headed to Mexico. After four days, a resident spotted Yuzo Ohashi in the Cashton vicinity. Sheriff Bert Johnson and Officer Hans Biegel approached and arrested the PW without incident. One of the few Japanese captured at Iwo Jima, Ohashi explained he feared being returned to Japan and thought himself close to the Mexican border. He had survived on berries and green tomatoes.[26]

To the consternation of the camp officials and distress of area residents, several Germans also managed escapes from McCoy. Sheriff Bert Johnson again picked up one such escapee on Highway 27, two hours after the radio broadcast his escape. Mrs. Forrest Richards observed the PW markings on Josef Karner's overcoat and reported him to Sheriff's office.[27]

Two MP's apprehended another German, Delbert C. Clark, in La Crosse on February 19, 1943, ending his brief period of freedom.[28] The third German PW to escape from McCoy came to the door of Mildred Knutson, seeking food. While she fed the guest, her husband went next door to call the MP's. The Knutsons believed the escapee had watched the house for some time.[29]

First reported missing by Camp McCoy on Saturday, April 14, Paul Nagorski was recaptured in Portage on April 15, two days after his break. The German prisoner later told investigators he hopped on a freight train at Sparta, got off at Portage, and failed to catch it when it departed. Like the others, he offered no resistance to the local arresting officer.[30]

A phone call from the Schaller farm quickly brought authorities who apprehended two more unidentified escapees in a railroad tunnel near the farm.

"Mother screamed and called for father, yelling: 'There is a man out the window!' Dad grabbed his double barrel shot gun, loaded it, and ran out the door in his long underwear. Finding no one, he came inside and called the Sparta police." Vera Schaller Olson still had a clear memory of that night because she recalled "I saw my Dad in his underwear for the first time. The man at the window was probably one of two German PW's on the loose from Camp McCoy. They were recaptured in the mile long Sparta-Elroy (railroad) Tunnel that cut diagonally through our property. That same evening, the neighbor girl, Betty Goatz, had been sent out to bring in the cows, but when she didn't return quickly, the hired man went out after her and the cows. He found her playing with green apples and sent her home. As the hired man rounded up the cows, he noticed two men getting water from the pump of a nearby unoccupied farm house about 150 yards from where Betty had played."[31]

Only prisoners identified as compliant went off base to work. As a result, few escapes occurred from the branch camps established for these contract workers. And the majority of these "escapes" were just adventure seeking excursions — to see the local sights, take a swim, visit the ladies, and pubs. These PW's usually returned undetected by morning roll call. Many of these incidents are detailed in the branch camp reports later in the book.

The military position proved correct, most non-Japanese prisoners easily accepted their lot; fair treatment, good food, a warm dry bed, medical attention, and no one shooting at them. In most cases, PW's ignored obvious opportunities to escape as they traveled to and from work stations outside the camps. A typical situation occurred with civilian driver Darwin Wosepka.

Wosepka recalled, "I was driving prisoners to the New Richmond Canning Company, carrying only a sidearm. One prisoner jokingly poked me in the back reminding me I had forgotten my rifle."[32]

Repatriation

The survival rate of prisoners held in captivity by the U.S. in WW II was unprecedented in history. With over 450,000 incarcerated in this country, only 477 PW's died nationwide. Of those, some 265 died of natural causes, 72 by suicide, 43 in traffic accidents, and 17 by drowning. Several work related fatalities also occurred. The death rate of American recruits preparing for battle exceeded that of the PW's.[1]

Quickly described by co-workers and neighbors as "the only civilian to kill an enemy Jap," Roger Young became a local folk hero around Sparta. As one of many civilians employed in the Camp McCoy motor pool, Roger drove a truck that took several prisoners on their scheduled work detail to pick up ashes from the camp buildings. One Japanese prisoner fell off Young's truck, striking his head on the pavement. In the base hospital the following day the PW died from the blow to his head.[2]

Partly a result of their exposure to American media, its people, and technology, and the humane treatment received throughout their stay, many German prisoners inquired about staying in America, rather than returning to their homeland. By the end of the war the PW's believed the war accounts presented by the American radio broadcasts, newspapers and movie newsreels. They understood the devastation and harsh conditions within Germany. Though many PW's requested permission to stay in the U.S., the military automatically denied each request. The postwar negotiated agreements established the policy of 100 percent repatriation of all prisoners, even when prisoners chose not to return to their native land.

Contrary to expectations of PW's and civilians alike, the PW's did not immediately return home after the signing of the peace agreements. By the end of 1945 fewer than 75,000 of the 380,000 German PW's had been returned to Europe.[3] Most remained working in the States into 1946. The last of the prisoners finally sailed to Europe in June of that year. The Secretary of Agriculture and some members of Congress insisted the War Department retain the prisoners for continued crop harvesting. In a compromise worked out between the two departments and the White House in January, 1946, President Truman announced a deferment of sixty days for contract PW's to stay for the ongoing harvest. However, he refused to extend that period and insisted on maintaining the schedule which required all PW's returned to their homeland by the end of June. Only the President's firm stand forced total repatriation at that time.[4] The military complied with the orders and returned all PW's to Europe or Asia by June 30, 1946, except the 141 Germans, 20 Italians and 1 Japanese, all serving sentences in U.S. penal institutions.[5]

American immigration policy then treated these former prisoners like any other prospective immigrant. They could seek immigration status from their homeland through the normal channels under the quota system of the period. An American sponsor and job offer provided preferential treatment for any applicants. And many Wisconsin farmers willingly sponsored and temporarily hired those prisoners that had worked so well for them during the war. As a result some did return to Wisconsin in the early 1950's.

Once the order came to evacuate the camp and prepare to return home, the activities within the camps quickened. Luggage had to be packed and tagged for shipment. Those without a home address sent their packages to the International Red Cross in Geneva. There the packages would be stored until claimed. The Army issued new clothes to the prisoners, this time U.S. Army uniforms dyed black and without the PW stencils. The camp authorities collected and returned all property on loan from the YMCA or other local organizations such as radios, sports equipment and musical instruments. Shortly before their actual departure the prisoners received their personal belongings that had been seized upon arrival in the U.S. and stored in individually sealed bags. The prisoners also redeemed any balance in their trust-savings account. Restricted from taking American currency with them, the repatriates received from the government checks for the amount saved. American authorities in Europe and Asia cashed these checks upon presentation. Most PW's went home with a sizable sum of money that helped not only them and their families but the European economy as well. The French, however, generally confiscated these checks along with any other valuables of the prisoners who passed through their country. [6]

A fact not widely known or remembered is that most of the prisoners who returned to Europe remained captive there for another two to three years. The German prisoners followed one of two routes home, one through England and the other through France. Passing through England usually provided a quicker and smoother journey than going through France. While sending some PW's directly on to occupied Germany, the British authorities detained other PW's only for a short stay to be "re-educated" before being transported to Germany. But the British also impressed many and required them to work within the country for another year or two. Perhaps a majority of the German soldiers repatriated through Le Havre, France remained captive there, kept as unpaid labor for up to three more years. In France, the PW's worked in the coal mines and at rebuilding the cities and farms.

During his three years of confinement in Wisconsin, PW Kurt Pechmann matured from a youngster of 120 pounds when captured to a formidable 185 pounds before he returned to Europe. However, Pechmann recalled that as a prisoner of the French, "I was fed poorly, sometimes only three beets a day. My weight dropped to 85 pounds before I escaped and walked home to Germany in late 1948."[7]

Willi Rau, who surrendered to American troops near Anzio, Italy, in July, 1944, had a similar experience. After his capture, he spent much of the remainder of WW II logging in Camp Au Train, Michigan, and in Wisconsin at Camps Barron and Rhinelander. In the spring of 1946 his group returned to Europe via Le Havre, France, where authorities impressed them to work in the coal mines for another two years. "Leaving America, each of us had gotten two black dyed sets of clothes without the "PW" on it. The French took these away from us as soon as we got there and provided us with rags full of lice. We were held like slaves. I was finally released in November, 1948."[8]

As prisoners arrived in Germany they found their receptions much a matter of chance, often determined by the situation in their hometowns. Some returned into the Russian Zone, only to be taken to the Soviet Union as slave labor never to be heard from again. Those that remained in Germany found the country destroyed and in chaos, their families now scattered, missing, or dead, their homes destroyed and their jobs lost. East German authorities generally considered them "contaminated" with Western ideas, untrustworthy, and suspect, and they treated them harshly.[9] Perceived as not having suffered like those on the German home front, many West Germans also discriminated against them. The repatriates often found existing jobs unavailable to them. And in the back of their minds, the vision of the democratic, economically abundant America they had experienced haunted many of them.

During their captivity, the U.S. military made a concerted effort to expose the prisoners to the advantages of democratic capitalism. Special "re-education programs" emerged at Fort Philip Kearney, Rhode Island, for selected prisoners.[10] The U.S. government hoped that those chosen prisoners would eventually become active leaders in the new governments and systems arising out of the ruins of Europe.

The Japanese repatriates also faced mixed receptions from family and community. Many families had held funeral services for them years before. The U.S. Army of Occupation attempted to persuade the Japanese people that they should welcome the return of their sons, husbands and sweethearts who had fallen prisoners to American forces, but the long standing and generally accepted belief that capture was a disgrace beyond redemption could not be easily overcome. The American authorities then attempted to convince the Japanese people that they had all surrendered to us when Japan accepted the peace terms of unconditional surrender.[11] Though never tried for treason by the Japanese military or legal systems, many returning Japanese prisoners endured discrimination in marriage, housing, and job opportunities. Perhaps worse, many suffered the personal anguish of never being able to reconcile their capture and survival with their earlier teachings of Bushido and patriotism.

Around the world, all those that survived WW II, have lived forever with that war. Its impact left permanent and often significant physical and emotional scars on the military personnel including the PW's. Those serving in the armed forces, as well as their families back on the home fronts, all experienced indelible changes in lives, attitudes, values and ways of thinking. For more than 5,000 German PW's these changes drew them once again to America, this time as immigrants.[12] Here they took up permanent residence and many eventually became citizens of this country they experienced during the war. No state by state breakdown of the numbers of former PW immigrants is available. We will never know how many returned to Wisconsin, but this state received its share. While a few of these immigrants are very open about their past, most have chosen to blend quietly and anonymously into Wisconsin's population.

Branch camps in Wisconsin

In 1942 substantial government purchases of canned food became a military necessity, and these military purchases demanded special handling. For military purposes, the canned food could not be labeled, needed a protective pre-coating that inhibited rust and had no bright surface that might be easily spotted from the air by hostile planes. At Wisconsin meetings held in Eau Claire, Appleton and Milwaukee in April of that year, military men and safety engineers explained these needs and directed canners to firms providing suitable equipment and paint.[1]

Further, because of national mobilization into the military and essential industries, few people, except local high school students, housewives and the elderly, were available for work on the farms and in other factories. The government deployed PW's to fill the labor shortages, especially in the seasonal agricultural jobs. From the approximate 10,000 captured soldiers of Rommel's Afrika Korps assigned to help in the harvesting and processing of canning crops in the Midwest, 3,959 worked in Wisconsin during 1944.[2] Branch camps established around the state housed the prisoners.

Many of the prisoners initially employed in pea packing remained in Wisconsin for later harvesting and processing of other crops around the state. The military established additional camps to house PW's for some of the later work. Historically, there has been some confusion as to the location and number of these branch camps in the state. Part of the problem stems from several camps being listed under two different names, such as Camp Fredonia also referred to as Camp Little Kohler or Camp Trempealeau also called Camp Galesville. Since not all the camps were open at one time, any published number included only those open at that moment, never the total of camps housing PW's around the state over the entire season.

The July 18, 1945, *Two Rivers Reporter* listed about 9,300 prisoners working in Wisconsin. This number was from an official statement released by Headquarters of the District II, Sixth Service

Stalag Wisconsin

Command, Chicago. Included under its command at the time were 7,900 prisoners working the pea viners and canneries, 400 in the cranberry bogs, cherry orchards and truck farms, and another 1,000 working out of the Hartford and Rockfield camps at eight various plants producing such things as dry milk, leather, hemp roping and tent poles.

With the world war raging, the military downplayed its use of the PW's, releasing minimal information about their numbers, location, employment and earnings. However, with the May 1945 surrender of Germany, information became more readily available, and in many areas the military provided press tours of these PW camps. Reported by Brigadier General Pierce of Fort Sheridan, the "total revenue from the state of Wisconsin for PW labor, all paid in cash by private contractors, amounted to $1,827,586.85 for the first eight months of 1945."[3] According to that same report, total income from July 28 to September 1 was $581,540.79. These prisoners, housed in thirty-three camps during the latter period of that year, worked in nearly 100 communities of the state. Since some camps did not close until the end of the year, subsequent news releases gave final total revenues earned for some individual counties while no additional information was forthcoming on other camps.

At the peak of the 1945 harvest season, the Sixth Service Command reported that "the number of prisoner camps under Fort Sheridan's supervision increased from fourteen to forty-one. This number includes those in Michigan as well as Wisconsin. During June and early July most PW's worked with the pea crop in Wisconsin. There are now close to 13,000 prisoners working in branch camps with additional requests for PW labor still being processed."[4] The economic impact of the prisoners' labor was monumental.

Most localities were understandably apprehensive about the possibility of enemy soldiers camped nearby. Some local areas seriously protested the placement of PW's in their communities. As a result, the military occasionally changed the locations of planned camps. For example, the camp scheduled for Manitowoc actually opened in nearby Chilton. Over time, these feelings of anxiety generally dissipated. Even in Manitowoc County, farmers began requesting PW help.[5]

The last section of the book details the thirty-eight branch camps in Wisconsin during 1944 and 1945. Listed in alphabetical order, each camp record includes a brief description and summary of its activities. Listed on the table on the following page are the dates and years each camp was operational. Not indicated on the table is the fact that at both Barron and Galesville the sites of the camps within each community changed from year to year.

Each camp record contains recollections of that camp from PW's, local civilians or guards who had personal encounters with them. These recollections demonstrate the variety of situations, attitudes and events occurring around the state.

Though these recollections are fascinating, it is well to remember that more than fifty years have passed between the actual events and the sharing of these encounters with the author. Over the years memories often become less accurate as they fade, blur or become embellished. Occasionally, conflicting stories were reported. The author attempted to establish the accuracy of the stories by comparing these conflicting reports with other sources and has included only stories she believes to be true.

POW branch camps in Wisconsin

Camp	Opened	Closed	Peak PW's
Antigo	7/45	10/45	150
Appleton	7/45	12/45	180
Barron**	7/44	9/45	422
Bayfield	8/45	11/45	125
Beaver Dam	6/44	8/44	300
Billy Mitchell	1/45	5/46	3,000
Cambria**	6/44	9/45	335
Chilton**	6/45	8/45	300
Cobb	6/45	9/45	176
Columbus**	6/44	10/45	575
Eau Claire*	7/45	9/45	143
Fond du Lac	6/44	8/44	300
Fox Lake**	6/44	9/45	350
Fredonia	6/45	1/46	330
Galesville**	6/44	10/45	450
Genessee	6/45	1/46	280
Green Lake	6/44	10/44	600
Hartford	10/44	1/46	600
Hortonville	7/45	12/45	305
Janesville**	6/44	10/45	600
Jefferson	6/44	7/44	180
Lake Keesus	6/44	7/44	250
Lodi**	6/44	11/45	250
Markesan*	6/45	10/45	637
Marshfield	7/45	9/45	243
Milltown**	6/44	9/45	325
Oakfield	6/45	12/45	238
Plymouth**	6/44	8/45	180
Reedsburg	6/45	8/45	137
Rhinelander	8/45	10/45	330

Camp	Opened	Closed	Peak PWs
Ripon	6/45	12/45	650
Rockfield	7/44	1/46	531
Sheboygan	7/45	12/45	450
Sturgeon Bay	5/45	8/45	2,140
Sturtevant**	6/44	12/45	350
Waterloo	6/45	9/45	310
Waupun	7/45	10/45	350
Wisconsin Rapids	5/45	11/45	200

*Closed and reopened during season.
**Closed for the winter/spring, 1944-45.

Camp Antigo 1945

CONTRACTORS HERE PAID
$31,730 FOR POW LABOR

— Antigo Daily Journal, December 15, 1945 [1]

This headline summarized the work of the PW's in the Antigo area in 1945. Up to 150 PW's worked in the Antigo canning factory and on area farms harvesting peas, beans and potatoes. Even with this help, hundreds of sacks of potatoes stood out in the field during a September rainfall because there was not enough labor to get them out in time.[2] The first thirty-nine prisoners and their equipment arrived in five trucks from Barron on the fifth of July, setting up camp on canning factory grounds. They used part of the warehouse for sleeping quarters and tents for mess and other facilities on the adjacent premises. A nearby field became the soccer area. Additional prisoners continued to trickle in throughout the season. The Antigo canning factory employed thirty-five of the PW's while the others worked at the viners and in the fields.[3] By September 12, 1945, the number of PW's in Antigo dropped to nearly 100. While some continued working at the canning factory until the end of the bean pack, harvesting potatoes on area farms occupied most of their time. Local farmers hoped to have more PW labor, but the corn packs around the state took priority over the potato harvest.[4] The camp facilities on the canning factory grounds were bursting, so additional housing had to be found. The forty PW's arriving on September 13 and the final group arriving later in the month were housed at the NYA (National Youth Authority) center dormitory on the northwest side of town. These NYA buildings included barracks, mess hall and gym. A central heating plant kept all structures comfortable as the weather turned colder. A parade grounds in front of the buildings completed the camp, all within the post and barbed wire fencing. Originally built at the beginning of the war, this center had been a school for glider pilots preparing for the Normandy Invasion.[5]

The community expressed little concern about personal safety as the PW's moved into the area. Perhaps Camp Commander Captain Barney B. Claghorne reassured the community when he spoke to a local Rotarian meeting. He acknowledged that the prisoners were not under constant supervision of guards with automatic rifles because "they are not eager to run away." He identified most as conscripts without any moral issue compelling them to fight.[6] With 138 prisoners now scattered and employed by 20 area farmers until October 19, 1945, the community continued to demonstrate little sense of anxiety or apprehension. Worry about future harvests escalated as the farmers read that as of January 1, 1946, PW labor would no longer be available. Where would the workers come from next season? Many employers in Wisconsin and throughout the nation lobbied for the PW's to stay in the U.S. longer. However, President Truman ordered them all returned to Europe or Asia by the end of June, 1946.

The only financial figures available on the work done by the PW's stationed at Antigo came from Fort Sheridan. In a September press release, the command reported the PW's at Antigo had completed $10,730 worth of work.[7] Private canners and farmers in the area had paid that amount to the military which forwarded the money to the U.S. Treasury. The PW's at Camp Antigo had been an economic godsend to the labor strapped area, one that also provided unique social opportunities.

For many years several local families continued contact with former PW's they had employed. As late as 1949 the Antigo Federated Garden Club was sending "CARE" packages to former prisoner Karl Schmidt of Rothendach, Germany. The parcels included seeds and clothing for which the club received warm letters of appreciation.[8]

RECOLLECTIONS
Elda Schrader. Antigo, WI -

During the potato harvest on the Emil Schrader farm, Mrs. Schrader made noon lunches for prisoners. She found the PW's to be grateful for the meals but refused the corn on the cob. They didn't eat corn on the cob in Germany since they believed it to be swine food. Daughter Elda recalled her parents keeping in touch with one PW for a few years after the war. She believed that August Goetz of Cologne, Germany, was their primary contact. According to Elda, "Mom and Dad sent them clothing. There was nothing in

Hans Arend, top, and fellow PW's bring in a load of hay on the Asa Littge farm in August 1945. Photo courtesy of Ruth Johnson.

Germany."[9]

Margaret Wendt. Antigo, WI -
Margaret recalled her family being "criticized by a lot of our neighbors for treating them so good." But her mother, hoping "our boys are being treated as well by somebody," continued to supplement the small sandwiches the prisoners brought from camp.[10]

Eugene Lukas. Antigo, WI -
Confident the Army would not send anyone dangerous out to work, Lukas filled his labor shortage with PW's. He recalled the remarkable circumstances of the times when these German prisoners were being invited into rural area dining rooms while newspapers were full of German atrocities and the Nuremberg War Crimes Trials. Very pleased with the work of his three prisoners who would keep the viner going all day, he was sure they outperformed any four or five high school kids he might have hired another time. Lukas remembered the guard dropping off his crew at 5:00 a.m. and then leaving. He understood the guard spent the day in a Neva tavern.[11]

Ruth Johnson. Pestigo, WI -
When the truck did not come to take the prisoners back to camp,

the Littge family of Shawano invited the PW's in for supper. Another day, niece Ruth bought a newspaper and a pack of cigarettes, planning to give these to the prisoners. She didn't see them, so she put the cigarettes on a fence post for the men to find.[12]

Jack T. Jilek. Antigo, WI -

Jack T. Jilek's father, Julius, hired two Germans to help on his potato farm. Jack claimed that Gottfried (Louie) Weigand kept the grader cleaner than any other employee before or since. Louie was friendly and talkative with family members that spoke German. However, the other PW, Rolf Kunze, was a captured pilot and seemed to be a true Nazi at heart. Jack recalled his surprise to find those German prisoners eating at their table unfamiliar with our German potato salad. The Jileks maintained correspondence with Louie and Rolf for several years. Both of these PW's returned to Germany by way of France and spent some time working for the French before getting to Germany in 1948 and 1949 respectively.[13]

Camp Appleton
1945

"200 men, 50 boys and some women for the patriotic, vital war job of picking peas," read the full page ads in the *Appleton Post-Crescent.*[1] Attempting to hire the seasonal workers necessary for the pea harvest, Fuhremann Canning Company purchased several such pages. Because they had very limited success in filling the positions, the company then contracted with the U.S. government for the labor of prisoners of war. Fuhremann also included with its own company request for prisoner labor the demand for workers from 176 Outagamie County farmers. After some of the labor shortage was filled with twenty conscientious objectors, and Mexican and Jamaican workers, 450 PW's arrived in the county. Housed in camps at both Appleton and Hortonville the prisoners were trucked by the military to canneries in Appleton, Hortonville, Shiocton, Shiocton Creek, Weyauwega, Bear Creek, and Clintonville.[2] In the Appleton area, Fuhremann Company took charge, daily deciding where the prisoners worked and their work assignments. As required, the canning companies paid to the military the prevailing wages of fifty cents to sixty cents per hour of prisoner labor.[3] In July alone the prisoners put in 24,673 man-hours of labor requiring the Fuhremann Company to pay the government $15,556 for their efforts.[4] Some PW's worked at the Fuhremann viners, including the one on County Road JJ. Though against international regulations, the prisoners put in the same fifteen to sixteen hour days the civilians did as they processed pea vines there. The peas were then trucked to the Fuhremann Canning Company on West Eighth Street for more processing by additional prisoners.

Located near the Fuhremann Canning Company grounds, Camp Appleton (Junction) averaged 180 PW's. There the men erected a tent city and outfitted a large garage (which still stands) with shower stalls and a mess hall.[5] When the city council refused to rent nearby Spencer Field, now Goodland Field, for twice weekly exercise breaks, the company set up a small yard on their grounds and eventually rented a pasture at the old City Home for use as a soccer field.[6] Commander Captain John G. Fitzpatrick, a veteran of the European Theater, organized Camp Appleton as a miniature military post with guard stations posted at each corner.[7] The forty-two enlisted men serving as guards attempted to keep the inquisitive out as well as keep the Germans in. Two of the guards enthusiastically accepted their orders for this assignment because they were hometown boys. Raised in Appleton, both Sergeant John Langenberg and Sergeant Roland Hanson still had families in town. Even the Germans seemed more content here. Having previously been held at a camp in Texas, the prisoners found the Wisconsin climate more pleasant and its terrain more similar to that of Germany.[8]

After the pea pack, some of the prisoners housed here moved to other locations while 137 remained. Those that stayed kept busy painting binders, weeding beets, and aiding farmers by threshing their grain until the beet harvest again put them back to work in the canning factories at the end of August.[9]

Because the war with Germany had been over since May, many local questions arose about repatriation of the prisoners back to Germany. Camp Commander Captain Fitzpatrick addressed those

Truck driver Donald J. Van Handel, far left, viner foreman Peter Dreissen (losing his hat to a playful PW), a company field man in dark clothng and three unidentified PW's at Fuhremann's pea viner. Photo courtesy of Richard B. Van Handel.

concerns in statements on the subject at an August Rotary Club meeting. He believed repatriation of German prisoners depended on three factors: "How long PW's are needed to fill the labor shortage in the U.S.; how soon they can usefully be absorbed in Germany and the availability of transportation." He believed they would remain in this country until those problems were solved.[10] With their work completed, the Appleton PW's moved on to Door County orchards and then Upper Michigan logging camps before heading home.

In September, Fort Sheridan reported the PW earnings from Appleton paid by private companies to the military during the entire 1945 season totaled $29,473,[11] making it a good season for all.

RECOLLECTIONS
Paul Wassenberg. Appleton, WI -

"I have vivid memories of seeing Army trucks loaded with Germans being transported to the fields. They passed within a block of where we lived on the south side of Appleton. I saw them almost every day as I came home from the 6 a.m. church service, where I served Mass. The trucks stopped at a stop sign and then made a right turn. The prisoners always seemed friendly, waving and yelling something in German, which I could not understand. I always wondered why they didn't jump off the back of the trucks when it stopped because I never saw any guards."[12]

Anthony La Loggia. Newburg, WI -

"If a guard saw you even talking to a PW, he came over and stopped the conversation. So we civilian workers at the Appleton Cannery kept our distance and didn't talk to the prisoners much."An impressionable 16-year-old, Anthony La Loggia remembered the huge scar from the bottom of the neck all the way down the back of a 19-year-old PW who worked nearby. In that section of the cannery the hot cans came out of the water bath so the crew, including this PW, took their shirts off, exposing this terrible scar. The prisoner explained with motion and sound that a machine gun had ripped him apart.[13]

Helen Van Handel. Appleton, WI -

"One day Mrs. Strick, a co-worker, came to me with a stick of gum and told me to write my name and address on the inside of the wrapper," recalled Helen Van Handel. "The guards at the Dundas

PW's working at Fuhremann pea viner shelling peas. Photo courtesy of Richard Van Handel.

Canning Factory seemed more lenient when the older ladies talked with the prisoners. Mrs. Strick then gave that stick of gum to one of the young PW's who had requested the information. Several of my high school girlfriends and I worked there but only during the pea pack. So an envelope from France about eight months later came as quite a surprise to me. In the note in the envelope, a priest explained he had a young man that came to his church regularly who wanted to correspond with me. The envelope also contained the first letter from that PW who had received my address on that gum wrapper. If I wanted to continue the correspondence, the note instructed me to send my letters to him (the priest) who would then give them to the young man. The letters came in German, so the jeweler I worked for at the time interpreted them for me. When the jeweler said, 'Oh, he seems to have serious intentions,' as he interpreted another letter, I became apprehensive. I had exchanged only a few letters before I stopped writing back. Several of my friends worked with me at Dundas. Since we all belonged to the Kaukauna High School Glee Club, we sometimes sang in harmony as we sorted the peas passing down the conveyor belt. The prisoners seemed to listen closely and smiled at us girls. Always very hot in the factory, one of my friends came to work in shorts one day. One guard quickly reprimanded her and told her never to wear them again. I'm not sure we really understood why at the time."[14]

Merlin Romenesko. Walworth, WI -
"I was a fifteen year old farm boy in 1945 working with PW's at the pea viner between our farm home and Kaukauna." Merlin Romenesko recalled that at the time his three oldest brothers were in the Army infantry, two in Europe and one in the Pacific, while two other brothers and he worked vining peas. "I had a German dictionary which I took to work and used to communicate with the German PW's with some degree of proficiency. I remember that we had a hard time understanding how we could work sixteen to eighteen hours a day but the Geneva Convention only allowed PW's to work ten to twelve hours; maybe their shift was even less, but not for the farm boys. Another memory is that my parents sent sandwiches to the PW workers, with the thought that if their sons ever became prisoners, hopefully someone would treat them with the same kindness. Fortunately, all three brothers came back uninjured even though all experienced combat. When my brother, Ray, came home that summer after being through Europe since D-Day plus ten we talked about my working side by side with the Germans. He warned me not to be misled by their friendliness and then told me how his unit was ambushed and one of his buddies machine-gunned. He cried as he told me about that ambush."[15]

Camp Barron 1944 & 1945

Camp Barron was unique in many ways. More open to the press than the others, this camp in northern Wisconsin housed PW's for both years and experienced two of only three "strikes" in the state. Selected as a site for a PW camp in 1944, Barron received prisoners again in 1945. Early news of the first arrival of these prisoners came from Milwaukee. Sixth Service Commander Colonel William H. McCarty announced the activation of Camp Barron on July 4, 1944, under the charge of Lieutenant Thomas H. Collier and Lieutenent Lorinz Sulzenfuss. The garrison arrived by train at noon on that date. The Soo Line stopped across from the camp to unload its human cargo.[1] In a following communique, McCarty asked that civilians refrain from visiting the camps, distracting the PW's from their work mission.[2]

On July 20, 1944, the editors of the Barron and Rice Lake newspapers received a rare opportunity which came as an invitation to visit the camp. The military placed a restriction against taking photographs of PW's, since under international law, photos could be construed as using the PW's for propaganda purposes. Leaving cameras behind, the honored guests took the only press tour given around the state in 1944, a practice common the following year. In their well censored joint release following the tour, the reporters described the camp as consisting of several dozen tents pitched on level ground on the east end of the city. Having a dirt floor, each tent had a drainage ditch dug around its perimeter to prevent flooding. In the small two to three man tents they saw a few photos of girls from back home. A few cheesecake pictures of pinup girls hung near the bunks as well. The prisoners had a life similar to U.S. Army service personnel. They arose at 6:00 a.m. to clean their tents, have breakfast and fall in formation for prisoner count at 7:30 a.m. Then off to work they went, usually transported by truck to their work station. Later, another truck generally took food to the work site where they ate lunch about noon while supper was served back at camp at 6:00 p.m. The final formation and prisoner count came at 7:30 p.m. with lights off at 10:00 p.m. Cooked by prisoners and served cafeteria style under a long tent, their meals were equal in quality to those received by their American guards. The food reportedly came to Camp Barron from Fort Snelling. The visitors noted that the ordinary barbed wire fence would not serve to hold anyone during an escape attempt and must have been there to serve only as a demarcation line. However, the reporters also noted the adequate guard facilities provided. During the tour the visitors saw prisoners involved in several forms of recreation including jumping rope, playing with a soccer ball and batting another ball. With a few American picture magazines such as *Life* and *Look* and several other magazines printed in German, reading and writing letters were other common pastimes. In the post exchange the reporters noticed a few cartons of cigarettes and a reasonable assortment of soft drinks and some beer. They were informed the beer was only 3.2 beer and limited to two pints per man per day when available. During short interviews with several prisoners, it became apparent that many still believed that Germany would win the war, and they (the PW's) would return to Germany victorious within the year.[3]

Several differences became evident between the two seasons the PW's were held at Camp Barron. The following year prison authorities announced the canteen would not sell cigarettes, beer or candy. Instead prisoners would be allowed to buy two ounces of tobacco a week and cigarette papers, razor blades, toothpaste, shaving cream, soap and some magazines.[4] PW's were kept in different locations, too. In 1944 they were housed on Highway 8 where the Jerome Turkey plant is now located. In 1945 the camp was relocated to the north edge of town, east of Highway 25 in the area now occupied by the Barron County Highway shops. Circled with woven and barbed wire fence, tents housed about 200 prisoners in 1944 and as many as 422 in 1945. While brought to Barron by train in 1944, they came in two large truck convoys the second year. Trucks transported these German prisoners from the camp to area farms, vineries and canning factories. In 1944, the prisoners stayed close to Barron and Rice Lake, but the following year the numbers of work locations and prisoners utilized expanded. The 1945 primary work stations still included 100 positions at the J. B. Inderrieden plant in Barron and 125 at the Rice Lake Inderrieden plant, but additional placements included 100 working for Stokely Foods in Cumberland, 25 at Clear Lake, 50 at Ladysmith

Cheesecake pictures near PW bunks. Illustration by PW W. Hoernchen, 1946. Photo courtesy of Willie Rau, permission U.S. Army, Fort McCoy.

and 22 at Chetek.[5] The area vineries including the Shanno Viner on P between Almena and Prairie Farm also employed PW's in 1945. And as Army regulations eased, PW's worked on canning company contract farms for harvesting as well. Through the use of news articles, the military encouraged farmers to hire the prisoners. The July 11, 1945 *Rice Lake Chronotype* noted "the War prisoners are being made available to agriculture" and listed contacts for area farmers who would like such help.

While very rare throughout the state, two different strikes or work stoppages took place at this camp. When the first PW's arrived in August of 1944, they had not received the pay earned at their previous work site. Because they were without the scrip to buy cigarettes and other treats, the PW's refused to work. The guards who had not received their pay either, sympathized with the prisoners, but quickly implemented the "no work, no eat" order. The following morning the prisoners returned to work and the payroll arrived in the afternoon.[6] Later in the season, a second strike quickly ended when the Army lowered the flaps on the tents the strikers occupied. The tents quickly became very hot and uncomfortable, convincing the strikers to return to work.[7]

Statewide, the military released no financial reports of the camps in 1944. But as the 1945 camp was evacuated the first week of September, Brigadier General John T. Pierce, commander of Fort Sheridan, reported prison labor figures. According to that report, in Barron County alone, the PW's had supplied about 50,000 man-hours of labor and earned for the U.S. government $48,057.[8] They had proved to be an economic asset to the community and the government.

RECOLLECTIONS
Charles Rieck. Middleton, WI -

Freed from a German PW camp, Chuck Rieck was now assigned to guard Germans at Camp Barron in late July of 1945. Rieck was shocked at the "Nazi" attitude of some militant PW's he found there. This particular group of prisoners from the early Afrika Korps still denied they had lost the war. Other prisoners were content to be there, awaiting their repatriation. One inmate in particular, Heinz, became the camp "pet," working in both the prisoner and guard sections of the camp. He became very familiar with the guards. When a problem with one of the stoves arose, Heinz simply took the grate from the stove and walked out of the camp down to the nearby foundry to have it fixed. The foundry called the camp and a detail was dispatched to pick the wandering PW up. When Camp Barron closed the first part of September, guard Rieck recalled how displeased the PW's were when they found they would be sent to upper Michigan to cut pulp. As the camp closed, Rieck also had a personal decision to make. With only twenty-five to thirty guards for the more than 400 prisoners, each man stood duty for twenty-four hours and then had off for forty-eight hours. During his free time, Rieck often worked for Charlie Jerome at his poultry processing plant down the street. Jerome offered Rieck a permanent position at the end of his enlistment.[9]

Kenneth McDonald. Barron, WI -

Ken was surprised to see the prisoners in a circle playing "catch" by bouncing a soccer ball from head to head. He remembered the entire family going down to see the PW camp on the north edge of town.[10]

Donald Neuenfeldt. Barron, WI -

The PW started to cry when he saw the month old baby in the crib in the living room. The German then brought out a picture of a house with white picket fence and another of his wife and two little girls. He had no idea what had happened to them. This German PW and three others worked two days on August and Helen Neuenfeldt's farm out of Turtle Lake and had been invited inside for a big dinner. Son Don remembered the PW's reaction to his Aunt Eva's baby and to not getting any pie that first day the prisoners were there. His mother had made only one pie, thinking the prisoners wouldn't know what it was anyway. But they saw and devoured it, leaving none for the others in the house. Don also remembered his mother's horror when she inquired where Dad was after it started to rain. Don had just brought the horses in, but the PW's and Dad were still in the field stacking the new cut peas and coming in with the car. Helen feared the prisoners would hit her husband over the head and take the car since there were no guards. Instead, they returned the next day to finish the job.[11]

Name Withheld. Eau Claire, WI -
The Rice Lake canning factory must have been a prized work station because it was right on the lake. After a hot day in the even hotter cannery, many of the PW's would take a quick dip in the lake before loading onto the bus to take them back to Barron.[12]

Stuart Hegna. Cameron, WI -
On a very lucky day Stuart Hegna found a perfectly good pitchfork buried in the silage. During the war years, he lived with his family on a farm outside of Chetek. In winter Stuart would go into town to the canning factory for a load of pea silage for the livestock. Stories circulated that PW's would sometimes throw their pitchfork into the silage, getting it buried and therefore gaining an extended break until another pitchfork could be found. The canning factory personnel quickly understood the game and bought a large supply of extra pitchforks to discourage this practice.[13]

Ronald Greener. Rice Lake, WI -
Managing the Osborne farm four miles northwest of Barron, Ronald Greener had a PW crew come several days to help with the oat harvest. Ron would run into town to the Highway 8 camp with his pickup in the morning to get the eight to ten man crew, returning them to Barron for supper. Contrary to American ways, these prisoners got down on hands and knees and loaded the oat

bundles rather than use pitch forks. No guards accompanied the prisoners to the farm. Ron's wife, Lenora, cooked a regular farm noon meal of meat, potatoes, vegetables and dessert for the prisoners as well as the other hired men on the farm. All ate together in the dining room. One day, one PW did come to the house in very broken English asking for the latrine. Another day, one prisoner asked Lenora the age of her two small children, sadly letting her know he had one about the age of her 2 1/2 year old at home in Germany.[14]

Joseph Oberpriller. Chippewa Falls, WI -
As a young boy, Joe Oberpriller rode his bike down to inspect the work at the vinery on Highway 8. There he got off and watched the PW's pitching peas. During one break he clearly remembered one of the PW's getting on his bike and riding it in circles after putting his own army cap on Joe's head.[15]

Floyd Thompson. Cumberland, WI -
Floyd Thompson remembered the *Rauchen Verboten* signs around the Cumberland canning factory. All workers, including the PW's, would have to go outside during breaks to smoke.[16]

Wilma Thompson Calloway. Pellston, MI & Carol Thompson Cormany. Chippewa Falls, WI -
Sisters Wilma and Carol Thompson could not get over how young the prisoners who worked with them at the Stokely factory were. When she accidentally stepped on a gunny sack a PW was dragging, Carol received a stare and a clenched fist, which she describes as an automatic reaction, from the youngest prisoner. He was only sixteen (also her age) at the time. The sisters noted how protective the other prisoners were of their young comrade. The Thompson girls also recalled lockets the prisoners had of their loved ones back home.[17]

Darwin Wosepka. Haugen, WI -
No one, including MP Darwin Wosepka, feared escape attempts by PW's at Camp Barron. With only his sidearm, Darwin once drove prisoners from Barron to the New Richmond Canning Company. One prisoner jokingly poked him in the back and reminded him he had forgotten his rifle.[18]

Harold Kringle. Barron, WI -

Near Brill, some local women worked in a rutabaga field several rows over from the German PW's. Hilda Gabriel overheard the men talking and laughing about the *dicke*, fat, woman. Fluent in German, she was able to tell the PW's off.[19]

Norman and Ruth Rydberg. Spooner, WI -
In a quiet spot along the Yellow River, the PW's took their lunch break. Norman Rydberg would bring out a big ten gallon cream can of hot coffee to go with his work crew's sandwiches brought from camp. During the bean picking season Stokely generally sent out two busloads of prisoners from Barron to Rydbergs pea crop. Occasionally Norm would also buy a crate of peaches or pears and treat the prisoners as well. He appreciated their good work.[20]

Camp Bayfield
1945

Was local government going out of business? Moving city and county government offices out, the military established Camp Bayfield in the Bayfield County Courthouse/Community Center. Set in a square block of shaded grounds, the building housed as many as 125 German PW's and 35 guards during the summer of 1945. Most prisoners slept in the second floor basketball gym area and used bathing facilities in the basement. The first floor accommodated the kitchen, mess, and quarters for the American guards. Camp commander, First Lieutenant Lawrence J. Distel, gave orders from his office, previously the site of the Bayfield City Council's chambers.[1]

The first seventy-five Germans arrived from Camp McCoy on Sunday, August 26, with another fifty expected to follow soon. Two guard stations were built near the streets in front, but only a snow fence in the rear of the building served to mark the perimeter. Actually, the purpose of the fence was to keep civilians away. On the back lawn, about a dozen tents also went up to house the excess MP's and PW's. As elsewhere, the prisoners did all the cooking and camp maintenance.

D. S. Knight of the Bayfield Canning Company made the arrangements with the military for the prisoner-laborers. They worked for his cannery and later for the Bayfield Fruit Growers Cooperative.[2] Initially the PW's worked picking beans. Knight and local farmers determined the number of pickers needed on each farm. The farmers then came in each day and picked up their new employees. The military provided transportation and guards only if a large group of PW's went to one location. The canners and contracted farmers agreed to a payment for PW labor of two cents per pound of beans picked with a minimum guarantee to the military of four dollars per day per prisoner. That meant the PW's would have to pick 200 pounds per day, which was high for the time. At the end of the first day of harvesting, an average of only 150 pounds per prisoner had been picked.[3] But most PW's gained speed with experience. From bean picking these men were then sent to work in the local Bayfield Fruit Growers Co-op's new apple grading and packing plant. There, the PW's filled round the clock shifts as the plant started a 24 hour-a-day operation.[4] Residents hoped the PW's would remain to help with the herring fishing later in the season, but without employment for the PW's between the apple and the herring harvest, the military moved them to awaiting jobs elsewhere.

At camp headquarters a friendly little Scotty mascot greeted local reporters and community leaders. On Tuesday, August 27, 1945, the Army offered a press tour of the camp and one of the bean fields. First Lieutenant Thomas Vickerman, the public relations man from the Sixth Service Command, and camp commander Lieutenant. Distel, led the tour throughout the buildings and then out to the Martin Erickson fields.[5] The guides also explained the daily routine of the PW's. When picking beans, they were transported to work at 7:30 a.m. where they worked up to twelve hours per day or until they met their quota. On this tour, the military emphasized that they tolerated absolutely no fraternization between the German prisoners and their guards or any civilians. To the visitors the prisoners seemed in good physical condition.[6] The prisoners also seemed content in their work but already looked forward to aiding in the apple harvest where they could reach instead of bend. When the tour returned to camp, they found a net across part of the parking space as the prisoners laid out a volleyball court. With space very limited at Bayfield most of the recreational pursuits of the captives included sedentary activities such as playing cards, reading, and listening to the single radio.[7] The tour confirmed the thoughts of Ed Erickson. Because many were fluent in English, Erickson, mayor of Bayfield, believed them to be upper-class Germans. Captured early in Africa, most had been part of Rommel's Afrika Korps. Having been in captivity for over two years, they looked forward to going home.[8]

The work record of these prisoners satisfied the farmers hiring them. Mrs. Martin Erickson, who had six acres of beans on her farm two miles northwest of Bayfield, said that "this bunch of prisoners has worked well. They didn't waste time in picking the beans."[9] Similar responses came from the apple growers. Fort Sheridan reported that between September 1 and September 29, the total earnings of the PW's in the Bayfield region was $6,965. By that time they had put in 10,163 man hours of work for the Bayfield Canning Company and another 1,237 for the Bayfield Fruit Co-op.[10] By working into November the prisoners added even more to the area economy.

RECOLLECTIONS
James Erickson. Bayfield WI -

Working at the Martin Erickson Farm picking beans, the PW's averaged 200 pounds picked per day per man at the going rate of two cents a pound. (Of course, this money went to the military and the men received their regulation pay of eighty cents per day.) Mrs. Erickson took lemonade in a five gallon milk can out to the field. This provided the beverage added to the lunch the prisoners brought with them. The eight to ten prisoners working in his father's fields would be accompanied by one guard with no noticeable weapon, according to son, Ed Erickson, who worked in the fields with them.[11]

Jack Erickson. Bayfield, WI -

Only eight when the PW's worked on the family farm, Jack Erickson clearly remembered the special seats they invented and wore. The prisoners took blocks of firewood and attached a plank to the top of each. Then they attached this seat around their posteriors with ropes and took their seats with them down the rows of beans as they picked.[12]

John Hauser. Bayfield, WI -

At Bayfield's Hauser Superior View Farm, the PW's picked and graded apples. John Hauser remembered that his father, Dawson, became friendly with one prisoner. After the war they exchanged correspondence and

Off-duty guard helps pick apples for Bayfield Fruit Growers. Photo courtesy of Ruth Moon.

his dad even sent the man some money to help his family. In the 1970's the former prisoner, Joseph Ruelick, and his family came from Germany, hoping to renew the old friendship but found Dawson in a nursing home suffering from Alzheimer's disease.[13]

Tony Wojak. Bayfield, WI -
According to Tony Wojak, current president of the Washburn Historical Society, local residents, including he and his parents, went up the hill to the Bayfield Courthouse to look through the fence at the prisoners. Sometimes they traded cigarettes for a German button or coin. The local residents had a common perception that the PW's ate better than the civilians.[14]

Harriet Haugen Johnson. Ashland, WI -
Since only the back of the building was fenced in, Harriet Johnson continued walking the shortcut across the courthouse square on her way to teach school each day. She walked past a guard station and regularly saw PW's in the back of the building being loaded or unloaded on their way to or from a day's work in the fields and orchards. While she had no looming fears about the prisoners, she certainly had no interest in getting any closer to them. However, she recalled that many of the high school girls were enamored with the guards stationed there.[15]

Merton Bruce Benton. Ashland, WI -

The Bayfield courthouse-community building housed Camp Bayfield with a guard tower in right foreground and military trucks near the building. Photo courtesy of Ruth Moon.

When his old van hauling the
PW's up to his farm couldn't
make the hill, Olaf Selfer attempted to back down but
rolled the vehicle on its side
into the ditch. One PW was
transported to the Washburn
hospital. Included in the con-
tents of the van strewn about,
Bruce Benton found the PW
lunches, sandwiches of bread
and mustard. Benton, who lived
about a block from the accident, noticed the sandwiches
when he went to see the com-
motion. Bruce soon saw those
sandwiches regularly. As he
turned thirteen, he became old
enough to work with them on
area farms. Hired by John and
Emma Krueger, he joined PW's
as they picked beans, raspberries, strawberries, and apples.
Kruegers spoke German and
conversed with the PW's who,
Benton recalled, seemed to

**Bayfield guard tower manned
by two guards and their mascot.
Photo courtesy of Ruth Moon.**

miss their families and wondered what had become of them back
in Europe. These farmers also brought extra food and provided
sandwiches and Kool Aid to all the workers, civilians and PW's.
Bruce understood that the guards brought out extra sugar from
the camp for the Kool Aid.[16]

With one guard dispatched from camp for every eight to ten
PW's, often four or five guards mingled on the farm at one time.
There always seemed enough for a good card game — the regular
pastime of the guards. Sometimes they played in the sheds, other
times under the shade of an apple tree. As combat veterans recov-
ering from their wounds, most of the guards bided their time until
released from the service. Some signs of physically handicaps
including limping and deformities were evident. Working with them
in the orchards, Bruce Benton remembered one guard sending a
PW back up the hill to retrieve his rifle. The guards seemed un-

concerned about escape or safety. [17]

The rowdy guards in the taverns became a local concern however. Bay-field's police force consisted of one man, Bruce Benton's father, Merton Vance Benton. Luckily, a sergeant stationed at the camp provided the lone officer some help in controlling the revelers. That MP would regularly patrol with officer Benton. Together one night, the two men caught young Bruce and a neighbor boy on a wood shed roof flashing their flashlight at the camp. Though the boys didn't know Morse code, they pretended they did.[18]

PW's Rudolph Thielicke and Ernest Schobert wear their military boots as they stand at the warehouse door. Photo courtesy of Ruth Moon.

J. A. Krueger. Minneapolis, MN -

The very first morning PW's arrived at the family orchard is still quite vivid in the mind of Reverend John Krueger. "I remember them standing around in the driveway in front of the log garage my father had built. The building had an upstairs (half-story) with a platform along the front on the outside reached by a rudimentary stairway. Dad was in the upstairs part getting out bundles of bushel baskets for the prisoners to collect apples in. I remember him coming out the door onto the platform with a couple bundles of the baskets, a considerable weight, if ever they landed on anyone. He held the baskets up, ready to toss them down to whichever prisoner would be able to catch them, so they could get started picking. Dad shouted, *Pasz auf!* (roughly translated, watch out!). As soon as they saw what he wanted, a couple of them immediately responded, turning toward him and held up their hands to catch the baskets. He tossed the baskets down and they were off to a good start for their first day. Over the years Dad often repeated the story of how relaxed the situation got out in the orchard with the guards not always very cautious about guarding the prisoners. Believing none of the PW's had any particular desire to escape anyway, a guard sometimes just propped his rifle up against an apple tree while he talked with his buddy. Once, when the prisoners happened to see the camp commander's Jeep coming up the road, one of them ran and picked up the rifle and took it to the guard in a hurry so the CO wouldn't catch the guard neglecting his duty and raise cain about it."[19]

PW Willi Fricke, "the musician of Berlin songs," plays an accordian in the Bayfield warehouse. Photo courtesy of Ruth Moon.

Mary Torbick McCarty. Bayfield, WI -
After the beans and apple crops were picked, several PW's continued to work on the Torbick farm. Now they dug a ditch for a water pipe for plumbing into the farm house. Mary Torbick McCarty recalled that while the prisoners were digging that ditch, her brother, John, returned home. Having served as a medic in Europe, he had seen too many mangled bodies of GI's. Very uncomfortable with the Germans around, he avoided them entirely.[20]

After the war, Robert Meyers, a Bayfield neighbor told the Torbicks about his experience while traveling in Germany. He stopped in a bank to exchange money. When the teller saw the name Bayfield on his papers, he immediately struck up a friendly conversation with them as he recalled his stay at a PW at Camp Bayfield.[21]

PW Rudolph Leithold, spokesman for Camp Bayfield prisoners. Photo courtesy of Ruth Moon.

Camp Beaver Dam 1944

They came by truck and left by train and did not stay very long. They caused no trouble and got the job done. They were the German PW's stationed at Camp Beaver Dam during the summer of 1944. The *Beaver Dam Argus* first revealed the possibility of German prisoners coming to Beaver Dam on June 1, 1944.[1] In trucks under heavy military escort, 300 German PW's arrived on the 17th of June. Commanded by Lieutenant. John B. Price and Lieutenant Lawrence J. Distel, they established a tent city camp in the midway of what at the time was the Dodge County Fairgrounds. (The Wayland Academy fieldhouse is located there now.) Using additional equipment the group installed night lights, showers, and cooking facilities. Only a wooden snow fence contained the prisoners who were otherwise lightly guarded.[2] The authorities closed the sidewalk adjacent to the fairgrounds along S. University Avenue to pedestrians and they blocked the street itself to all vehicular traffic for the duration of their stay. Further, the city council issued an ordinance that prohibited stopping or loitering on both streets facing the camp including Highway 33, which passed on the north side. Despite the council ordinance, the curious quickly congregated at the fairgrounds fence. The following week, Colonel William. H. McCarty, commander of the Wisconsin and Upper Michigan District of the Sixth Service Command, issued his usual warning against civilians fraternizing with the prisoners and asked local citizens to stay away.[3] Before the bans, a Watertown resident who stood near the fence observed prisoners lining up in rows, locking arms, and singing German songs.[4]

Both the Stokely Foods plant and the Central Wisconsin Canneries in the city utilized the labor of these prisoners. These prisoners joined the imported Jamaicans in the pea and corn packs.[5] The prisoners themselves stayed only for the pea pack, breaking camp August 4, 1944, their destination unreported.[6]

Military trucks lined up outside Camp Beaver Dam with rows of tents behind the trucks on left, summer 1944. Photo courtesy of Dodge County Historical Society.

RECOLLECTIONS

Robert Frankenstein. Beaver Dam, WI -

Dodge County received war awards for the big increases in food production that year, with the PW's major players in that harvest and canning season. Bob Frankenstein recalled that he always had a certain amount of fear whenever he went near the prisoners. Nevertheless, as a young boy, he often stood by the fence of the fairgrounds to listen to the Germans sing their songs and watch them play soccer.[7]

James Hammitt. Eau Claire, WI -

"I'm ashamed to say it now, but it was sort of like going to the zoo when I and several other grade school boys would go down to the fairgrounds to look at the prisoners. Our first couple of trips were a little tense, but any fear quickly dissipated as the friendly PW's seemed as interested in us as we were in them. On each visit, several prisoners quickly assembled near the fence where we stood and tried out their limited English on us. On several occasions, they gave us change to go to the little neighborhood store to purchase candy bars for them."[8]

Gilbert Bleck. Greendale, WI -

"As a 14-year-old boy living on East Mill Street in Beaver Dam, I saw the PW's often and had several contacts with them that summer of 1944. The end of our long garden abutted against the south side of the Dodge County Fairgrounds. The fairgrounds has since moved, but we had a fascinating view that summer. Two of the tents in the PW camp had red and black swastikas (flags) hanging on them. These PW's came from Rommel's Afrika Korps, and word spread among the local German speaking farmers that several Nazis were in the bunch. Perhaps, they flew those Nazi flags. The PW's played around with a soccer ball, keeping it in the air among several of them using head, shoulders, feet and legs. In the evenings around dusk, some of the Germans often gathered at the fence along Highway 33 near University Avenue and sang as a choir. Local residents came from miles around to listen. Other encounters with the PW's came while I worked with them. A neighbor, Stan Rissman, owned several farms. About five of us teenagers worked for him in the fields, generally cutting thistles in pea and oat fields. One day we worked in a large field on Rissman's main farm on Highway 151 several miles north of Beaver Dam. While we worked in one part of that field, about ten German PW's worked in another, with Jamaicans in the other corner of the field. We never

Soccer match at Camp Beaver Dam, summer 1944. Photo courtesy of Dodge County Historical Society.

saw more than five of the ten Jamaicans standing and working at any one time. Like us, the Germans always worked. Most of the local farmers spoke German and communicated well with them. Another day, Rissman had a lot of dry hay on the ground needing to be put into the barn before the approaching storm hit. He promised each German a bottle of beer and a cigar (against the rules) to rush and get that hay in. They really flew and beat the storm, earning their rewards. Later in the season, I worked a field next to a tavern along Highway 151. I remember an Army truck parked in front of the bar, standing in the hot sun, with PW's packed in the back of it. The GI guard (s) was in the tavern sucking booze. My final encounter came the night the prisoners left. Our American Army kept marching cadence by having a GI call it out. In contrast, the Germany Army sang to maintain their marching cadence. That cadence was sung for the last time in Beaver Dam one August evening as the German PW's pulled up stakes and left the fairgrounds. It was dark, about 9:30 p.m., when the Germans marched north up University Avenue about a mile to the train depot on N. Spring Street. They marched double file, singing the entire way. We teenagers tagged right along. They boarded the troop train waiting for them. I still remember the steam engine at the front of that train, its fire box glowing red in the night. It was all quite exciting for curious teenagers."[9]

Camp Billy Mitchell Field 1945

On January 4, 1945, the Milwaukee County Board agreed to lease Mitchell Field to the U.S. War Department for one dollar. Shortly thereafter 1,500 German soldiers marched from their barracks to an adjacent hangar where two battery assembly lines had been hastily set up. Within months, the number of PW's there swelled to more than 3,000. Added to that number were the fifty U.S. Army officers and 250 enlisted men running Camp Billy Mitchell Field. During the next fifteen months, an ongoing parade of prisoners passed through the gates. The authorities officially closed the camp on April 1, 1946. On that date, the last remaining prisoners were sent to Fort Sheridan on their way home.

Although barbed wire fencing surrounded the grounds, it took only days for two prisoners to make their escape on the night of January 13, 1945. After lights out, Willi Lepil and Carl Heinz Zoeller left their barracks and followed the fence until they found a location they could crawl over. During their short escapade, they stopped at a dance hall to watch some polka dancers. The prisoners were surprised to find not only the large German population but also so many people of Polish nationality in Milwaukee. Lepil later remarked to investigators, "Looked like we were in enemy territory without realizing it." Recaptured quickly, the first two escapees had not yet been missed back at camp. Milwaukee police detectives Charles Hurst and Walter Duray thought the two looked like suspects they had been seeking in a mail theft case. Both agreed the two certainly looked suspicious anyway. The bareheaded escapees wore their jackets turned inside out and had cut or torn the red PW's from the legs of their trousers. When the two officers asked Zoeller for his draft card, he answered, *"Vass dat?"*[1] During their interrogation the escapees maintained they were just going to Milwaukee for an exploratory trip and, hopefully, for some of Milwaukee's famous beer. The pair claimed they intended to return to their barracks by morning. The investigation also found both Germans had seen combat — Zoeller at Anzio and Lepil at Stalingrad and in Finland. Lepil had been wounded five times. They had been captured together during a German retreat outside Rome in August of 1944. As their interrogations ended, they both "thanked the detectives for their kind treatment."[2] Perhaps the PW's had expected to be shot as escapees. Camp officials quickly tightened security as a result of this initial escape. By the end of January, watch towers had been erected and equipped with floodlights to watch over every section of the camp.

Camp Billy Mitchell Field opened as a separate command which supervised branch camps at Rockfield, Hartford and Sturtevant. But reduced to the status of a branch camp on June 5, 1945, Billy Mitchell Field and its three subordinate camps were all placed under the Fort Sheridan command.[3]

Colonel W. C. Bechtold, the officer in charge, conducted a press tour of the camp and battery facilities. As usual, Fort Sheridan sent a public relations officer, Major Lynn Fairbanks, to lead the tour this time. The press corps witnessed the operation of one of the largest battery assembly lines in the nation at the time. In the National Guard Armory building on the airport grounds facing Howell Avenue, a modern conveyor system of production turned out thousands of small batteries for the Assembly Battery Company of Milwaukee. Attempting to comply with the Geneva Convention, owners established this new company as an affiliate of Ray-O-Vac to handle this special production. Our Signal Corps used the batteries produced here for practice training in communications. Reporter Leo Stonek from the *Cudahy Reminder* noted that some of the prisoners still wore the famous white Rommel hats they were wearing when captured.[4] Reporters found the grounds well secured by a tall fence topped with barbed wire and guard towers spaced throughout the compound. A second fence within the grounds encircled the barracks area. With no guns allowed in that section, even the officer in charge left his Army pistol at the interior gate as he walked among the prisoners.

In this camp a few dogs were permitted as pets. The reporters were also shown a copy of the *"Lagerzeitung"* (Light News), a camp paper written and published by the prisoners themselves. The mimeographed publications, usually about five pages in length, included a serial story, cartoons and educational material. One copy was distributed to every twenty-five men. Some of the few Germans that could read English translated the news of the *New York Times* for the rest of the contingent. With radios also available for their use, the prisoners started to believe the news reports about the war.

Camp authorities identified a variety of activities made available to occupy prisoners' free time. Common entertainments in the camp included singing and painting/drawing. The two tour guides reminded the press corps of the art exhibit held by a dozen or so prisoner artists earlier in May. Held at Billy Mitchell Field and open to the public, the art show included many paintings for sale.[5] Other recreation included American movies for which the PW's paid a small admission fee. Highly anticipated Red Cross packages from Germany caused much excitement when distributed. The reporters also learned that the camp allowed visitations from U.S. relatives one day a month. Limited to one hour per visit, many relatives came repeatedly.

Touring the barracks converted into a chapel, the press learned that a Catholic priest assumed the responsibility of permanent chaplain on the base. The priest, assisted by an area Protestant minister, provided religious opportunities for these prisoners and the GI's stationed there. Noting measures the camp authorities took to meet the personal needs of the PW's, the press corps seemed reasonably satisfied with all they saw.[6]

While at Mitchell Field, PW's handled 10 million battery cells and assembled them into 202,000 batteries. The Battery Assembly Company paid the U.S. treasury $165,000 for their services. Other PW's were transported daily from Mitchell Field to the Nestle Milk Products Co. in Burlington where they made cans for condensed milk. That work netted about $7,200 for the treasury. The PW's did extensive maintenance work around the field itself, the value of which was later estimated to be $150,000.[7] A few prisoners worked for a short time at the Frank Pure Food Co. in Franksville, assisting with the spinach pack.[8] Additionally, some were trucked daily to Oak Creek to work at the A.C. Spark Plug factory there. Probably the largest area farm to hire PW's as field hands, the nearby Tehan Farm had railroad tracks crossing it, providing the greatest opportunity for PW escapes. Several other area farms and manufacturing plants also utilized the labor of the PW's. Fort Sheridan reported collecting over $265,296[9] from private companies for wages of Billy Mitchell Field PW's in 1945, but did not report the additional earnings added to the treasury in 1946.

Although Milwaukee County had been promised the return of its airport six months after the war emergency ended, Camp Billy Mitchell did not close until April 1, 1946, when the last prisoners pulled out. Then, after two more years of bickering, the federal government finally relinquished control of the facility in February 1948.[10] The military had certainly gotten its dollar worth.

RECOLLECTIONS
William Michaelis. Crivitz, WI -
"We kids were fishing in a pond in McGovern Park when a siren went off. Later, we were scared to death when men came out of the bushes with guns in their hands. These were soldiers looking for an escaped prisoner." Bill Michaelis and his friends often saw Army trucks pull up to the stop sign at Silver Spring and Hopkins with ten to fifteen Germans in back on their way to work on farms for the day. The prisoners would wave and holler to the kids in their strange language.[11]

Gerie Peter Sobocinski. Cudahy, WI-
Constantly hearing the song "Rum and Coca Cola" drove Gerie Peter to distraction. As secretary to the post surgeon at the station hospital, she had to listen to medical assistant Sergeant Tiltz daily and repeatedly singing that song while the PW's in the ward hummed along. Most of the patients here were PW's from the base. Some PW's who had been medical students before the war worked as the medical assistants, including assignments in the operating room.[12]

You might think you were in the Louvre or another European art gallery while you walked through Camp Billy Mitchell. Talented prisoners had created beautiful copies of the great paintings of Europe and offered them for sale. F. Herbst, a German PW, painted a Duncan impressionist piece that was purchased by Gerie Peter as the field closed. The 16 by 26 inch painting still hangs on her living room wall and over the years has been identified as the real thing by several guests.[13]

The authorities carefully watched Gerie's neighbor, Millie Molkelke. Millie, a WW I war bride from Germany, and her husband were members of the German *Bund,* a friendship league in the Milwaukee area. Because of her background, Millie, like so many others, had to report regularly to the military. The fact that she lived very near the camp also meant that her phone was tapped, like other German families nearby. The military feared escaping PW's would seek out such German nationals for assistance.[14]

Carolyn Anich. West Allis, WI -

"Across the field from our home in South Milwaukee was a small 'crick' where my girlfriend Marilyn and I would run off to. There we would 'walk the rocks' seeing who would successfully make the most daring crossing after a rainfall without falling in. It was located partly inside the fence of the Badger Malleable Foundry. Well, weren't we surprised one summer day to find many young men sitting on the opposite bank of 'our crick.' They were all dressed alike in pants and loose jacket-type tops that had large PW letters on the back. They didn't look scary to a couple of innocent and naive school girls. We tried talking to them, but we don't think they understood us and we couldn't understand them. They were dirty from foundry work and hot and tired. They could have gotten away the same way we got in, swinging on the gate over the water. We don't know if they ever tried. That summer we would snitch cookies or cupcakes off the window sill from our mothers' kitchens and take them to the men. Only one came forward to accept

PW on a bunk in Billy Mitchell field barracks, 1945. Photo courtesy of Milwaukee Public Library.

our offerings and take them back to the others. They laughed and smiled just like regular people. When old man Hazeldeck's peaches were ripe we would sneak into his orchard and take those in to the men. Likewise with farmer Diehlen's apples."[15]

Harry Hetz, M.D. Kenilworth, IL -
"About once a month four fellow prisoners and I were invited for a meal with the George Tesch family on Sundays. Tesch would pick us up at camp and return us in the evening. The five of us worked for him on his farm the other six days a week. The most memorable of those Sunday trips was the big Christmas party we attended. Our holiday brightened as we enjoyed all the food and merriment in a house so beautifully decorated throughout."[16]

Jerry Zimmerman. West Allis, WI -
"I lived only four blocks from the Wisconsin State Fair Grounds which was a most interesting place for me throughout my childhood days. When I was about 14-years-old, neighborhood friends and I watched German prisoners of war work in the vacant animal barns. Trucked to the fairgrounds from their barracks at Billy Mitchell Field, their tasks were to unload and store large quantities of potatoes, beets and carrots, which were harvested locally and temporarily placed in the cool of the barns. These fresh picked vegetables remained in the barns until the prisoners bagged them for shipping to canning and processing centers. Occasionally, depending on the attitude and judgment of the armed Army guards, we children were allowed to talk with the prisoners without supervision. Even my 11-year-old sister and her close girl friends of that age were permitted to walk to the park by themselves and visit. We found it of great interest that those prisoners looked nothing at all like the terrible men we had learned to picture. To our curiosity and surprise they looked no different than other young men in the neighborhood. But they did have the white PW crudely painted on their clothing and spoke in a very broken, heavily accented English. My focus was so much on the PW's that I have little memory of visiting with any of the guards. I am also surprised that all of our parents had no serious concerns about our accessibility and exposure to these prisoners."[17]

Carol Wilinski Jungbluth. Hartland, WI -
"I was sent to bed just because I watched a movie. We lived on

Conflicting salutes as PW's leave the hangar and head to the barracks at Camp Billy Mitchell, 1945. Photo courtesy of the Milwaukee Public Library.

the south side of Grange Avenue, which was the southern border of Billy Mitchell Field. Almost directly across the street from our house, a gate in the chain link fence opened into the camp. We could see the barracks and movement within. I don't recall ever seeing a guard by that gate. One summer day I noticed the gate was open and walked in. As this 9-year-old wandered around, I peeked into one of the buildings and found a movie being shown. It seemed I was not unwelcome, and as the room was not too crowded, I stayed to watch. When my mother found out where I was, she was very angry. From hindsight I can understand why. I never again wandered through that gate until after the PW's left."[18]

Carl L Mueller Jr. Milwaukee, WI -
"I stopped in the bar directly across the main Gate on Howell Avenue several times during my short recuperation period. Each time I recognized some 'privileged' Germans (PW's) who would come in for a beer. I was sure I had seen a few of these customers in the common mess hall. As a B-17 pilot returning from Eye, England, I had some R & R (rest and recuperation time) before heading to Drew Field in Tampa, Florida, so I went to Milwaukee to see my mother. Swimming with friends at the Bay View Beach, I

stepped on a broken bottle and seriously cut my foot. I ended up in the hospital at the PW camp in Billy Mitchell Field. Walking on crutches, I recuperated there for about a week. I ate in the same mess hall as the PW's and watched in amazement as they each devoured a half or whole loaf of bread with their meals. On several evenings, including VJ (Victory over Japan) night, I hobbled over to that tavern. Each time I noticed those same few familiar faces. Those PW's sure had it made, as I'm certain they never had it so good in the German army."[19]

Richard R. Figlesthaler. Greendale, WI -
"My brother returned from the South Pacific with recurring malaria. While on furlough he had a serious bout with it and was sent to the hospital at Billy Mitchell Field. His girlfriend and I went to visit him there. She was quite the looker and as we walked through the compound, many German prisoners made lewd gestures and comments to us. My brother's fiancee went up to the wire and spit in the face of one of the German prisoners."[20]

Mel Leonard. River Hills, WI -
"One hunt I will always remember came in the fall of 1945. Not

PW's pose in the Camp Billy Mitchell kitchen, 1945. Photo courtesy of Milwaukee Public Library.

quite old enough for military service, I took my hunting dog 'Fritz' to the Hamm farm, just into Ozaukee County. There, perhaps as many as 160 acres were in cabbage. But also on the property was a large marsh with many pheasants. On opening day of hunting season, the marsh seemed surrounded by hunters and shotguns. When the action started, my dog took off, so I called him back yelling, 'Here Fritz! Come here Fritz! Get over here Fritz!' It was then I noticed several heads popping up out of the field nearby. They had cabbage knives in their hands and PW stenciled on the back of their shirts. What a sight! The final humiliation of the day came just before we headed home, Fritz managed to get too close and personal with a skunk."[21]

Gene Haas. Milwaukee, WI -
"Immigrating from Germany to Spring Green in the 1920's, my father, Joseph Haas, moved to Milwaukee to work in a defense plant during the war. He received word that a first cousin, Louis Windmeiser, had been captured and imprisoned at Mitchell Field. Over the several months of Louis' stay in Milwaukee, Dad received permission to visit him. Occasionally I went along, and sometimes Louis' brother, Herman, from Spring Green would come with us. We would meet Louis in the social center where the PW's would be playing cards, listening to the radio, and/or reading. Dad often took packages that might include cigarettes, cookies, candy or fruit to his cousin. It was always a pleasant visit."[22]

David Reimers. Brookfield, WI -
Here they come again!! What excitement for a small boy! Military Jeeps with mounted machine guns racing across the open field headed to the little woods. We lived at the end of a long dead end road out near the woods not far from the U.S. Disciplinary Barracks and Hospital. Escapees from the disciplinary station always headed for the woods since it was the only cover around. And, of course, that is where the MP's would recapture them. My father occasionally wandered over to that compound to visit through the fence with German speaking prisoners."[23]

Robert. T. Heldt. Chicago, IL -
By the early months of 1946, the war was long over and discipline was quite relaxed at Camp Billy Mitchell Field — a little like a reversed "Hogans Heroes," according to guard R. T. Heldt.

"At that time we had only about 30 or so guards for about 2,300 prisoners. Attempting roll call every morning and evening, we never seemed to get the same count. Occasionally, after morning roll call someone would bring in a drunken PW we had missed. We had no machine guns there, just M-1's. Although we ate in the same mess hall, we ate separately and had different menus. About all the PW's were getting by this time was organ meat — boxes and boxes of frozen livers were trucked in. When the camp finally closed at Billy Mitchell Field, the military did it in style. A military band was imported from Fort Sheridan and the PW's were given a ceremonial send-off back to their native lands."[24]

Gerie Peter Sobocinski. Cudahy, WI -

The PW story does not end when the camps are closed in Wisconsin. In 1947, on one of Gerie Peter's first dates with Harvey Sobocinski, he took her dancing at the Tic Toc Club. In the middle of a set, Harvey asked her to sit down at their table and wait for him. He left, and she waited and waited and waited — for almost two hours. She had first come in contact with him while he was the Statistical Control Officer of Billy Mitchell Field over two years earlier. He had returned from duty with the Flying Tigers in China and worked at the camp headquarters. Later, he returned to China and eventually was involved in assisting the escape of Chiang Kai-shek to Formosa. That evening, when he finally returned to her table, he explained he was still undercover with Special Forces. While he was dancing with her, he and an escaped Nazi recognized each other. Harvey had gone to a phone, called for back up and then followed the Nazi into the honeycomb sewer of Milwaukee where the escapee was eventually captured."[25]

Donald Meyer. Oak Creek, WI -

Torn down board by board, transported to Oak Creek and reassembled, one Mitchell Field PW barracks is now the Ole Schlaeger-Dallmann American Legion Post #434. Two others are similarly used by Greendale and Bay View VFW posts as clubhouses.[26]

John Flynn. Glendale, WI -

"In 1963 we were sitting in the Nantes, France, train depot drinking coffee with friends and wondering what that man outside was doing pacing up and down. Someone said he was the local gendarme. When he came in, he heard us speaking English and approached our table asking where we were from. Our friends replied they were from Illinois. When I said we were from Milwaukee, he really got excited. He tore off his jacket, then shirt and showed us his tattoo, the name Milwaukee. He said that as a PW he had worked in the state fair race track stables and could still list just about every tavern along Greenfield Avenue."[27]

Camp Cambria 1944 & 1945

Preparations for the swell of prisoners and Jamaican migrant workers started a couple of weeks before their June 10, 1944, arrival. Camp Cambria was located on the W. H. Manthey property west of the Cambria village limits. Army personnel first arrived, charged with erecting buildings and making arrangements for sanitation. In fact, they erected only tents to house the PW's, their guards, a mess hall and kitchen. To supplement the field stove and oven, a PW later built another oven out of bricks. Heated with a fire in the oven and then cleared of the fire and ash, this oven worked as a retained-heat oven. Using its boiler to heat the water, a converted old steam tractor provided hot water for kitchen and bath purposes.[1] Approximately 675 Germans and 358 Jamaicans moved into the county during that canning season.[2] Of that number, the 197 Germans housed in Cambria worked in Pardeeville and Friesland, as well as the two Cambria canning factories.[3] This unique labor force filled shortages during both the pea and corn packs. The camp remained activated until mid-September when the PW's were shipped to Fox Lake, then on to logging camps in Michigan for the winter.[4]

During that first season, *The Cambria News* circulated a request asking the local population to support the young American soldiers guarding the camp. Specifically, laundry services were being sought by the MP's. The article also encouraged additional friendly gestures to provide some social activities for the guards.[5] Later in the month the paper included a harshly stated warning from the camp against any fraternizing with the enemy. The editorial reminded readers that these prisoners were, until very recently, carrying out the will of the Fuhrer and were the same sort of men killing our boys in Normandy and butchering civilians in Norway, Greece, France and Poland. It also suggested that here is "no indication that any great numbers of these prisoners have experienced any change of heart since their capture . . . they are still true to Hitler." The editorial ended with this plea: "There is one, and only

Camp Cambria, July 1944. Photo courtesy of Mona Ferris.

one, proper attitude of civilian men, women and especially girls toward the prisoner of war. That is to ignore him."[6]

Before the 1945 arrival of 335 German PW's, the military issued similar calls for local citizens to again extend hospitality to the forty-five guards and two officers. A second statement warned that no fraternization would be tolerated. This year the German prisoners would be assigned as follows: "175, Cambria Canning Company; 90, Richland Canning Co., Friesland; 30, Pardeeville; 40, Columbia Canning Company; 27, camp maintenance."[7]

By mid-August, a total of 53,204 man-hours of work had been performed by the Camp Cambria prisoners of war on four PW work contracts. Their labor brought in revenues of $28,483 to the U.S. Treasury according to Brigadier General John T. Pierce, command-ing general of Fort Sheridan. He had released the work summary in August, 1945.[8] These prisoners continued their efforts until pulling out in September. By the time they departed, their earnings had nearly doubled, confirming their importance to the local industry. When Fort Sheridan released the later figures, the PW earnings paid by private companies to the military in 1945 from Cambria had increased to $41,439.[9]

RECOLLECTIONS
Thomas Williams. Cambria, WI-
Sixteen year old Tom Williams and many of his co-workers re-sented the fact that the PW's working with them in the Columbia

Canning Factory worked only eight hour shifts and got a ten minute break each hour. The civilian workers got no such breaks and
worked much longer hours. Attempting to quiet the discontent
among civilian employees, one of the company board members
who spoke German tried to convince the PW's to forgo their breaks.
After that "discussion," the PW's and their guards marched back
to camp. The prior agreement between the company and military
prevailed, preserving the regular breaks for the prisoners. A less
irritating memory Tom had of the PW's involved the weekly afternoon parade. Each Sunday the prisoners marched down the middle
of the road from camp to Lake Tarrant for a swim. The prisoners
swam on the opposite side of the lake from the community swimming hole. The whole community could hear them singing on their
way to and from the lake.[10]

Margaret Williams. Cambria, WI -
At Cambria, company officials feared the Germans might attempt
to poison the food or sabotage the equipment, so they refused to
allow PW's to work around open food. Instead, they employed the
PW's at labeling, boxing and loading assignments.[11]

Mona Lloyd Ferris. Lannsdowne, PA -
Those military requests for local residents to extend hospitality to the MP's ultimately resulted in wedding bells. The Hughes
family, owners of the *Cambria News*, invited one of the guards to
dinner after church services. Daughter, Dorothy Hughes thought
her best friend, Mona Lloyd, should meet this nice young man
who weekly came to dinner. During a later visit by the guard to
the Hughes home, Mona did drop by. Sparks must have flown immediately as Pfc. James Ferris jumped up and introduced himself
to Mona as "Jimmy" Ferris. After the Cambria season, Ferris accompanied these prisoners to Michigan for the apple and cherry
harvest and later to Alabama to pick cotton. But correspondence
with Mona flourished. The following year Ferris was sent off to
Germany but not before putting an engagement ring on Mona's
hand. Mona's mother cooked for the PW's at the Cambria Canning
Factory and her brother worked with them in the warehouse for
a month in 1944. All three remembered the PW's singing as they
marched between the camp on the other side of town and this
canning factory.[12]

Camp Chilton
1945

Desperate for workers, the area food processors undertook a search for employees. John Hume, manager of the U.S. Employment Office, helped organize a canvassing of local civic groups and clubs. Lakeside Canning Company alone needed sixty full time workers. But on May 19, 1945, the *Manitowoc Herald Times* reported no responses from that areawide survey. The use of PW's seemed the only solution to the labor shortage. Because of local objections to camping prisoners at the Manitowoc Fair Grounds, the military decided to house the 500 to 600 prisoners at Chilton instead. These PW's would assist the pea pack in Calumet, Manitowoc and Brown counties. In June 1945, 300 prisoners arrived from Camp McCoy and billeted at the Chilton fair grounds, under the supervision of commander Captain David Fine. The local press expressed the reluctance of the community to have the prisoners in their midst and emphasized that the use of prisoners was a last resort measure to prevent the produce from literally rotting in the fields.[1] In just one month, these prisoners proved their worth, putting in 43,721 hours of labor, saving the crops and earning for the U.S. Treasury $23, 242.[2] These PW's had been employed by the following canneries: Valders (20), St. Nazianz, (10), Hilbert (20), Chilton Canning Company (40), Dundas (60), A. T. Hipke at New Holstein (40), Calumet Dutch Packing Company at Brillion (50), and Lakeside Packing Company at Manitowoc (55).[3]

Partially to offset the expressed local concern, the military invited area newsmen to visit the camp in July 1945. The press found in addition to the reported PW's, the camp also housed two officers, thirty five enlisted men and two medics. Inside, the visitors found what was commonly reported in PW camps around the state: Most PW's slept on cots in the permanent buildings of the fair grounds, while the overflow slept in a few tents, prisoners maintained their own camp including the cleaning, laundry and cooking of their own meals as well as those of the guards, they wore discarded military clothing and had opportunity to spend their eighty cents per day pay in a small canteen. On Sundays some PW's played soccer inside the race track while others busied themselves with woodcarving or other handicrafts. The *Chilton Times -Journal* reporter noticed two large cook stoves outside the kitchen building. Too large to go through the doorway, they were temporarily covered with canvas until the planned wooden roof could be erected. The fair office building had been converted to shower and laundry facilities at the expense of the canning factories. The "Cattle Barn" sign still hung above the doorway to what now served as a PW dormitory. Upon inquiring, the reporter learned that the religious opportunities provided within the camp included Lutheran services held each Thursday and Catholic services held each Wednesday.[4] Although on the same tour, a *Manitowoc Herald Times* reporter saw things a little differently. In the August 2, 1945 edition of that newspaper the reporter suggested that Camp Chilton was a little more structured than many others. He noted that Chilton commander Fine required his prisoners to wear the regulation GI two-inch haircut. His article also mentioned the individual search of the prisoners as they returned to the camp from their cannery work detail. Apparently, such a search was designed to prevent PW's from bringing any restricted articles into the camp. Both reporters agreed that the prisoners were not coddled by the Army or their employers.[5]

In a later press interview, Captain Dettmar, the spokesman for the 6th Service Command, noted that all the tough and troublesome Nazis had been screened out of the prison camp at Fort Sheridan and sent to a special camp. Camp Chilton housed only prisoners who had no criminal records and who were willing to work. Nonetheless, the only people allowed to talk to the PW's included those that needed to speak to them regarding work performance. Dettmar warned against other attempts to talk to prisoners, mail letters or do any other favors for them or to give them food. And he warned, "We don't want any young girls hanging around the place where they are housed."[6] As a precaution against such fraternization, a snow fence surrounded the compound. It had been installed as much to keep the curious out as to keep the prisoners in.

A potentially fatal accident occurred in the Manitowoc Lakeside Packing Company on Sixth and Jay Streets. Prisoner Eber Werner received a fractured skull when he fell twenty-five feet from a stack of cases onto the cement floor. Taken by ambulance to Holy Family Hospital, this very lucky prisoner recovered quickly.[7]

Mixed feelings about this influx of prisoners abounded in the area. The Manitowoc paper continued to allude to the local lack of enthusiasm for having prisoners, even as it also reported the request to keep them. County Agent Carl Neitzke filed the county's request for permission to keep 100 prisoners for the late harvest.[8] But, since the County Fair would be held at the fair grounds, the issue of where to house any remaining PW's became a big unsolved problem. As the 1945 pea pack slowed down, the PW's gradually transferred to the cherry orchards at Sturgeon Bay and other canning facilities near Appleton and Sheboygan for the bean, beet and corn harvests. During the five and one half weeks at Chilton, the PW's packed more than a half million cases of vegetables. Their stay also contributed to the Fair Association improvements valued around $2,500. The camp closed August 10, 1945.[9]

RECOLLECTIONS

Donald E. Bonk. Appleton, WI -

Donald E. Bonk was a teen working for his father/manager of the Chilton Canning Company during the war. He remembered picking up PW's and guards at the fairgrounds and driving them by bus to the cannery. As he recalled, there was one guard for every 10 PW's early in the season, but by the "end of the summer, two guards with trained dogs controlled up to 250 prisoners." As elsewhere, he recalled local gals flirting with the guards and the prisoners through the fence. Many area people also stopped by to visit, seeking information about family still in Germany. Bonk believed the most trouble the community had was with the guards on payday when they stopped at the local taverns. His father considered the prisoners good workers and some were good mechanics, too, fixing the machinery in the cannery.[10]

Richard Hipke. Manitowoc, WI -

"Guards were walking around our plant with submachine guns," according to Dick Hipke, an owner of the A. T. Hipke & Sons Canning Factory in New Holstein. The prisoners were fed well the first year, but their rations were cut back the second season. As a result, empty cans were often found hidden in the factory, left by prisoners who had opened them and consumed the veggies from the cans. Hipke also believed a couple of American girls working in the plant fell in love with German prisoners and continued correspondence with them after repatriation. But he knew of no resulting marriages.[11]

Ronald Tordeur. Green Bay, WI -

As a young boy, Ronald was "sacred to death" of the "Nazi"

I don't care about millions ... five
cents would do it

"Ich brauche keine Millionen ...
mir genuegen 5 cents zur Milch"

Illustration of a PW needing more scrip by PW W. Hoernchen, 1946. Photo courtesy of Willi Rau with permission of U.S. Army, Fort McCoy.

prisoners that came by truck each morning to harvest beets on the family farms. One day, while watching his father and uncle repairing a Caterpillar tractor, his Aunt Liz came running over. She said the prisoners had quit working. The guard told her they wouldn't work because the coffee was cold, "No hot coffee - no work!" Ron remembered Aunt Liz in the pickup going over a little bridge out to the field headed toward those prisoners with fresh HOT coffee in a milk can.[12]

Elroy Kandler. Lake Fire, WI -
Another youngster was frightened by the shotgun toting guard. Elroy Kandler would walk with his grandmother, Margaret Meyer, down the gravel road to the field where the PW's worked. Hired by the cannery, she would take sandwiches and apples to them for lunch. With the water jug nearby, the civilian guard sat on the stone wall overseeing the work. Kandler remembers, "When one prisoner handed me an apple, saying in broken English; 'Boy, take apple,' the guard got mad and rushed over, making me return the apple."[13]

Genie Williams. Green Bay, WI -
"Our neighbor, Leo Reel, was in charge of the Stokely Pickle and Kraut factory in Duck Creek at the time. When large groups of prisoners were being transported, perhaps from one camp to another, he would ride in a vehicle behind the buses. Concerned

about possible trouble, he generally asked my father to ride shotgun. All Dad ever took for a weapon was his .45-caliber pistol without the clip. No one really expected trouble and what could one or two men do anyway?"[14]

Mary Hipke Frisch. New Holstein, WI -

The prisoners often sang as they worked. They missed going to the opera on Saturday night. At least, that is what they told Mary Hipke Frisch when she worked in the Hipke Canning Factory warehouse with them. The girls made boxes, cutting the cardboard and gluing it to shape. As a result, they had knives or "toad stabbers" as they called them, but the prisoners heard "tote" stabber, meaning dead in German. As a result, the PW's were a little cautious around these young ladies.[15]

Laverne Hutterer. Manitowoc, WI -

"Germans or no Germans, we children continued to go to the vinery and beg our supply of fresh peas for snacking. We had no fear of the prisoners there, as they willingly handed over vines of peas to us."[16]

Mary Ann Gruber Ignera. Manitowoc, WI -

"My mother, Clara Burg Gruber, was born on the Mosel River in Germany and emigrated as a young woman, living with her older brother and family until she married. She always kept close contact with her relatives back in Germany. When the war started, her nephew, Heinze Burg, was captured in North Africa and imprisoned in England for a while before being shipped first to Alabama and then Mississippi. Another nephew was also drafted, captured and spent the rest of the war in a PW camp in Texas. Mother continued correspondence with these two nephews throughout the war. When prisoners arrived in the Chilton area and started to work in the pea vinery at Rockwood, she decided to become involved with them. She helped organize the ladies of this tiny community, who then took turns cooking a soup or stew and carting it off to the vinery to supplement the sack lunches provided the PW's at noon. Mother hoped her nephews were being treated with equal kindness."[17]

Camp Cobb
1945

Where is Cobb? For readers unfamiliar with this tiny community in the southwestern section of our state, Cobb is located four miles due west of Dodgeville. Or, as the crow flies, it is about fifteen miles due north of Belmont, our first state capital. Cobb is just a blink along Highway 18 today, not much larger than when the PW's came to town. Because the small community could not support a local newspaper or radio station, information about Camp Cobb is almost nonexistent.

During the war Cobb Canning Company was the largest business in the community. In cooperation with its neighboring Lancaster Canning Company and Mineral Point Cooperative Packers Company, the Cobb cannery contracted with the government for the use of PW labor. This group of canners requested 210 PW's to fill their labor shortages in the fields, at viner stations and in the canning factories.[1]

The number of prisoners that arrived never filled the canners' request. After opening on June 23, 1945, only 75 to 176 PW's ever stayed at one time in the barracks at the rear of the Cobb Canning Company. But even with their limited numbers, by September 1, these men had already put in a total of 29,881 man hours of labor. That work earned $35,376, much more than the cost of their keep for the U.S. government.[2] With ninety-three to ninety-eight PW's remaining at Cobb, their work continued through September as the prisoners put in an additional 8,354 hours of work at the Cobb Canning Co., 2,701 hours at the Mineral Point Cooperative and 1,563 hours at the Lancaster Canning Co.[3] With no other man power available, these prisoners saved much of the crop in the region and allowed the local canners to profit.

RECOLLECTIONS
Elsie Masters. Dodgeville, WI -
" 'Follow Your Heart' was Mom's motto when she let the PW's save their sack lunch for an afternoon snack and invited them into

our dining room for a big, home-cooked, noon meal. She had two sons-in-law in the service at the time, and this was her assurance that if they or her own sons were ever prisoners of war in an unfamiliar land someone might return the kindness." It was daughter Elsie's job to wait on the table. Elsie Masters remembered one young prisoner in particular— with his curly blond hair and blue eyes, she thought he was especially handsome. That PW confided in her brother that the feeling was mutual. "I don't think the ice water had ever flowed as freely, and in spite of my brother's teasing, I made trip after trip around the table, pouring and serving, serving and pouring." Working along with her father and four brothers, the four or five prisoners quickly became comfortable with each other, taking off their shirts in the heat of the day, guzzling cool water from the common earthen jug, cooling their bared feet in the mud puddles and learning to enjoy eating fresh peas. The prisoners ate all they could and then carried clumps of vines back to the barracks for an evening snack. Elsie also had special memories of camaraderie developed between the prisoners and her brothers, exemplified on the day it poured so hard. Since the men were in a secluded field, they all took their clothes off to load the last two trucks. Grateful for the willingness of the PW's to work in the downpour with his sons, Elsie's fathers knew these peas would have otherwise been lost.[4]

Thomas Everett. Cobb, WI -
"We had just bought a new wagon and needed to drill holes to adjust for the wheel spacing. One of the hired PW's corrected

"artists" at work

"Kunstmaler" am Werk

Illustration of PW painting "PW" on a comrade's pants seat, drawn by an unidentified PW, 1946. Photo courtesy of Willie Rau with permission of the U.S. Army, Fort McCoy.

our efforts at drilling, telling us we should drill a small hole first, then the larger hole. His suggestion worked much better than our original attempt. The prisoners all seem to be very exact in their work. Born in Germany, my grandfather readily talked with all the prisoners that came to shock grain and paint the barn."[5]

June Billings Nagel. Cobb, WI -

"One PW was riding on the wagon I pulled as I drove my stepfather's tractor out to where the crew would be pitching peas. This attractive blond young man said something to me in German, so I said, 'I can't understand you.' He quickly responded in English, 'If I say I like you, do you understand me?' I was 15 at the time and got so flustered, I took off on that tractor until we got out to where the work began."[6]

Name Withheld. Cobb, WI -

One PW was a barber in civilian life, so in camp he cut hair, including that of the guards. When the local barber found out, he complained to the camp commander because he thought he was losing many potential customers. The camp commander intervened and the guards were no longer given the free haircuts. Fuming and vengeful at having to pay for their haircuts, the guards drove to the next town to get their hair cut, leaving the local barber without his expected additional clients.[7]

Norman Nagel. Cobb, WI -

Also blamed on the barber's complaint was the loss of PW labor to finish the digging of a new septic system on Harold Nagel's place. He had hired a couple of prisoners and they had gotten a good start. But, for no apparent reason, the order came that PW's were no longer to be used for anything but food production.[8]

Evelyn Mueller. Cobb, WI -

During lunch break, tomatoes were secretly pushed into the toes of the high rubber boots worn while filing the silo. This was one of several "tricks" played on each other as prisoners worked on the John Mueller farm. The PW's quickly joined family members participating in these jokes. Mueller became well acquainted with one special prisoner who had taught himself English. After the war they kept in touch through letters. In the 1970's, the families exchanged visits and still maintain correspondence today. In the first letter from the repatriated Erich Verhoeven, dated December 21, 1948, he told of his long journey home. From Cobb, in October 1945, his group of PW's went to Arizona to pick cotton until February of 1946. In March, they landed in Belgium and were on severely limited rations for eight weeks until shipped to England. For the next fifteen months Erich and comrades worked outside Bristol in the woods and on farms. In August of 1947 he was off to Scotland, where he worked on farms there until February of 1948 when he was finally released and sent home to Viersen-Dulken, Germany.[9]

Cal Lambert. Lancaster, WI -
Only 14 at the time, Cal had contact with the PW's. Cal recalled for two to three days a week, two big olive-drab Army trucks would rumble in, raising a cloud of dust. Out of each truck would jump twenty to thirty PW's ready to work in the fields, bundling and stacking the cured hemp. It was backbreaking work, but they seemed to enjoy it. "Sometimes they'd holler to one another and laugh, other times they sang. Only one American Army sergeant guarded the two truckloads of prisoners. One evening as I walked through the field to get the cows for milking, I was looking down trying not to step on the sharp hemp stubble. Suddenly I found myself face-to face with one of the prisoners! He said something to me, but I didn't understand his language. 'What?' I said. Again he tried to speak. Finally, the MP came over and smiled. He questioned the PW in German then turned to me and said 'Hans wants to know why you aren't in the Army?' 'I'm only 14!' I blurted. Did he think I was a coward? 'Hans is 15,' the sergeant said. 'He was wounded and captured when he was your age.' Ever since Pearl Harbor I had dreamed of getting into the fighting. After that conversation, war never seemed like so much fun."[10]

Camp Columbus
1944 & 1945

Almost a week passed before the *Columbus Journal-Republican* finally reported the arrival of 370[1] German PW's set up in a camp on the Columbus Foods Corporation grounds.[2] At Columbus, the 48' x 320' sheep sheds had been remodeled with the addition of a concrete floor, installations for cooking, shower and toilet facilities. The prisoners erected tents for sleeping. These prisoners joined Jamaican migrants working in the Columbus Foods Corporation canneries in Columbus, Fall River, Cambria, and Stokely Bros. at Astico. While the Jamaicans stayed at the canning factories at which they worked, the military bused the PW's to and from the canning factories daily, returning them to the camp each night.

The community had barely learned about the arrival of the prisoners when an escape occurred. The news quickly spread. Thoughts of two Nazi soldiers loose in their area terrified the residents. After only eight days at Columbus, PW's Otto Gorschluter, 19, and Wilhelm Ermeling, 30, escaped from a warehouse at the Columbus plant. Camp officials didn't miss them until check-in time shortly after midnight. The following day a local posse of men in eight cars toured the area within a five mile radius of town. Joining Sheriff Arnold of Dane County and Deputy Sheriff Bill Orth of Columbia County, the posse covered the highways, notified farmers and gave descriptions of the escapees. The local radio also broadcast a warning and descriptions. Then, even before the FBI could arrive, Gorschluter approached a resident in Rio, identified himself and asked that the camp be notified so he could be returned. Village Marshall Thomas Smith quickly accepted the surrender and took him into custody. Not long after Gorschluter's arrest, his comrade was apprehended. Ermeling stopped at a farm house asking for a drink of water. The farmer recognized the description of the prisoner and gave Marshall Smith another call. Again Smith took the second escapee into custody as he walked out of the farm yard. Transported to Columbus, the fugitives spent the night in the city hall jail. The following day Smith turned the two over to the FBI and military authorities who interrogated them and then sent them to Camp Grant.[3] No additional incidents of attempted escapes from Camp Columbus occurred that year.

Warily, the community accepted an even larger contingent of German PW's the following year. The military allayed any fears of the civilians, reminding them the war in Europe was over. Since the PW's were expecting to be returned to Germany soon, they presented their best behavior. Furthermore, the military had warned prisoners that additional disruptions would delay their return to Germany. Furnished with this information, anxieties eased as any trouble would be highly improbable this year. In June of 1945, 550 PW's moved onto the Columbus Foods Corporation Plant property again. Four officers and seventy-five enlisted men supervised this detachment of prisoners. Similar housing and sleeping arrangements were made this second year. The sheep shed remodeled the previous year had been thoroughly cleaned and disinfected in anticipation of the arrival of the prisoners.[4] In 1945, the Fall River Canning Company hired the largest number of prisoners on a daily basis, 175. Others worked at various locations: 150 worked at the Columbus Foods Corporation; 102 at Stokely Goods, Inc., Astico; 61 at Stokely Foods, Inc., South Beaver Dam, and 25 at the local Borden Company.[5]

During the previous year, the area media cooperated with the military, giving minimal coverage of the PW's. But now the war with Germany had ended and on July 18, 1945, the commander invited area press to tour Camp Columbus. The PW's amused Madison and Columbus newspaper reporters by turning their backs to the cameras. Reporters found the camp population had risen to 575 according to figures given them by Commander Capt. M. Steinacher. That meant Camp Columbus ranked as the second largest of the thirty-one branch camps then operating in Wisconsin.[6] The press raised concerns that the prisoners were fed too well. Steinacher responded by explaining the prisoner's diet included carp, pickled herring, fruits and vegetables and other non-rationed food stuffs. Curiosity satisfied, the press and readers seemed content with the arrangements in the camp.

Because the 1945 pea crop was the largest on record and the local labor supply so short, even soldiers from Truax field were recruited to work in the area canneries during their off hours. "Five months ago I was shooting at them Krauts in France and here I'm working with them," cracked one veteran. "And it's good to see all the 'sap' out of the supermen." Both soldiers and prisoners worked within twenty feet of each other in Columbus and other Dane County canning factories.[7] Miraculously, no confrontations between the two opposing armies were ever reported.

The camp temporarily closed after the pea pack as all prisoners headed for the cherry orchards at Sturgeon Bay. Later, 275 PW's returned to detassle, pick and can corn. With the corn pack completed, Camp Columbus closed for good in mid-October. While 170 cheerless PW's headed to Michigan for more work in logging and wood pulp enterprises, the rest joyfully headed to Fort Sheridan, IL on their way home.[8]

Surprisingly, the large number of prisoners held at Camp Columbus only earned $59,420 for the government,[9] but that was the figure reported by the Sixth Service Command at Fort Sheridan in mid-September with only a couple of more weeks of work remaining before the PW's pulled out.

RECOLLECTIONS
Bill Shephard. Columbus, WI -
There were real artists among the prisoners including one who had actually worked painting the mural on the ceiling of the Reims Cathedral. Another interesting PW held in Columbus had been a minister. These two and the other prisoners were fascinated by the cows. In Germany, a farmer who owned two cows was wealthy. Across the road from the Stokley plant lived a farmer with thirty cows. Shepherd, working in the personnel office at the time, remembered the PW's would go outside on their breaks, sit and just watch those cows. The cows amazed them. Shepherd also told of the PW's being hired out to the farmers. On one such job, after the PW's filled the silo for an elderly farmer "the old guy came out at 10:00 p.m. with sandwiches and beer for them all."[10]

Howard Hong. Chicago, IL -
As YMCA liaison officer, Hong inspected the Midwest camps and regularly reported to Fort Sheridan. In his September 4, 1944, report he wrote "Because of the good work record, the camp (Columbus) enjoys local favor which has been expressed in the loan of a piano, one organ, two violins, one guitar, one saxophone, one drum set, and one French horn. An orchestra is now being organized. I was able to fill in the gaps with a banjo and trombone." Hong also re-

ported that classes would begin when sufficient numbers of books arrived. The PW's showed a great interest in the English language textbook, *Sprachlehre*, dictionaries and other books reprinted by the YMCA. Although the camp owned a projector, no money was available to rent movies because of the withholding of camp funds. Hong repeatedly reported the problem with the canteen profits, not being available for general camp use. He wrote that "in a local bank an account of over $900 was accumulating, but Capt. M. Steinacker, the local commanding officer, is not authorized to use these funds. This problem is common in all branches in Michigan and Wisconsin. No supplies for recreation, barbering, etc., have come from the base camp and Columbus would like to use said money for such."[11]

Wilma Black. Columbus, WI -
Wilma Black remembered orders not to feed the PW's working on her father's farm during the July, 1945 pea harvest. But since the prisoners seemed so hungry, she and her mother ignored the rules and fed them. By October, military orders had been reversed, and now the family was told to feed the PW's lunch as they worked in their corn fields.[12]

Thomas Mount. Sun Prairie, WI -
Workers often found swastika designs on the bottom of the boxes of canned goods going out of the Oconomowoc Canning Company at Sun Prairie. PW's working on the box stitch machines sometimes added the Nazi symbols to the boxes. Tom Mount also remembered being fascinated by the acrobatic exercises some of the PW's did as they dangled from the 1/2 inch iron sway bar in the factory. They would perform "skin the cat" and many other tricks. This 1944 bunch of prisoners he worked with surrendered during the North Africa Campaign — tall, blond, husky, very physically fit, and well disciplined. They marched in step to and from the canteen where the factory provided meals to all employees. Captured during or after the Normandy invasion, the PW's who worked there the second year weren't so cocky. Tom couldn't forget the terrible smelling cigarettes the prisoners often smoked, provided, he believed, by the German Red Cross.[13]

Camp Eau Claire at Altoona 1945

The loud outcry of protest from area residents near the planned Camp Eau Claire site forced the military to reconsider establishing a camp there. Originally the army planned a tent city in Eau Claire near Mt. Simon but hastily found another location. Camp Eau Claire was actually located within the city limits of Altoona on Enterprise Street. The prisoners and their guards billeted in some military tents and the 4-H buildings at the Eau Claire County Junior Fairgrounds which border both communities.[1] The advantages of this location quickly became apparent. The camp utilized several buildings and facilities on the premises. The 4-H Fairgrounds opened in 1941 with two new dormitories furnished with bunk beds, a kitchen/concession area, two barns and an open shed. A water faucet located near a cemented area allowed 4-H contestants to wash and primp their livestock before showing. A tent placed over this cattle bathing area converted it to PW showers. The dorms were utilized as they were found.[2] To accommodate a mess for over 175 men, authorities erected another cook tent adjacent to the 4-H kitchen. Camp Eau Claire was quickly activated. The Altoona press did not seem very interested in its new neighbors. The only article published on the PW camp by the *Altoona Tribune*, dated July 12, 1945, reported the special water main laid from the Eau Claire water system to the fairgrounds providing sufficient water for bathing and cooking purposes.[3]

Not so indifferent to the establishment of the camp, many area residents regularly walked or drove by. Under command of Captain Hodges and Lt. J. B. Price, the 143 PW's and 35 supporting GI guards arrived in Army trucks. Most of these prisoners were accustomed to the routine of camp life and work. They had been in the United States for two years following capture in Tunisia early in the war.

Most of the guards had also experienced combat duty overseas. An Eau Claire native returning from action in New Guinea, Sgt. Edward Ludwikoski, happily accepted orders which assigned him to guard duty in his home town.[4] Security at the camp included a wire fence enclosure and two guard towers on opposite corners. In the evening the prisoners accompanied by guards walked across the street to the open field between Fairfax Avenue and Highway 53. There they usually played soccer.[5] Local spectators often parked along the highway to witness this strange sport. Also visible from the road was that open kitchen tent where, under the watchful eye of a mess sergeant, the PW's cooked for themselves and their guards. Though less visible, other camp duties included doing laundry and keeping the camp clean.

A shortage of available labor for the pea harvest became evident early in the season, but both the AFL and CIO protested the suggestion of bringing in prison labor. However, because local manpower was not forthcoming, the labor unions compromised and allowed the military to determine the necessity of importing PW labor. Locally, the military purchased about 43 percent of the pea pack and 44 percent of the corn pack and determined these crops must be harvested and processed.[6] With no alternative labor supply, the military established Camp Eau Claire. From the camp, prisoners were trucked to and from their work shifts at the Lange canning factory on West Madison Street and to farm fields outside the city. During the July pea pack, Fort Sheridan's commander, General John T. Pierce, reported the PW's had put in a total of 16,913 man-hours of work for the Eau Claire Lange Canning Company and earned the U.S. Treasury $8, 805.02.[7] Even with all of this assistance by the PW's, the cannery was unable to harvest over 150 acres of peas because of manpower shortages.[8]

Once the local pea pack was completed, the military moved the prisoners out to other work locations. They left in time for the annual Eau Claire County Junior Fair to be held at its fairgrounds in August as scheduled. Then, in early September under Capt. Richard J. Tierney, seventy-five PW's returned to Camp Eau Claire. These were not the same prisoners stationed here earlier. This second group of PW's had been captured during or after the Normandy invasion. This smaller crew worked in the cannery only until the corn pack concluded at the end of the month.[9]

RECOLLECTIONS
Shirley Hoff. Eau Claire, WI -

Shirley had her eye on the young American guards with whom she often stopped to chat. She collected autographs of eleven of the guards as well as Capt. Jack Hodges. Since she worked at the Hoff Produce, Poultry and Egg Plant across the street from the camp, she saw the prisoners daily. Shirley recalled that a large pig fence but no barbed wire surrounded the camp. The prisoners often walked around in the yard, but she does not remember them smoking or playing ball of any kind.[10]

June Linse Knudtson. Fall Creek, WI -

"As young members of 4-H, my friends and I took special interest when the PW's took over our new fairgrounds. While much of the area was enclosed with a fence, our ball park remained outside the PW area, so we still could play softball there. After a game, we kids commonly wandered over to the fence and visited with the prisoners. While I could understand some German, one PW spoke English well enough to get his point across. He told us he and many with him had been drafted, did not want to fight a war and were happy to be here no longer involved in the fighting. I can still remember how blond all of this group seemed to be. I came from a German background, but we didn't have any blonds in our family."[11]

Lucille Schultz Welter. Eau Claire, WI -

When the arm of a young German prisoner became entangled in the machinery at the Lange canning factory on Oxford Avenue and West Madison Street in Eau Claire, a German speaking female civilian employee acted as interpreter. Mary Schultz talked to the prisoner, calming him and reassuring him until rescuers extricated him from the machinery. This was a rare exception to the strict policy of segregation between civilians and PW's at that plant.[12]

Mary Wagner. Eau Claire, WI -

Mrs. Wagner remembered as a youngster that she and her friends ran to the boulevard to yell and jeer at the PW's riding past her family's Water Street home. Transported in open trucks, these prisoners were probably on their way to Huntsinger's Farms to pick peas or corn.[13]

David Foster. Eau Claire, WI -

How can a man eat his lunch and chew tobacco at the same time? Before going into service himself, Eau Claire's Dave Foster worked in the cannery. There he often observed PW's in the yard unloading produce. He marveled at one German who would eat and chew at the same time, with juice running down his chin.[14]

Lorraine Robillard McFarlane. Eau Claire, WI -

Though publicly unreported, at least one escape from Camp Eau Claire occurred. Lorraine McFarlane repeated her father's version of the incident. While walking his beat as a patrolman, Police Chief Guff (Godfrey) Robillard noticed a man who looked out of place walking down the street. He sought backup before he approached this individual who was found to be a lost German prisoner. Robillard arrested the German and returned him to the PW camp. It is not clear whether this prisoner walked away from the Oxford Street canning plant or from the camp in Altoona.[15]

Rachel Kaeding. Fall Creek, WI -

"When our peas were being shelled I went to the viner to pick some up for canning. I was driving my in-laws' classy, gray and blue De Soto. As I parked the car, the PW's quickly circled me all a buzz (sic). By their smiles and gestures and use of the word '*wagen*,' I knew they were very much in awe of the car. Inside, I felt a little resentment for the good time these PW's seemed to be having. I was concerned about my brothers in the Pacific Theater and Jim Zell, a kid from Fall Creek. The military reported him as captured by the Germans, but his family was unable to communicate with him."[16]

Camp Fond Du Lac 1944

The GI's in New Guinea became very upset when they heard about the PW camp back home in Fond du Lac. Newspaper headlines about PW's enjoying a local tavern and reports of prisoners being well fed really irritated them. Even more devastating news came in letters from friends about the local girls constantly visiting the camp. These reports were incomprehensible to them as they tried to survive the ferocious action in the Pacific. Before the summer ended, the *Fond du Lac Commonwealth Reporter* received and printed an interesting letter from the five hometown boys then stationed in New Guinea. As spokesman, Sgt. Kenneth Blitzke wrote the polite letter asking local citizens to treat these Nazis as "Prisoners of War," not new neighbors. In the letter, Blitzke wrote that reports of local girls going to the camp with candy and treats for the enemy particularly troubled him and his buddies. He also questioned why the PW's were allowed to sing their way down the street to work, noting that if American soldiers home on leave did that they would probably be picked up for disorderly conduct.[1] Perhaps this response from local GI's explains why no camp existed at Fond du Lac the following year.

The German PW's arrived by train in Fond Du Lac and marched along Macy, Court, Main, and Fourth Streets to Fond du Lac Avenue, then on to the fairgrounds. They carried their few personal belongings in little back packs attached to their waists.[2] The prisoners marched in close formation singing a song which sounded similar to "Pack Up Your Troubles," creating a flurry of interest in the community as they opened Camp Fond du Lac. Cooperating with censorship regulations, local news and radio ignored their arrival and employment. The press finally revealed the number of PW's held locally only after their departure. Residents learned that nearly 300 PW's had been housed at the fairgrounds and worked at the canning plants in the area. In August First Lt. Harold V. Smith still held command of the camp and PW's when he marched them back the same route they came, singing their way out of town. The captives seemed to take little notice of the few armed guards marching at their side and rear.

After they left, one local beer distributor lamented a substantial reduction in business. He reported delivering twenty-five cases of beer to the camp shortly after the arrival of the prisoners and making regular deliveries every other day during their stay.[3]

During their stay, the community extended its hospitality to the thirty-nine enlisted men guarding the group. The Association of Commerce provided booklets showing places of interest. Designated as the local USO center, the YMCA opened its facilities for the servicemen for lounging, swimming, boxing and racket sports. The Teen-Kan-Teen hostess, Mrs. H.Gard, also invited the guards to visit the Kan-Teen. Encouraged by local leaders, residents offered transportation for the troops as well.[4]

The community remained tranquil until a news story broke. Readers were startled by this *Fond du Lac Reporter's* July 22, 1944, headline: "WAR PRISONER DISCOVERED IN RURAL TAVERN." The article reported that on the afternoon of July 21, one prisoner did not return with his work crew from a pea viner near Marblehead. When his absence was later noticed back at the camp, authorities broadcast the escape alarm. All guards immediately reported back to camp, and a general alert and search was initiated. Deputy Sheriff Leo Flaherty and an FBI agent took the prisoner into custody as he left the Solanuta Tavern in Marblehead. Sheriff Arnold Sook said that the PW who had been at large no more than an hour or two offered no resistance.[5] But many residents remained concerned.

In mid-August, the military abandoned camp and quietly transferred prisoners elsewhere. Workers dismantled and set aside the temporary improvements for possible future use. As if nothing unusual had been there, local crews prepared the fairgrounds for the annual county fair to open on schedule, September 9.[6]

RECOLLECTIONS
Charles Scheilbach. Fond Du Lac, WI -

The city dump caretaker, Charles Scheilbach, reported a "terrible waste of fuel" when he noticed sizable amounts of partly burned coal mixed with the ashes coming from the prisoner camp. Scheilbach's complaint received prompt action, and the military quickly stopped this fuel waste. Over the season, Mr. Scheilbach had several opportunities to talk to the prisoners as they hauled their refuse to the dump. On one such occasion he asked a prisoner if he would he run away if given the chance? The prisoner replied: "What, run away from this? Why, this is heaven. The war is over for us and we are getting much better treatment than we ever would get over there."[7]

Edward Ucker. Waupun, WI -
The possibility of sexual encounters between local young girls and the prisoners always concerned the military. Keeping the girls out of the camps was a primary function of the camp fences. Guard Ed Ucker remembered seeing girls lined up at the Camp Fond du Lac fence, occasionally one with her back to the fence and skirt up in the air. Stopping clandestine meetings within the canning factories proved even more difficult to monitor. Ucker also recalled that the boxcars at the Rosendale canning factory offered some privacy during scheduled breaks. At least one young woman reportedly got pregnant in a boxcar.[8]

Lloyd Hatch. Rosendale, WI -
"*Harsh Neiden*" (short hair cut) became an effective threat Rosendale Canning Factory foreman James R. Hatch used when PW's working in his plant got surly. Occasionally, they intentionally mixed up the grades of peas. This would ultimately cause very unhappy customers when they opened a can of "tender young peas"

if you take a side-step, you've got to pay the "Price"

Wer Seitenspruenge macht, zahlt oft einen hohen PRICE

Illustration of PW haircuts by PW W. Hoernchen, 1946. Photo courtesy of Willi Rau with permission of U.S. Army, Fort McCoy.

and found old peas hard as bullets. Lloyd Hatch recalled his father saying that if he reported such problems to camp authorities, the PW's head would be shaved. The threat of this punishment usually kept the prisoners working appropriately.[9]

James Magellas. Satellite Beach, FL -
Not only in the Pacific but also in the European Theater, local boys became upset with what they read in their local papers. Lt. James Megellas, a paratrooper who jumped in Holland, had been under constant fire for some time. Finally, during a break in the action he read his latest home town papers. From them he learned of Camp Fond du Lac and how well the prisoners were being treated. He shared the article with his foxhole mate, Lt. Murphy, who became equally incensed at the reports of good food provided to the prisoners and local girls hanging on the fence flirting with the prisoners. Such images demoralized both men. The pictures forming in Megellas' mind so haunted him that he wrote a letter to the *Fond du Lac Commonwealth Reporter* editor expressing his dismay about how demoralizing such reports were to the troops on the front line. American troops were being slaughtered by the German troops "cut from the same cloth" as the PW's. Jim never received a response to his letter and thereafter never received another complementary paper. Back home, his sisters watched for but never saw his letter to the editor in print.[10]

Donald Marschall. Rosendale, WI -
"Had any of them ever seen Adolf Hitler? That was the big question, the one I should have asked my father to ask the prisoners when he stopped to visit with them at the fairgrounds. My friends and I were all fascinated with Hitler, Tojo and Mussolini, our great enemies. We kids saw the PW's at the Rosendale factory and sometimes went over to the fence and offered them a piece of candy. Although they didn't speak English and we didn't know German, their smiles said they appreciated our gestures of goodwill."[11]

Camp Fox Lake
1944 &1945

Major General Aurand, the Sixth Service Command's ranking officer, selected Fox Lake as one of very few PW
Camps to be personally inspected. Accompanied by other
top military brass, his special visit to Camp Fox Lake occurred on
August 24, 1944. During that visit he also toured the Central Wisconsin Canneries plant in town.[1] After his stopover, he expressed
satisfaction with both sites. Recording his visit, the area newspaper
finally made its first reference to the camp. The article took many
readers in the neighborhood by surprise as they learned of these
special neighbors. While the paper never listed the numbers of
PW's held there, Fort Sheridan records the military deployed 284
PW's to Fox Lake in 1944.[2] With Lieutenant Krajewski as commanding officer, the GI's occupied a dance hall, the basement of which
became the kitchen and mess hall. Large tents behind the building
housed the prisoners. Perhaps this was the "Community Building"
mentioned in the press the following year.

After his visit, YMCA inspector Howard Hong reported almost
nothing to fill the leisure time of the PW's. He noted only one basketball and one volleyball available to these men who preferred
to play soccer and fist ball. Despite the lack of leisure activities
available at Fox Lake, the morale seemed acceptable to Hong. His
report also mentioned that while two Protestant services and
one Catholic mass were offered each Sunday, the attendance was
always low. The shift systems used in Fox Lake staggered the one
day off throughout the week and resulted in most PW's assigned
to work on Sunday.[3]

On July 1, of the following year, 535 German prisoners arrived
in Fox Lake by way of the Milwaukee Road. While some were distributed to nearby camps 350 remained in Fox Lake.[4] A snow fence
enclosed the camp that was built around the Community Building
Park. With the building as headquarters, the PW's again slept in

tents on the grounds. The prisoners ranged in age from fifteen to sixty-five and, as elsewhere, seemed glad to be there.

Brigadier General John T. Pierce, Commanding General of Fort Sheridan, released a work summary in August, 1945. During July alone two Fox Lake work projects produced $21,166.18 for the U.S. Treasury. That represented PW pay for 40,423 man-hours of work during the month.[5] By the end of the season, Fox Lake earnings had risen to $41,255, according to a second press release.[6]

Negotiations for repatriation continued with the new German government for several months, but the war with Germany had ended in May 1945. As a result, the local command relaxed fraternization rules. The friendly interaction between the PW's and local citizenry at the camp, in the canneries and on the farms resulted in quite a farewell scene. A large crowd of local people congregated at the train station as the PW's marched to the depot on their way home at the end of this season. It became a strangely sad farewell for old enemies. Camp Fox Lake had been not only monetarily profitable, but a huge success in human relations as well.

RECOLLECTIONS
Erwin Scheinast. Heidenheim, Germany -

Josef Scheinast and his fellow prisoners played several jokes on their captors at Fox Lake. One incident involved cutting the heads off their rations of matches, collecting them for months in a discarded metal ammunition box. Once they had the box full, their fun began. In the dark, a couple of the PW's crawled out to a nearby hill with the ammo box. There, they lit a home made fuse then ran back to watch the big bang. The ammunition box detonated with a loud explosion and lots of smoke! The startled American guards sounded the alarm assuming an attack of some kind, and quickly opened fire on the burning box. When the GI's cleared the area, they found the PW's doubled up with laughter. The consequence of this fun was one week of half rations and no more matches. However, the PW's kept their cigarettes burning by using the glass on their flashlights to focus the sun rays on paper. Perhaps the guards wondered why the PW's smoked only on sunny days. The second joke on the guards took place as the prisoners felled trees. Somebody shouted to warn his companions of a falling tree. After it crashed down, the crew started cutting the branches off the trunk with their axes. They found a big skunk that had been killed by the fallen tree. So they buried the skunk and put a provisional cross on the grave. As the guards came around, the PW's circled the grave, took their hats off, folded their hands and looked to the ground as one of them read from a pocket Bible. The approaching guards saw the scene and assumed one of the PW's had been killed. They hurriedly started to dig the victim out of the grave. As the GI's pulled the skunk out of the grave, the PW's again burst out in a peal of laughter and got another week of reduced rations. On another day, however, the joke was on the prisoners themselves. The Germans liked to wear their hair longer than the GI's and needed something to style it with. There was no hair tonic or gel at the canteen. One of the older PW's thought the juice of the birch trees standing along the road was often used in many hair lotions. So the PW's set to work, cutting some bark off the trees and collecting the juice. Once they smeared it on their heads they could easily comb and style their hair. But when the pitch dried, their hair looked like a helmet, totally plastered over. The only solution was to shave the whole head. Now Scheinast's work detail itself became the focus of much laughter at the camp.[7]

Robert Frank. Beaver Dam, WI -
Bob Frank, whose family lived just east of the camp, remembered many evenings when he and his dad strolled across the pasture to the camp. There they joined other neighbors to watch the nightly soccer game. Since his father spoke German, a conversation over the fence with the prisoners often took place. On Sunday afternoons, the PW's often marched to the local theater for a special movie showing. Later in the season, Bob and his father joined four PW's on a threshing crew for Uncle Bill and Aunt Julia Frank. At the noon table, a memorable conversation in German took place. When finally translated, Bob became stunningly aware of his own advantages. For one of the prisoners, this had been his first meal in a private home in twelve long years. At age ten he had joined the Hitler Youth and went off to camp. From there the youngster entered the army.[8]

Virginia Steinhorst Phelps. Fox Lake, WI -
Of German heritage, Delmar Steinhorst spoke the language fluently. As a result, the three PW's hired to help with his grain harvest and shocking had a pleasant, friendly environment. The PW's welcomed their noon meal eaten at the table with the family. A friendship with Heinz Bieback evolved and continued after

the war. Delbert's daughter, Virginia, remembered soap being an important item the Steinhorst family included in several "care" packages sent to the Biebacks. One photo of Heinz and his wife included in a thank you letter from them survives among the family photographs.[9]

Camp Fredonia at Little Kohler 1945

Captain Ray Thill got "home" early as he took command of the PW camp set up at Little Kohler. Originally from nearby Belgium, WI, for Thill this assignment was just a few miles from home. Arriving in the little village on Friday, June 15, 1945, Thill and his 330 German PW's started work on Sunday. Accompanied by an Army medic and dentist, forty-six combat veterans, and two officers, they staffed the camp. The local Glunz hall, "Danceland" and general store, became the Army headquarters. Next door, the kitchen of the Century Tavern became the camp mess. Tents quickly erected housed the prisoners, and a snow fence went up to mark the perimeter of the camp.[1] These enemy German soldiers substantially outnumbered area residents at this tiny crossroads just out of Fredonia, so little information about Camp Kohler exists.

Saint Mary's Catholic Church, located directly across the road from the camp, became the religious center for the PW's. Prisoners interested in attending church simply marched across the street for a special service held immediately after regular Sunday Mass. A guard escort accompanied the PW's, one in the front and another in back of the group. The two guards just stood in the rear of the church with their guns in hand during Mass. With the body of the Mass still in Latin, Father Oscar Winninghoff, officiating at the time, gave his homily in German for them.[2]

Available for twenty-four hour shift work, most of the prisoners were employed harvesting and processing the local pea crop, but some assisted canning spinach. In 1945, these area canning factories contracted the labor of the PW's: West Bend Canning Company, 40 men; A. Neiman Company at Thiensville, 80; Fredonia Can Goods, Inc., 60 prisoners; Canned Goods, Inc. at Saukville, 60;

and Krier Preserving Company at Belgium, 60 PW's.[3] Later in the season, harvesting sugar beets became an important task as sugar was in short supply and severely rationed. In fact, as winter came early in 1945, the PW's actually chipped the precious sugar beets out of the frozen ground.[4]

Although Little Kohler continued operations until January 1946, Fort Sheridan included the camp earnings in the mid-September press release. In that statement, the military reported PW earnings paid by private companies to the military from Little Kohler totaled $60,090.[5] The military never publicly released the amount of their earnings during the last four months of their stay.

RECOLLECTIONS
Leona Klemp. Grafton, WI -
Leona Klemp worked the full 1945 canning season at the Fredonia Canning Factory. During the corn pack her work on a husker needed a strong man to pull the corn down from the chute. Speaking German herself she communicated easily with Ludwig Mauder, the PW assigned to her husker. They never spoke of the war or his capture, but he seemed sure his family had all been killed. The most common topic of conversation was food, what was eaten in Germany, in America and served to the PW's. The prisoners mentioned lots of marmalade and some corn, too. Since (field) corn was pig food back in Germany it always surprised the PW's, including Ludwig, to find our sweet corn actually good and sweet. Ludwig expressed his craving for chicken, so against the rules, Leona occasionally brought him a leg of chicken or a piece of cake. Each time, she left it wrapped on the window sill, and he took it with him when he went to lunch. Not known in Germany at the time, American Jello provided the most unique food experience for these PW's. Leona recalled "Ludwig always had a smile and talked a lot." Soon he had his eye on Leona's 16-year-old daughter Evelyn, who worked with her mother. Afraid of the big, black, Jamaican workers, Leona said she and the other civilians never feared the Germans. Leona received correspondence from Ludwig as he journeyed home. From Little Kohler, his group of PW's first made a stop in Florida and then in England on their way to Germany. The Klemps and Mauders still continue to exchange greetings and photos. For many years, Leona commonly included several boxes of Jello in her Christmas greetings to the Mauders in Germany. Several years ago, daughter Evelyn and her husband, George Tetzlaff, stopped to see the Mauders during their European

trip. They had two wonderful meals with the Mauders, who also provided their overnight lodging in Schweinfuert.[6]

Arthur Schmitz. Port Washington, WI -

Night foreman Arthur Schmitz remembered that prisoners made up the majority of his crews at Krier Foods. Hired by the company, two local ladies came in and cooked meals for the prisoners, promptly serving them at midnight. Arthur sometimes ate with the PW's because the ladies cooked such tasty meals. The prisoners traded cigarettes to co-workers for candy, keeping both groups in better spirits. One night, a heavy lightening storm knocked out all the electricity in the area for a good half hour. Schmitz said he stood in a doorway and during the flashes of light saw the prisoners just standing at their stations waiting for the storm to pass and/or electricity to be restored. Not one made an attempt to run. One prisoner later said, "there is a lot of water between here and Germany."[7]

Ronald Schmit. Little Kohler, WI -

"Several of the prisoners that helped Dad with the farm work were gifted in woodworking and made their own tools such as wood planers, levels, and saws. In exchange for cartons of cigarettes, they gave several such items to my father."[8]

Frank Deutsch. Cedarburg, WI -

At least one "escape" attempt from Little Kohler went unreported. The Deutsch's owned a cottage along the Milwaukee River on Blueberry Road near Fredonia. Eleven year old Frank, his father, and two uncles saw "three strange men coming down the gravel road." They wore the same type pants and same style jackets and were not speaking to each other. Walking three abreast when they got to the river, they did not stop, just stepped right in, shoes and all. Wading across the river, they walked out on the other side heading south and disappeared. About fifteen minutes later, an Army Jeep appeared carrying two MP's. The officers asked if the family had seen anyone or anything unusual, and specifically "had we seen two or three men?" One uncle spoke up saying three men had crossed the river. "I remember the Jeep turning around going back up Blueberry Road toward Fredonia. I have no idea whatever happened to the escapees."[9] (If no local authorities became involved, the military seldom reported such incidents to the local residents.)

Camp Little Kohler commander Capt. Thill supervises MP's cleaning their weapons, July 1945. Photo courtesy of Stella Thill.

Betty Allen Ewig,. Port Washington, WI -
Seeing the PW's and guards in the canning company yard "made the war seem so close" for Betty Ewig. Her family lived adjacent to the Knellsville Canning Company at the time.[10]

Josephine Gantner. Port Washington, WI -
"What a waste of time fixing stuffed peppers for the prisoners' lunch when they just ate out the stuffing and left the peppers." That recollection came from Mrs. Nick Johannes, wife of Knellsville Canning factory owner and her neighbor, Alice Offerdahl, who cooked and served lunch to the PW work crew each day. Once they also gave the PW's each a can of beer, but quickly reprimanded by the guards, they never did that again.[11]

Laverne Janeshek. Port Washington, WI -
Some of the PW's evidently became very desperate for a drink. Commander Thill told his niece of the impossibility of keeping lemon extract or vanilla on the shelf in the camp kitchen. It immediately disappeared and Captain Thill assumed the PW's swiped it for its alcohol content.[12]

Roger Mueller. Fort Atkinson, WI -

Roger Mueller recalled one lazy and very foolish PW pitching peas on his farm outside Random Lake. Walking four on each side of the wagon, the crew of eight prisoners pitched the pea vines onto the flatbed. On the outside row, this foolish PW pitched them the other direction to the next row rather than across the three rows onto the wagon. When the group turned and came back down the next section of land, the same PW now had twice as much to throw and the same distance to throw it because he was still on the outside row.[13]

Harriet Scholz Knapp. Sussex, WI -

Strange as it may sound today, the PW's who worked at the Fredonia Canning Company ate at the local Legion Hall there. Hatte Scholz filled in as a substitute cook for them. She and her husband also sold bushels of melons to the local cooks for some of those lunches.[14]

Stella Thill. Oceanside, CA -

Though her husband commanded Camp Little Kohler, Stella Thill never went inside, viewing it only from the road. One of the stories Captain Thill often repeated to her and others over the years concerned a very homesick young PW. One day the prisoner went berserk and jumped the fence. He ran to the neighbors who were an elderly couple. He grabbed the old man and hugged him, thinking of his own father. It took some time to calm both men down.[15]

Andy T. Dieringer. Cedar Grove, WI -

"One of the prisoners had his eye on one of the gals that worked with me at the Fredonia Canning Company. She happened to be Mary Ivy, wife of Don Ivy, one of the owners of the plant. Mary felt uncomfortable around that PW and requested that I be sure that I or some other civilian male would always be around in the warehouse whenever the prisoners were there. We never had any overt trouble with that prisoner or any other. I also remember talking with another PW often. In his fluent English he told me that as a 45-year-old he had a good business before being drafted. He was not very happy about losing his business or the war and expressed his intense dislike for Hitler."[16]

William Parnitzke. Fredonia, WI -

"The two PW's on the flatbed of my brother-in-law's 1936 Ford 1 1/2 ton truck were not very ambitious. Working on the Bley farm, they had not moved the load of peas up toward the cab of the truck like they should have done. On a hilly field as the truck made its assent out to state highway 33, the poorly stacked load hanging out the rear of the platform shifted the balance of the truck. The Ford flipped up on its rear end with the cab up in the air. An *Ozaukee Press* photographer came to take a picture but the Saukville Canning Company field man ran him off. The field man complained he had enough trouble without it being published in the paper." Another incident shared by William Parnitzke concerned two prisoners who got into a squabble and started using their pitchforks as weapons against each other. The PW's were supposed to be stacking vines for cattle feed. Parnitzke recalled that the guard used a ladder to get up on the stack and went sneaking up from behind. "He used his rifle butt to beat the PW's up a little to prevent them from really hurting each other."[17]

Lawrence Slavik. Saukville, WI -

While employed as timekeeper at Knellsville cannery, Larry Slavik also drove a truck that picked up the prisoners at Little Kohler in the morning and delivered them back to camp each evening after their work shift. His socializing with a few guards became more intense as the race for the baseball pennant heated up. An avid Tigers fan, one guard from Detroit sat in his car listening to the baseball games whenever possible. Larry and a couple of other guards often joined him in the car rooting their team on.[18] The Tigers whipped the Cubs in that 1945 World Series.

Camp Galesville 1944 & 1945

Adaily swim in Lake Marinuka became the favorite feature of Camp Galesville. The military selected Trempealeau County Fairgrounds, adjacent to the lake, as a site for a PW labor camp serving canning factories in Galesville, Blair, Holmen and Onalaska. With barb wire attached atop a double height snow fence, military and local workmen enclosed a square on the lower part of the grounds, but the lake always offered a possible escape route for determined prisoners. The large pavilion at the fair grounds became the mess hall and sleeping quarters for some PW's. The prisoners also equipped and occupied the main exhibition hall. The American soldiers utilized one of the new buildings outside the fence for their barracks. Coming from Duluth, camp commander First Lt. Stanley J. Krajewski brought his wife and her sister with him but housed them in the nearby Hilda Olson home.[1]

Only open 30 days in 1944, this camp became home to 120 prisoners and their 30 guards and a point of considerable interest to local residents. From the fence they viewed prisoners at leisure, gathering in groups, playing handball or exercising, and playing what looked like chess. A phonograph, a violin played by one prisoner, and bursts of song also entertained the PW's and local spectators. The very irregular dress of the prisoners included a wide range of styles from trunks to overalls with shorts predominating. The limited headgear consisted of a few straw hats, some service caps and one lone derby. Always visible, the guards with rifles added the sense of reality to the situation.[2]

After lowering the flag, the military vacated the camp on July 19. Some of the PW's moved to Camp McCoy, the rest to Camp Janesville. As they left, Superintendent L. S. Montgomery of the Gale Packing Co. praised the work of the prisoners at the pea plant. Similar reports came from the other canning plants employing the PW's. In return, Lt. Krajewski offered thanks to the community for all the courtesies extended to him and his guards.[3]

Stalag Wisconsin

The number of PW's housed at Camp Galesville tripled the following year. The 1945 pea crop set records and needed even more labor for its harvest. During this season, the 450 Germans housed at Camp Galesville worked in the area: 125 at Galesville, 40 at Blair, 125 at Holmen, 100 at Onalaska, and 50 at West Salem. Employers also utilized some of these prisoners at the viners and as general farm labor. Expected to operate well beyond the date of the county fair, the military sought a different location for this second camp. After selecting Reception Park,[4] they allocated the curling rink and surrounding area for the encampment.

Gale Packing Co. paid the community to sink a well in the park as an advance force of prisoners erected four-man tents and enclosures for the incoming prisoners. The new well provided water for four lavatories and showers for prisoners and for similar facilities in a separate building for the officers and guards. An improvised tractor engine supplied hot water. The camp included a two bed dispensary under the supervision of a young Viennese, a medical student before entering the German army. Converting the curling rink itself into the headquarters building, the observation room provided a lobby and desk room for the commander's aides. Partitioning off a separate room, this year's camp commander, Captain Stuart A. Evans, gained a private office. The rink itself became the mess hall and kitchen while another partition created the camp canteen. Supplies arrived daily by truck from Camp McCoy. *The Arcadia News-Leader* noted in a July 12, 1945, article that seventy Army tents, many of them bearing numerous patches, housed the PW's. Eventually this camp housed 500 Germans. The Army enclosed the entire compound with a fence topped with barbed wire and on each side of the compound built sentry stations occupied by guards day and night.

Designating July 6 as "Press Day," the military invited area newspapers to tour the camp. Before the tour actually began, Commander Evans and Lieutenant Paul Alfonsi from Camp McCoy opened an hour of questioning. Surprisingly, most of the questions dealt with the war in general not the PW's.[5] During the tour, some journalists watched two different sandwiches being prepared for the PW's. The first consisted of slices of unbuttered white bread with thin pieces of boiled side pork. The second type of sandwich had a mixture of mashed potatoes, milk, onion and a bit of lard spread on unbuttered whole wheat bread.

In the sparsely supplied PX, Capt. Evans explained to the

press that profits from the PX went to rent movies, purchase some reading material and to pay local clergymen brought in for weekly services. Evans mentioned Father John Leies of Marynook at Galesville and the Rev. George F. Muedeking of Arcadia as clergy holding weekly services at camp.

The press learned that this group of prisoners had come from the 8th Service Command out of Dallas, Texas. Similar to the terrain and climate of their native land, the Galesville area made the PW's feel more at home.[6] During this press tour, Mary Ferris, a *La Crosse Tribune,* reporter, was introduced to a prisoner who represented the camp's professionals and also acted as camp medic. He had been a medical student in Vienna before the war and now studied American medical books which "impressed him terribly." He displayed a new American medical book costing fifteen dollars. From his daily work allowance savings this student had purchased the text. Ferris also met the spokesman for the prisoners. Fluency in English elevated the prisoner to this important position as representative for the PW's whenever any problems or misunderstandings arose. A baker before joining the Nazi air corps, now he and three assistants kept a record of the work done by the prisoners.[7]

Between the pea pack and the lima bean and sweet corn harvest the prisoners worked to clean, maintain and change machinery, move viners to bean areas, and work for area farmers. To hire PW's on a private farm, a farmer needed to file a request to Mr. Jens Klavestad, the farm labor agent, for a specific number of prisoners he wanted to hire by 2:00 p.m. the day before he needed them. The farmer then picked up the prisoners the following morning, worked them for up to 10 hours, and returned them to camp that evening. The area farmers paid to the military the prevailing wage of fifty cents per hour for the time each PW actually worked. Transportation time to and from the farm was unpaid. No guards accompanied these prisoners. The PW's carried their own noon lunch while the farmers provided the water. It wasn't long before farm laborers wearing clothing stamped "PW" were seen all around the county. Although they usually worked in small groups of two to four, larger groups went into La Crosse County for hand tilling of cabbage, corn, and beans for the canning factories.[8]

In 1945 the prisoners remained at Galesville until the end of October, helping with the rest of the season's canning and a variety of farm work. Through September, the PW's at Galesville had earned $43,255 for the government.[9]

RECOLLECTIONS
James Cram. Clearwater, FL -

The military's worst nightmare nearly erupted in June of 1945 when Staff Sgt. Jim Cram finally returned home to Galesville on a six-day pass from a military hospital in Chicago. During the Battle of the Bulge, he and his company had been overrun. Even though badly wounded he was one of only 16 of the 287 men in his unit to survive the entire ordeal. His treatment as a prisoner of the Germans during the last months of the war violated most of the Geneva Convention rules. He weighed about sixty pounds when he escaped, only to be captured by the Americans who thought he was just one more German posing as an American. Very lucky to be alive, he was finally recognized as an American and began his four months of recovery in European hospitals. When he eventually returned home to Galesville, he slept most of the first two days. Rested and having visited with family, he decided to walk down to see the town. After stopping to visit with his old employer, he went next door to one of his old hangouts, the Coffee Cup. There he was astonished to find German PW's drinking beer and having a good time. Army guards sat nearby with their rifles standing against a wall. Cram became incensed as memories of his captivity and all his dead buddies swept over him. He rushed home and returned with his loaded 30/30 Winchester rifle. With rifle poised, he pushed open the door and ordered all civilians to get out. Then he ordered PW's and guards to line up and at gun point he marched them back to their tent camp. After a heated discussion with the camp commander the incident ended peacefully. But no more prisoners were allowed in downtown Galesville again.[10]

Vava Norwood. Hixton, WI -

The canning factory asked Vava Norwood to furnish water and sandwiches to the PW's sent from Camp McCoy to pick their corn. Her husband had contracted a field of sweet corn with the Blair Canning Factory and the cannery provided the labor. An open cattle truck full of smiling, waving PW's came to the farm. A guard instructed the family not to go near the truck or prisoners. At lunchtime, the driver took the food Vava had prepared to the PW crew and guards. The prisoners picked the field in one day and never returned.[11]

Audrey Fillner. Galesville, WI -

Using a mirror to flash dots and dashes across her back fence to the PW's in the ball park, Audrey Fillner received a quick reply of flashing signals. Unfortunately, this 15-year-old didn't know the Morse code. She quickly decided maybe she shouldn't continue, especially since she had no idea what she was flashing or what was coming back.[12]

Boyd Relyea. Blair, WI -

Fifteen year old Boyd Relyea drove the family car to Blair Canning Company every morning to pick up four to six PW's and their guard. His father, Elwood, had two farms about three miles east of Taylor at the time and was short of help. One of his father's hired men had joined the Army and been killed in Europe. Now German PW's would take his place helping on the family farm pitching peas and threshing the 200 acres of oats. Boyd stopped in Taylor on the way back to Blair to get tobacco for the PW's, but he doesn't remember how they paid for it. None of the Relyea family nor civilian hired help spoke German, but a couple of the PW's knew a little English. Each day Mrs. Relyea insisted the PW's join the family and the other hired help inside to eat the lunch she had cooked. She knew they had only marmalade sandwiches and thought they needed more to do the hard work her husband asked of them. The PW's seemed tickled with the home made meals. Sensing the war now finally over and that they would go home soon, the PW's hooted and hollered when the radio broadcast the surrender of the Japanese.[13]

Rod Van Vlect. Hastings, MN -

Though probably only 6 at the time, Rod Van Vlect still remembered the fun he had when he rode with his father in the pickup through the cornfield. About a dozen or so PW's walked along the sides of the vehicle, picking sweet corn, tossing the ears into the bed of the truck. With rifle in hand, the guard sat on top of the cab dangling his feet down across the window.[14]

Harry Hetz, M.D. Kenilworth, IL -

"Backed up against the river, the camp had only a snow fence on the other three sides. The main entrance was an open area in the fencing with a small shed, a table, and, usually, a guard. Once, as I wandered around the compound I came to that gate and found a gun on the table with no guard in sight. So, I sat down and proceeded to look the M1 over, disassembling it as I explored. The guard eventually came around the shed and unconcerned asked how I, one of the German PW's, liked the gun."[15]

Lynn Rall Olson and Gerald Rall. Rochester, MN -
His cartooned picture of Hitler framed in a toilet seat hung on the office wall of Gerald L. Rall, owner of the Rall Feed Mill. One day, Wilber Sulky, one of his regular farmer customers, stopped by to have some feed ground. He had with him a couple of PW's. All was okay until Wilber went to the restroom, leaving Gerald alone with the prisoners in the office. Even then Rall thought nothing of it until he suddenly remembered the picture and became concerned about the reaction of the prisoners if they noticed it. Notice the cartoon they did, "they pointed at it and laughed like hell," Rall recalled.[16]

Ruth Emmons. Galesville WI -
One PW working on their farm helping harvest the peas expressed through the interpreter that the house reminded him of his homeland. The farm of Ruth and Ralph Emmons had a stone barn and a very large old stone house. The thirteen room, two story house was built into the side of a hill, permitting one to walk out the second story onto the hillside. At noon, Ruth fed the PW's with the family and hired hand in the huge kitchen of that house.[17]

Illustration of a "toilet seat Hitler." Replica courtesy of Gerald Rall.

Name withheld. Mondovi, WI -
George was 15 at the time German PW's worked on his family's farm. The Norwegian neighbor translated the conversation among the prisoners when word arrived of the Japanese surrender. The Germans suggested that the Americans would be smart to keep on marching into Russia, as they would be the next big problem.[18]

Camp Genesee 1945

Imagination might initially question the appropriateness of holding 280 men in two barns. But these two barns of the Brookhill Farm (now Pleasant Valley Farm) on Highway 59 two miles north of Genesee were very large. With lots of windows on the second floors, they easily converted into rather pleasant barracks. On June 20, 1945, 100 PW's arrived at Camp Genesee.[1] This camp quickly grew to 280 PW's under Captain Richard Vreeland, who promised local citizenry the prisoners would be under constant guard and there would not be coddling of them. While twenty-five prisoners remained at camp occupied with various maintenance chores, one hundred twenty were employed at fifty-five cents per hour by the Oconomowoc Canning Company, another eighty worked for the Hipke Food Company in Merton at sixty cents per hour, and the Waukesha County Farm Labor Association employed eighty men at fifty cents per hour. The prisoners' pay went to the U.S. Treasury while the PW's themselves received the regulation eighty cents per day in canteen coupons. Of the forty guards with them, most were combat veterans returned from the Pacific, European, and Mediterranean theaters.[2] Until August 3, PW's working in the pea harvest and pack helped complete the season's bumper crop which was a 25 percent increase over the previous year's harvest. The canning factory spokesmen all agreed the PW's did a fine job in getting the crop harvested. The military purchased about 45 percent of the year's canned peas, the rest went to civilian consumption.[3]

Excitement erupted at Camp Genesee when a chimney caught fire in one of the barns used as prisoner barracks. The PW's themselves helped the Waukesha Fire Department extinguish the blaze, which resulted in negligible damage.[4] In a separate incident at the Oconomowoc canning factory, one prisoner burned his hand on one of the giant pressure cookers. He didn't work for several days, but spent his time painting. When he returned to work he brought with him a painting of the cooker room.[5]

While most camps closed at the end of the canning season, Genesee Depot remained open until January 1946, when the prisoners began their repatriation back to Germany.[6] During this later season, some of the PW's worked at beet processing in the Merton canning plant, others with sugar beets at a Menomonee Falls cannery, and the rest helped local farmers. One of the biggest dairies in the state, the Wern Farm Dairy, also hired many prisoners. Lt. William DeLong replaced the camp commander in time to oversee the camp vacated.[7]

Near the end of the 1945 season, a Fort Sheridan press release reported Camp Genesee Depot PW earnings paid by private companies to the military totaled $36,860.[8]

RECOLLECTIONS
Clarence May. Oconomowoc, WI -

Clarence May described the PW's painting of the cooker room as "very realistic." Having finished the painting while healing from a burn received working on a pressure cooker in the Oconomowoc canning factory, the PW showed his artistry to Clarence, who was in charge of field operations there. May also recalled the work and politics of the PW's he supervised. At the end of the night's work, "not a single pea was left lying about — they (the PW's) were that efficient." While talking politics to English speaking prisoners, May heard several times, "We are not your enemy. It's too bad we're fighting. Russia is our real enemy."[9]

Richard Kraus. Whitewater, WI -

Though not uncommon among civilian employees, eating the tomatoes out of hand before they were canned was stealing, wasn't it? That's what it was called when a PW ate a couple of tomatoes at the J. G. Cox Canning factory in Whitewater. Although reprimanded by both the foreman and Mr. Cox himself, the PW continued to work there.[10]

Gerald Herrmann, Genesee, WI -

What is a Catholic church without a place for social activities? Father Conrad Altenbach faced that serious problem when he took over St. Paul's Catholic Church in Genesee. Father Altenbach happily took confessions in German or English, as he was fluent in both. When Camp Genesee opened, he became the priest ministering to the prisoners, holding regular Masses in the compound.

Eventually, the priest struck a deal with the camp commander, and in the fall, PW's took the challenge of raising St. Paul's church building and putting a basement under it. The church hired a contractor to put up the block after the PW's raised the building onto beams, then dug the basement by hand. Young Gerry Herrmann took his pickup truck to camp each morning and returned with eight to ten prisoners. The Christian Mothers, parish ladies, took turns providing lunches for the crew and looked forward to the new basement where they could soon entertain with additional lunches and other social events.[11]

Prisoner Gunther Boehmer had been away from home twelve or thirteen years by the time he met Gerry Herrmann. With Gerry, he shared his experiences in the Spanish Civil War as a member of the German Luftwaffe. Herrmann also became friendly with another prisoner to whom he mentioned his problem of obtaining an inner tube for his Model A Ford. The PW told him there was one hanging on the wall back at the compound, but Gerry noted that was military property. However, it wasn't long before the PW presented Gerry with a deflated inner tube, and, very grateful, Gerry asked no questions.[12]

John Tehan, El Cajon, CA -
"My brother, four sisters, and I would all crowd around the two windows of my parents' bedroom to watch the large flatbed stake truck parked in front of the house, not more than twenty feet away. The twelve to twenty prisoners and a dog were on their way to the 2,000-acre Shangri-La Gardens outside of Palmyra. My father, William Tehan, managed the farm at the time. The guard came to the house to get the day's instructions for his PW work crew. While the truck was there, we were never allowed to go outside, but when we waved, the prisoners would smile and wave back at us peeking out the windows."[13]

Beverly Reinders. Waukesha, WI -
The Maule family outside of Dousman thought the single sandwich sent with the PW's was not enough for the hard physical work they put in on their farm, so Mrs. Maule always invited them to the kitchen table to eat with the rest of the family and hired help. "After lunch, the prisoners would often drift across the road to the our place where Mom often provided cookies or some other treat while Dad conversed in German with them. All of a sudden the PW's

stopped visiting. We learned that the Maules had been criticized for treating the prisoners too well, and the camp implied they should stop providing the extra food and treats." Criticism or not, friendly contacts had been made, especially with two prisoners, Ernst and Reinhold. The Maule family continued correspondence with Reinhold for several years after the war, even sending clothes to help his family.[14]

Arthur Mayo. Genesee, WI -
"In the fall, the neighborhood thrashing crew was joined by two PW's, one a slightly built blond, the other a brawny, dark-haired man. Both prisoners were a little reluctant to put out much effort the first day until Grandmother Tessman spoke to them in German during the big thrashing crew meal. Of course, when we all had a beer about mid-afternoon and Uncle Tessman gave the prisoners one, too. That put them in a friendlier frame of mind. For the rest of the harvest, these PW's worked with the thrashers as they went from farm to farm. Each evening, as they were returned to Camp Genesee, Uncle Charles Tessman gave the prisoners a little bonus — cigarettes."[15]

Arland Krummroy. Oconomowoc, WI -
One young PW brought to the Edward Krummroy farm was thought to be a true Nazi. He didn't want to work. So Edward put him on the straw pile next to the thrasher where he would have to pitch the straw or get buried. Two other prisoners worked willingly, even late in the day after the milking began, and enjoyed cups of fresh warm milk as a special treat. One lone sandwich was all the prisoners brought for lunch, so at noon they joined us at the family table. Since they were not supposed to be eating with us, all kept an eye out for the returning officer. One day the officer did drive in, and son, Arland, remembered "the PW's quickly huddled in a corner of the kitchen to be eating by themselves." Some of Arland's clothes went to Germany after the war as the folks corresponded with one repatriated prisoner who had no clothes for his own son about the same age.[16]

Dale Burnell. Waukesha, WI -
Dale Burnell had PW's shocking oats on his family farm just south of Waukesha. Dale's favorite memory recalled how "the PW's relished the cabbage slaw my German grandmother made with vinegar." Down the road a couple of miles, several lasting friendships

developed on the Gygax strawberry farm as PW's picked strawberries during the season. The Earl Baumgards, owners of Gygax
and future in-laws to Dale, exchanged correspondence with two
repatriated prisoners for many years after the war. The Baumgards
sent several care packages to the George Kauftmann family. Letters
kept by the Baumgards not only expressed much gratitude for the
gifts but also described the deprivation in defeated Germany.[17]

John Rohrer, Watertown, WI -
    "Since our assigned PW's came rain or shine, we occupied them
with odd jobs such as pitching manure and scouring milk cans, as
well as haying and regular field assignments. One PW circulated
among the farmers because he was a butcher by trade. About
twenty different PW's worked by twos or fours at our place out of
Nashotah that summer. During that same time a cousin of mine
who had been captured as a German soldier died in an Oklahoma
PW camp. Born in Germany, my folks often spoke of their homeland with the PW's they hired. German friends from Milwaukee
drove up to visit with the prisoners, too. My mother fed the PW's
well and if the crew had a beer, the PW's were included. One PW
felt bad about eating so much when his family back in Germany
was starving. Another prisoner, Franz Rittinger, a school teacher
before joining the German army, worked for us often. His cousin
from Milwaukee came up to visit him several times, bringing liquor,
cigarettes, and other treats for him. Getting such items back into
camp became a game. The camp cook became the key player, as he
was the only PW allowed outside the perimeter of the compound
— to take out the garbage. If a very well wrapped bottle of liquor
was thrown into the ditch near the garbage, the cook retrieved
it for the prisoners. After the war, my family kept contact with
Rittinger and the folks eventually visited him during their trip to
Germany in 1953."[18]

Ruben Herrmann. La Crosse, WI -
    Ruben Herrmann rode with his father in the farm pickup as he
delivered several big black roasters full of baked chickens to the
camp. They were covered with bales of hay, whether to keep them
warm or hidden is not clearly remembered. His mother, Anna, had
baked this treat special for Thanksgiving. In December, the family accepted an invitation into the compound for the Christmas
pageant presented by the PW's. While it did have some religious
overtones, the painted backdrop and the beautiful voices were

most memorable to the guests. Ruben's father, Jacob, like many neighboring farmers, hired the Germans as day labor around the farm.[19]

Leslie, Hendrickson. Waukesha, WI -

The bottles of wine, the six or seven bottles of liquor, and about one hundred and fifty dollars in Christmas tips were gone when Leslie Hendrickson came out of the office back to his milk delivery truck. Since this was the week before Christmas, Leslie had found many nice gifts and tips left in the milk boxes and chutes by his route customers. As he always did when he completed his route, he stopped in the office of the Wern Farm Dairy to check his deliveries and get any additional orders for the next day. While he was in the office, the PW's working at the farm helped themselves from his unlocked truck. One rather talkative PW, called Fritzy, reluctantly acknowledged that was what happened, noting that was the only way the PW's could get such things.[20]

Camp Green Lake 1944

By the time of the September corn pack, Camp Green Lake had become one of the biggest in the state. And it had also experienced its share of trouble including a strike, the removal of an officer and an escape. In June, the military established this temporary camp at Lawsonia, a huge private estate outside the village. Mrs. Lawson kept a prized herd of cattle in her several large barns. The military converted one of those barns into the enlisted men's bunkhouse and the chicken house into the officers quarters. Other buildings also housed prisoners and the overflow of prisoners slept in tents.[1] While the orderly tent and canteen tent had electricity, candles illuminated all the other tents. After connecting water and telephone service, the Army erected a flood lighting system that would light up the entire compound at night. The prisoners listened to the radio, read American newspapers, even foreign language papers printed in the U.S. The authorities also posted on bulletin boards, translations of German communiques printed in the *New York Times*.[2]

Curious, many area residents waited at the depot on the evening of Monday, June 19 to watch approximately 250 prisoners get off the special train of the North Western Railroad. They arrived dressed in a mix of uniforms, some even wearing shorts.[3]

It wasn't long before rumors concerning the camp and prisoner activities spread wildly around the area. In mid-July, the rumors circulating concerned the cause of the German prisoners' "strike," reportedly staged to protest management of the camp. The community knew the camp had quickly returned to order because the prisoners went back to work in the nearby canning factories the following day. *The Ripon Commonwealth* investigation confirmed that a one-day strike had occurred on July 12, 1944. Some of the PW's themselves complained to cannery officials that second in command Lieutenant Behrendt was being transferred. Further inquiry suggested that the 32-year-old officer, a German born naturalized citizen, had been excessively lenient with the prisoners which displeased many of the guards and several local residents. Some even called him pro-German. Two specific incidents surfaced. The previous Sunday night, the prisoners began singing German war songs at camp. Their music attracted a crowd of about seventy-five townspeople who gathered along the road outside the prison fence. Some demanded to be let inside. The guards refused, citing the Geneva Convention rules. But Lt. Behrendt appeared and ordered the gates opened. The second incident occurred the previous week when Lt. Behrendt was returning a small group of PW's back to camp from work. The truck stopped at the Nautical Inn, a Green Lake tavern operated by Fred Hoth. Lt. Behrendt asked to bring the prisoners in for a beer. Hoth indignantly refused. These two actions of Lt. Behrendt prompted his replacement by Lieutenant Francis Walsh. Walsh quickly took control and the camp again settled down and went back to work.[4]

A committee of four from the local Frank H. Brown American Legion Post also interviewed Lt. Walsh and Camp Commander Lieutenant John W. Scott on the rumored laxity in guarding the German prisoners. The camp officers admitted some fraternizing between civilians and the prisoners at first, but reported the practice had been ordered ceased. Guards had been given additional training in methods of handling the prisoners. Both the Legion representatives and the camp officers agreed that civilians should be prevented from talking to the PW's except as a necessity.[5]

Less than two weeks later, more excitement spread through the community when two prisoners went over the fence. On July 20, 1944, the two grabbed a local youth, Rex Ritchie, near Hattie Sherwood Park and asked for directions to a beach. In their broken English, the men told him they were from "der camp" at Lawsonia and wanted to know where to go for a swim. A very frightened Ritchie gave them directions and watched them walk away. Ritchie then ran to his nearby employer H. Eaton who phoned the sheriff, Al Christensen. When the sheriff and the Eatons found the prisoners with their spotlights, the pair obediently climbed into the car and returned to the camp headquarters without any resistance.[6] Authorities believed the pair were not attempting to "escape" but really were just looking for a cool relaxing swim. However, many in the community remained unconvinced and frightened.

With the end of the pea pack, the military temporarily vacated the camp during the last week of July. Another Northwestern train took the entire complement of 250 prisoners and guards to Michigan.[7] As the group of PW's marched from camp to the depot that day, the residents noticed several bore musical instruments and one held a small dog under his arm.[8]

Additional accommodations had to be made at Lawsonia in August as local canners anticipated up to 600 prisoners to return for the corn pack.[9] Many more tents quickly went up. This second company of prisoners stayed until early October. Under another commander, Lieutenant Hesselman, they were transported to the many corn canning plants within a twenty-five mile radius. This second camp had no incidents that the public became aware of, but the community still breathed a sigh of relief when the camp finally closed with little fanfare in early October, 1944.[10]

RECOLLECTIONS
Edward Ucker. Waupun, WI -

A 16 year old Milwaukee native was a PW at Green Lake. His folks had immigrated to the state and ran the Deutschland Dairy in Milwaukee. His mother had taken him and his baby sister back to Germany to visit the grandparents. There, the Nazis grabbed his passport and drafted the youngster into their army. He quickly became a paratrooper, ultimately jumping over Cypress. At his first opportunity, he surrendered to the Americans but was held as a PW for the duration of the war. At Camp Green Lake, the prisoner convinced MP Ed Ucker of his citizenship and background by listing most of the towns between Milwaukee and Eagle River where the family had a cottage. This American prisoner was being beaten by two other German prisoners when he discovered them sabotaging a truck. Ed and another guard stopped the beating, but not before Ed himself had received a fist in the face and had cracked the back of his head against a truck bumper.[11] This Milwaukee native became the spokesperson and translator for the prisoners while at Green Lake.[12] (After the war, he was forcibly repatriated with all PW's. The U.S. Army did look into his and several similar claims, eventually providing these special draftees visas back to America.)

After climbing out of a staff car, two smartly dressed, crop-wielding Nazi officers gave a pep talk to PW's in a farm field outside Markesan. Telling the young prisoners the war was not over yet and suggested that they would fight for Germany again, the Nazis demanded to be saluted, but the PW's turned their backs on the enraged Nazis. One officer then went to guard Ed Ucker and de-

PW's at the depot heading to trucks on the way to camp, 1945. Photo by W.C. Schroeder.

manded a salute from him. He replied in German, "I don't salute Nazis." The officer then shook his fist in Ed's face suggesting that if he were in his army the German would fix him. But Ed, clasping his rifle tighter, reminded the Nazi who had the gun. As the angered Germans sped off, the prisoners cheered and yelled. Ucker quickly declined their suggestion that he would make a good German soldier. The German officers were official visitors, inspecting the condition of the camps and working conditions.[13]

Sitting in a line of trucks loaded with prisoners headed for the day's work detail, a German officer sat beside 17-year-old MP Ed Ucker. The officer criticized Ucker's attempts at double clutching the truck. Willing to improve his skill, Ucker took his truck out of formation onto the nearby parade grounds where the prisoner quickly taught him to double clutch the truck. This skill proved useful to Ed for the next two years. Ucker's greatest fear was the possibility of a local sniper using his hunting rifle to see what damage he could cause a truck full of Nazis. Luckily, no such incident actually occurred, though there was a great deal of anti-Nazi hostility in the community.[14]

Jeanette Weber. Fond du Lac, WI -

As a 13-year-old traveling to Grandma's house, Jeanette Weber and her mother passed Lawsonia often. Jeanette remembered being uncomfortable as she stared through the fence at the two story barracks and saw the men looking out the windows. With the car windows down, they could also hear what they perceived as shouting among the men — perhaps at them as they passed.[15]

Russell Clark. Princeton, WI -

The canning company provided rain coats to the PW's as they harvested the sweet corn in the rain on the Clarence Clark farm five miles north of Markesan. Son Russell Clark also remembered the guards with guns in the field and at the viner, and he recalled food trucks bringing lunch to the prisoners out in the field.[16]

Ruth Smith Allison. Green Lake, WI -

"If the military knew we were married, my husband would have been washed out of the Army flight training program, so we kept our little secret. The first person I actually told was a PW named Franz Beck. I was working at the canning factory with prisoners on our machine. This young man must have taken a special liking to me, because he brought me an ice cream cone to the window as a treat. I decided I better tell him *verheiratet* (I am married). Undaunted, he then quickly fell in love with my good friend and co-worker Norma who corresponded with him even after the war."[17]

Earl Hoth. Ripon, WI -

While his brother was serving overseas fighting the Germans and his uncle, Fred Hoth, was throwing German prisoners out of his Green Lake bar, Earl Hoth quietly worked at the Silver Creek Canning Company in Ripon. He recalled the fascination of the PW's there as some kids on rollers skates went zipping by the factory. Break time that year also provided interesting memories as one of the PW's had been a professional circus acrobat in civilian life.

The acrobat often performed for all, doing flips, head and hand stands, and swinging from the rafters.[18]

Robert Tabbert. Lac du Flambeau, WI -

"All of my walking, hiking, running, basketball, football, mountain climbing, working as a field geologist, and wading in trout streams, the ability to use my legs relate back to that summer day in August, 1944. It was then a German PW jumped up and rolled me off that truck bed and saved my legs. As a crew assigned to the Umbecht brothers, three of my high school buddies and I pitched peas onto their two old Reo flat bed trucks. Falling behind in the harvest, the Silver Creek Cannery applied for PW help. Sent from Lawsonia, PW's joined us still wearing their Afrika Korps uniforms including the shorts, heavy hobnailed boots, knee socks, rolled up shirt sleeves, and mussete bags slung over their shoulders. They all wore funny looking, peaked, army caps covered with various army insignias. No guards, no prison uniforms, no PW stenciled on their shirts. As they tumbled out of the yellow school bus, they formed up and stood there, like an army squad waiting for orders. These PW's quickly realized that our harvest crew was made up of boys who needed help, and the PW's took on all the harder jobs in loading the trucks. They brought us fresh black bread baked daily at their camp by their own cooks. We furnished the water. At noon we would pull the truck into the shade of the barn, eat lunch together, and take a nap. One noon, after pitching heavy wet pea vines and eating my peanut butter and jelly sandwiches, I stretched out with my legs dangling over the edge of the flatbed on the down hill side of the truck and I quickly fell asleep. The next thing I remember is that I was rolling around on the ground wrestling with one of the 'kriegies,' short for *Kriegsgefangenen,* prisoners of war! Not knowing what had happened, I pushed and kicked at the German. Carl Umbrecht, the truck driver, pinned me down and said, 'Whoa, whoa, take it easy Bob, he just saved your legs!' The brake on the old truck had slipped. As the truck headed toward the milk house, that PW had jumped up and rolled me off the truck onto the ground before the flat bed could crush my legs into the milk house wall. Helping with the harvest in Wisconsin, that PW changed my life with his quick thinking and bravery. I still regret not keeping in contact with him. I never saw him again."[19]

Roger Tornow. Oshkosh, WI -

"My parents evidently made the arrangements with their friends who owned the Pickett Canning company. I was to have a very unique and memorable experience. Only 9 years old, I was sent down our long drive way to wait for the bus in midsummer. When the bus stopped, I got on to find it full of PW's and two guards. The guards each had "tommy" guns, one stationed in the front and one in the back of the bus. I spent the day with this group of men. We went out to a pea field where the PW's pitched the peas onto the wagons. At lunch time, we all got back into the bus and headed into town to the canning factory cook shack for lunch. Then we headed back to the pea fields. I didn't work, just wandered around and watched. Some of the PW's spoke to me in their broken English. When one patted me on the head, a guard immediately came over to check things out. I believed the pat to be a friendly gesture, the PW was smiling and talking with me, but the guard wanted to be sure. It was a day I still remember."[20]

Jack Thrall. Fond du Lac, WI -

Farmer John Flanagan of Pogan contracted his crops to the Winneconne Canning Factory. But in 1944, he absolutely refused to allow his peas to be harvested. He had lost a son fighting in Europe

This wooden plaque by Josef Fritz depicting his North African experience was presented to Alvina Albrecht in 1944. Photo courtesy of Twilah Deboer and the Brandon Historical Society.

and would not allow a German on his property. According to Jack Thrall, owner of the plant, the PW's were the only men available to harvest the peas, so Flanagan's crop went to waste.[21]

Alvina Albrecht. Brandon, WI -
The Brandon Canning Factory bused twenty-two prisoners into Brandon each day to help in the canning of peas according to Alvina Albrecht, a cook at the bunkhouse. She quickly noticed these good-looking young men had hearty appetites. What's more, they were very appreciative, saying *"Danke schön"* often. They had much better manners than most of the American workers brought up from the South. The American crews ate at noon and the Germans ate at one o'clock, never eating together. Only two of the PW's talked frequently to German-speaking Anna, who with her husband, Bob Spaulding, managed the canteen. Alvina didn't talk to the PW's because she thought her German wasn't good enough and she'd make a fool of herself. The PW's learned from Anna that she could speak German. One day when Alvina served them, one held the salt shaker over his cup of coffee as if to pour it in. Without thinking she said, *"Nein! Das is salz."* (No! That is salt.) The PW knew he had tricked her and laughed heartily saying, *"Du kannst Deutsch sprechen"* (You can speak German.) That same prisoner nicknamed her *der kleine* (little one) and a co-worker, who was rather plump, *dicke* (fat.) He made a plaque by burning the design into wood, then painting over the scene and asked Anna to give it to Alvina. His name, Josef Fritz, was on the back. The plaque is currently on loan to the Brandon Historical Society Museum. Alvina recalled another PW as a real cut-up who loved to make people laugh. One day the prisoners sang several German songs. It was so beautiful, remembered Alvina, the building almost rocked. Later in the season, Mr. Spaulding went downtown and brought back a bottle of beer for each one of the PW's, who were delighted with the treat. The last day of work, before the prisoners pulled out, everyone shook hands. Alvina recalled that one of them squeezed her hand so hard it hurt for an hour. A feeling of sadness swept over the civilians and prisoners alike. "Even though our countries were at war, we could put that aside and think of each other as fellow human beings."[22]

Camp Hartford
1944 - 1946

Lawrence Welk, Benny Goodman, Woody Herman, the Dorsey Brothers, Duke Ellington, and Guy Lombardo all played to packed houses. In fact, all the "Big Bands" played at the lovely Schwartz Ballroom in Hartford. The beautiful octagonal parquet dance floor had a huge fireplace at one end of the room. The ballroom was truly impressive, measuring 130 feet across with a 65 foot ceiling. Hanging from the center of that ceiling was a 16-foot, two-ton chandelier.[1] A large bar and eating area was attached. People came for miles around to dine and dance, but in October, 1944, the dances abruptly ended. Why the abrupt change? Nazi prisoners moved in. The Schwartz became Camp Hartford. To the dismay of many music lovers the big bands never returned, not even after the war.

During the 1944 pea pack, the military filled labor shortages in the Hartford area canning factories by transporting PW's from Camp Lake Keesus.[2] Later that year, Hartford got a camp of its own. Unlike most branch camps, which operated only during the summer months, the Schwartz Ballroom at Hartford held prisoners year round. Expecting to exist for only a couple of months after its October, 1944, opening, the camp actually housed prisoners continuously until closing in January, 1946. The prisoners worked in the many area canning factories including the Clyman Company at Clyman, Hustisford Canning Company at Hustisford, Baker Canning Company at Theresa, Columbus Foods at Horicon, Mayville Canning Company at Mayville, and the local Libby, McNeil & Libby canning factory. As usual, they also worked on area farms that contracted crops to those canneries. But these inmates also worked in more diverse work settings. With hemp the source for rope at the time, hemp production was encouraged by the government. Prisoners were employed at the Atlas Hemp Mills, the War Hemp Industry, and the J. LeRoy Hemp Mills, all located in the area. The Dairyland Cooperative Association Inc. in Juneau, The Borden Company at

Columbus, and Belmont Cheese plant at Mayville employed them in dairies. With the help of PW's, Oconomowoc's Carnation Company made cans for shipping canned milk. Prisoners also tanned hides at W.B. Place & Company, Inc. and did various tasks at the McKay Nursery Company outside Madison. One prisoner even worked as a baker in a local bakery. Since many of these companies needed year round employees rather than just the seasonal help in food harvest and processing, Camp Hartford did not close.

The sixty-three acre camp took over the entire premises of the Schwartz Ballroom and Park. A fence surrounded the compound. One hundred fifty double bunks erected around the perimeter of the ballroom slept 300 men. But when the numbers swelled to around 600, the Army recruited volunteers to sleep in tents just outside the side entrance.[3] Former-prisoner Kurt Pechmann enjoyed his tent as the best of both worlds. Each tent had its own electric lights and iron stove, so those volunteering to sleep in the tents found them warm in winter and much cooler in the summer than PW's in the ballroom. The prisoners installed wooden floors in the tents before winter set in. Perhaps best of all, those in the tents didn't have the fog from all the cigarette smoke and ongoing noise of men on other shifts to contend with. All used the latrines, showers and laundry installed in the basement of the ballroom.

The Hartford soccer team Jan. 1, 1945. Kurt Pechmann is far left, second row. Photo courtesy of Kurt Pechmann.

The prisoners ate in the dining room while their own cooks used the modern kitchen facilities there. Many guards regularly chose to eat with the prisoners because of the tasty German style meals served.

YMCA representative, Howard Hong, in his November 22, 1944, inspection report for Fort Sheridan, described Hartford as "an unusually fine dance hall at the edge of the city." Although still a "good camp," Hong found some trouble spots. He reported that thirty-five prisoners captured in the North African and the Italian campaigns had become a disruptive factor. Hong also noted that the school was the weakest part of the activities programs, and he recognized some tension in the relationship between the camp and local churches. In 1944, the camp became too crowded to hold church services within the compound. At the request of the prisoners, they were permitted to attend services in two churches within walking distance. On November 5, about eighty Catholic prisoners attended mass at St. Killian's officiated by Father Stehling. However, due to some community criticism, St. John's Evangelical Lutheran Church decided against allowing prisoners to attend their regularly scheduled services or a separate service. So Pastor Taylor of the Methodist Church made arrangements for the prisoners to have a separate service there. When the military approached Reverend A. F. Selmikeit, pastor at United Church of Christ, for help, he chose to preach to the prisoners at the ballroom after his regular services. The local American Legion post finally passed a resolution supporting the work of the pastors and churches, and the local newspaper printed a supporting editorial, easing tensions. Later, Peace Lutheran Church provided a minister as well.[4] The following January, 1945, Inspector Hong counted 274 PW's housed there for the winter. Noting that the trouble makers had been removed, the religious issues had been settled and an excellent program of courses had been initiated, he now reported Hartford one of the best camps he inspected.

The prisoners enjoyed all the privileges and advantages that they would have in a base camp because of the interest of their commanding officer, Captain Joseph Atkins. This commander regularly received high praise from military and Red Cross inspectors as well as prisoners. A monthly newspaper, *Die Brucke* , was regularly distributed from the base camp at Fort Sheridan. Articles for the paper were contributed by prisoners throughout Sheridan's branch camps. Other papers of great interest to the PW's usually available included copies of *Der Ruf* (a national paper written by and for German PW's) sold in the canteen and the *Milwaukee Deutsche Zeitung* (an area German language paper) often accessible as discards from guards and other local contacts. Usually tuned to local polka stations, radios regularly played in the background here as well as in many branch camps. Kurt Pechmann and George Hall, former Hartford prisoners, claimed to have had a short wave radio hidden under the furnace there. The camp regularly offered to show prisoners two American movies per week. To help overcome the language barrier, an English speaking prisoner generally previewed each movie and periodically during the showing stopped the film to explain the action.[5] Because of the newsreels before each movie, the radio broadcasts, the newspapers, and the weekly news bulletin, the pending outcome of the war became evident to the prisoners. Other entertainment included cards, chess and other board games. A seven piece band and male chorus were active, each giving periodic concerts. The band often performed concerts in the community band shell on summer evenings, and the chorus sang at the St. Kilian Christmas Masses.[6] Other talented prisoners including several comedians organized additional performances for the enjoyment of the internees. Weather permitting, football (soccer) became the major sport of choice and physical outlet for the men. The prisoners actually organized leagues and played intramural games often.

The camp commander even allowed a local photographer to come into the camp to take group and individual pictures. He justified the photos noting how useful they could be to local authorities in case of escapes. The photographer then sold the pictures to the individual prisoners.[7] As with most of the camps, there were no incidents of escape attempts ever reported by the guards. However, fellow prisoners knew Oskar Schmoling often went over the fence at night only to return before roll call in the morning. According to his fellow comrades he was only looking for adventure. Captured at age 16, he celebrated his 17th and 18th birthdays as a PW at Camp Hartford. Schmoling was one of the youngest German prisoners held in Wisconsin, certainly the youngest at Hartford.[8]

Allowed one scheduled visitation day per month, many prisoners looked forward to visits from relatives living in Wisconsin who traveled to the camp for the visit. A butcher in Ripon received permission to regularly pick up his PW nephew Adolf Jesse, taking him home for day long visits. However, authorities denied the uncle's request to keep the nephew home to work as a full time butcher for him.[9]

Consistent with current policy, the military did not make public any 1944 financial records concerning the PW's, but the military reported in 1945 that the Camp Hartford earnings in September alone amounted to $27,465. Hartford PW's had earned a grand total of over $250,182 for that year to that report date.[10] The PW's remained and worked in the Hartford area until January, 1946. As a result, it became one of the most financially lucrative camps in the state.

RECOLLECTIONS

Amy Parent Fissel. Oshkosh, WI -

Hartford boasted the Schwartz Ballroom, which was a beautiful ballroom for a town of its size. Amy Parent often attended dances there. Then word came that the Germans were here and would be quartered in the ballroom. The following Sunday, a large truck pulled up and about forty prisoners marched to the front of St. Killian's Catholic Church. Since Mass was still in Latin, Amy assumed they understood all but the sermon. Amy was so frightened at her first sight of the enemy, she fled up to the choir loft where

Several PW's assigned to W. B. Place Company. Oskar Schmoling is at far right, middle row. Photo courtesy of Kurt Pechmann and Gerald Indermuehle.

PW's and civilians share lunch at the Dairyland Cooperative in Juneau, Wis., 1945. Photo courtesy of Kurt Pechmann.

she'd be safe. When she finally looked down to the first floor, all she saw were "blond, rosy cheeked, young lads of 20 or so." Her fear left but to her chagrin, the big bands dances never returned to the Schwartz after the war.[11]

Mary Von Rohr Whritenour. Wauwatosa, WI -
Reverend Adolph Von Rohr of Peace Lutheran Church tended to the Lutheran flock at the camp as he regularly went out preaching and ministering in German. He often spoke of this unique episode of his ministry.[12]

Lucile Selmikeit Lechner. Brown Deer, WI -
"My father, Reverend A. F. Selmikeit, minister for the United Church Of Christ, was criticized and called a 'Nazi sympathizer.' After his regular services, he went to the ballroom and preached to the prisoners. However, since he was requested to do this by the camp command, he felt he was just fulfilling his Christian duty by giving them religious support. Reverend Von Rohr cut short his duty — why, I don't know. Father Stehling and my dad continued to serve the PW's to the end of their stay."[13]

Ted Komp. Hartford, WI -

"We snuck up on the camp approaching from behind lilac bushes," recalled Ted Komp. As a youngster, he and several friends went out to see the PW's soon after their arrival. Eventually the boys got the nerve to approach the fence to see these enemy soldiers up close. When someone down the fence tried to give or exchange something with a prisoner, a guard quickly came and chased the civilians away. Ted recalled a lot of hostility in the community against these Germans. Several families had lost one or more sons in the war in Europe already. After the prisoners moved out, the dance floor was in rough shape and the place became a skating rink for a while.[14]

Gertrude Indermuehle. Hartford, WI -

As a teen, Gertrude Indermuehle worked with prisoners at the W. B. Place & Company. Walking on her way to work one morning, she slipped and fell just as a truck full of prisoners drove by causing them to hoot at her. Though unhurt, her embarrassment all but kept her from going to work.[15]

Kurt Pechmann. Madison, WI -

An unnamed area farmer requested twenty prisoners to work in his onion fields. Rolf Wlasak and nineteen fellow PW's could hardly believe their unique experience at that farm. Stomping down

Hartford PW's on the B. Zwiebeck onion farm. Photo courtesy of Kurt Pechmann and Gerald Indermuehle.

the onion stalks took only about an hour, and the prisoners were quickly on their way back to the farmhouse. The farmer told the guards to stay in the kitchen while he led the prisoners into the dining room. There, spread on the table was what looked to be a wedding feast. The prisoners enjoyed the grand meal and wine, while the old German immigrant farmer enjoyed the stimulating conversation in his native tongue.[16]

Rolf Wlasak. Dresden, Germany -
It was in the fall of 1944 when a conveyor belt broke down at the Juneau Dairyland Cooperative. PW Rolf Wlasak offered to help with the repair. Having been a toolmaker at home, he was able to help the "shop master," who himself had been a mechanic in Germany. Rolf's job quickly went from helping unloading boxes from a train to mechanic. Learning the U.S. measuring units was the biggest problem Rolf faced. Satisfaction with his work and trust in him quickly developed. He became the plant mechanic for the second shift and was actually given the keys for the storage rooms for spare parts, materials, and tools. He spent most of his work time on the 2:00 p.m. to 10:00 p.m. shift alone in the shop. Secluded there in that remote shop he seldom had a visit from a guard. If he planned to work on a forbidden project for himself or the camp, he always had the electrical welding device ready to create fireworks for any guard that might just show up.[17]

Armond Lackas. Hartford, WI -
A local farmer regularly picked up the camp kitchen garbage for his pigs. When the camp learned of the farmer's public criticism of the "waste of food" at the camp, something had to be done. With the approval of Commander Captain Atkins, Armond Lackas, the Provost Marshall, went to the local county fair and bought 10 little piglets. The local farmer had nothing more to pick up or complain about, and the prisoners ultimately feasted on the pork they raised.[18]

George Hall. Beaver Dam, WI -
Camp authorities distributed Red Cross packages as they became available. German candies, cigarettes, cigars, shirts and reading material generally came in those packages. At the Schwartz Ballroom camp, the prisoners suspected their prisoner spokesman of keeping much of the Red Cross donations for himself. The

A Hartford soccer team identified by fellow PWs Kurt Pech-mann and George Hall as all SS men later transferred out. Photo courtesy of Kurt Pechmann and Gerald Indermuehle.

PW's knew him as a "snitch" who was reportedly allowed by the guards to keep a pistol under his pillow for his own protection from fellow prisoners.[19]

David Lau. Watertown, WI -
Most workers at Clyman Canning Company came from a German background. Almost naturally, the civilians referred to the PW's as *"landsmann,"* or fellow countrymen. The first couple of weeks there, security was tight, the guards very watchful and heavily armed, but that quickly eased. The first season most of the prisoners assigned there were captured with Rommel. They exemplified the young strong examples Hitler liked to brag about. Often wearing shorts and tank tops, these prisoners exposed their muscular builds. The second year most of the PW's were older, captured as a result of the Normandy invasion. The watchmaker among them willingly fixed any watch at work or camp.[20]

Dorothy Weise. Hales Corners, WI -
"During 1944 and 1945, I was a high school senior employed at the Hartford Coffee Shop. There we made huge pots of soup and piles of sandwiches that the guards picked up for the PW lunches. I do not remember any prisoners with the guards, but we were always so busy it was hard to notice details."[21]

Rev. Herber Stelter. Sheboygan, WI -

"You don't talk like most of the others," a PW told civilian Herbert Stelter. The two men worked together at Aunt Nellie's Canning Company in Clyman. At the time, Stelter also attended divinity school at the Thiensville Seminary. Because he grew up speaking German, he became the straw boss for a detail of PW's stacking boxes on the shift. Needing an interpreter, a guard once brought a prisoner to Herbert. The guard wanted to know who this PW was and why he didn't have a PW stenciled on his shirt. The prisoner convinced both that he had been issued the shirt at the camp just that way, missing the PW designation.[22]

Name Withheld. Columbus, WI -

Ice cream was a common dessert for the PW's at the Borden milk plant in Columbus. On the night shift alone seventy-five to one hundred PW's would load two railroad boxcars with cans of ice

A ring made by a PW from a nickel and dime for Jim Schinderle. Photo by Jim Widmer, courtesy of Jim Schinderle.

Camp Hartford PW Choir. Photo courtesy of Kurt Pech-mann.

cream powder, most headed for the Navy. The test samples were regularly distributed to the employees including the prisoners. At that time, Borden's processed about 200,000 pounds of milk a day into the powdered ice cream mix. In addition to the local product, railroad tanker cars from across the country arrived daily full of the powdered ice cream to be canned there as well. The prisoners worked two shifts a day seven days a week helping to keep the factory going year round. This plant fed the prisoners their noon meal or a midnight lunch. At one such lunch sweet corn was served. The Germans just sat there until finally someone grumbled "*swine fütter.*" So the night foreman buttered a cob and started to eat saying, "*Schmeckt gut!.*" First one, then the rest of the prisoners picked up an ear and tried it. They quickly came to enjoy the corn enough to ask for seeds to take home to Germany.[23]

Stuart Grulke. Fairhaven, NY -
"'*Heil Hitler!*' the German lieutenant loudly proclaimed as he spat at my father, Emil Grulke. Dad had a truck for hauling peas and managed the viner station about three blocks from our place, Elm Terrace Bar & Dance Hall. After the incident the lone guard told that German to sit down and stay there until it was time to leave for the day. That PW never returned to the viner. The other fifteen to twenty prisoners came each day, ready and willing to work. I often climbed up on one of the several stacks, hid behind a chute, and visited with the PW's. They asked lots of questions

about America and our farming practices. One of those PW's actually gave me his flight 'wings' as a gift. At lunch time, the PW's lined up and marched to our place, entered in single file, and sat at a large table in the dance hall. There my mother served them a delicious noon meal each day. I also remember the PW's being impressed with my father's Lincoln. It had twelve cylinders and a radio. The neighbor's corn cultivator attracted their attention too. He allowed them to take the reins of the horses and cultivate a row or two, going over the hill and out of sight each time. The prisoners always came back and with big grins on their faces."[24]

Ellen Place Schuette. Bradenton, FL -
"My family owned the W. B. Place & Company in Hartford which hired PW's to help in the tannery during the war. I was in high school and really had no contact with the prisoners at that time other than to see them in the trucks. After college, I spent the summer waiting on trade in the company show room. One day a man came in and said that at one time he had been in Hartford as a prisoner of war. He came back to buy a leather jacket from us. I also sold him a pair of our leather shoes to take with him back to Germany."[25]

Camp Hortonville 1945

Although farmer opposition to the plan had been expressed rather vehemently, nearly 500 Germans soldiers invaded Outagamie county on June 25, 1945. Perhaps because of local resistance, the security and surveillance at Camp Hortonville was initially extremely tight with guards posted every twenty feet along the perimeter of the compound. However, security quickly lessened, with guards eventually posted only at the corners of the compound. It also quickly became clear that the fences surrounding the camp proved most useful in keeping sight-seers away and unwanted visitors out. While many local residents continued to detest the presence of these German PW's, other area residents looked at the situation differently. Those of German descent came seeking news of relatives back in Europe. Sight-seers and visitors often clogged the road to the camp on Sundays.[1]

The Army described this invading force of PW's as "meek, unarmed, and well guarded." While some of these prisoners were seasoned soldiers captured early in North Africa, others surrendered as recently as March and April of 1945. Of this large contingent of 500 PW's arriving at Hortonville, 175 continued on to Appleton Junction. The remainder camped on the Earl Buchmann property east of town across from what is now Dynes Country Club. At the time Dynes was a supper club on the lake with a toboggan hill across the road. At the foot of the toboggan hill Camp Hortonville emerged.[2] The camp housed about 305 prisoners including forty who remained at camp assigned to cooking, the motor pool, and mechanical and maintenance tasks. Seventy of those Germans not assigned to camp duties worked for the Fox Valley Canning factory at Hortonville. The balance worked for canneries in Clintonville, Shiocton, Shawano, Seymour, Winneconne, Bear Creek and Manawa. Pay in those canneries ran from fifty cents to sixty cents per hour.[3] These prisoners continued to fill labor shortages as the canneries packed peas, corn, and tomatoes.[4]

The daily schedule for utilizing PW labor at Clintonville's canning factory was similar to all the canneries out of Camp Hortonville. Six days a week, fifty PW's regularly rode buses from Hortonville to the Clintonville Canning Company for the 7:00 a.m. to 3:00 p.m. shift. Retrieving this work detachment, the bus dropped off replacements for the 3:00 p.m. to end of run shift. Fed a hot meal back at camp, each prisoner took a sandwich sack lunch to eat during their work assignment break. The military sent no beverage, but the cannery provided water.[5]

With only one small permanent building used for the PX/canteen and officers' quarters, the rest of the Hortonville brigade lived in a tent city. As in many other camps, even the cooks worked under canvas. Camp Hortonville had a unique feature. Built by the prisoners early in their stay, a "Murphy" type walk-in fruit cellar provided refrigeration.[6]

Base camp, Fort Sheridan, reported satisfaction with the work and earnings of the Hortonville PW's. By mid-September they had already earned $28,503 in wages collected by the military from the area canneries.[7] While the contracts between the government and canneries ended October 1, the military did not abandon the camp until December, 1945.[8] The Army did not report the final earnings of the PW's at Hortonville to the public.

RECOLLECTIONS
Arthur Kalchik. Hortonville, WI -

"The fences around Camp Hortonville were very poor and non-existent in some areas," recalled Art Kalchik, an MP there in 1945. But he and fellow guards had no fear of prisoners or their escape while working in the camp, canneries and farms nearby. Other recollections of Art included his claim that Hortonville farmers fed PW's working on their farm, but not the guards like himself. According to Art, camp food was transported from Green Bay with the PW's doing the cooking. The PW's played volleyball on Dynes Country Club grounds across the road. On his days off, Art himself often worked for Elmer McKevver at his lumber business for a wage of $5 a day. Like Art, six other MP's met and married local girls and settled in the area. Among these buddies of Art who found brides and stayed were James Adams, Larry Durnill, and Orville Williams.[9]

A guard relaxes at Camp Hortonville in 1945. Photo courtesy of JoAnne Buchmann Schwarz.

William Ratzburg. Hortonville, WI -

As a boy, on many hot summer days Bill Ratzburg hiked from town out to Dynes Lake at Dynes Country Club across the road from the PW Camp. On each trip he saw the tent city on the hillside, with the driving lane down the middle of the camp. Bill remembered hearing that the PW's were issued rubber suits to protect them from the dampness when in the fields breaking off the corn and loading the picked corn onto nearby trucks headed for the canneries.[10]

Nellie Krueger. New London, WI -

A local fellow repeatedly attempted to climb over the fence to get INTO the camp, evidently seeking sexual favors. Nellie Burns heard this and many other stories as she drank coffee at the camp gate while visiting with her boy friend. Meeting him in her brother-in-law's Hortonville restaurant, Nellie Burns eventually married camp Sergeant Orville Williams. He and the other guards held at least two private dances at the Community Hall in Hortonville during that summer. At these dances select PW's served the lunch to the GI's and invited guests. Nellie remembered PW's being transported to local and area fields and factories including the Flanagan Kraut Factory in Bear Creek and Hamilton's Kraut Factory in New London and perhaps Shiocton. After the war one ex-prisoner who returned to the States called on her, seeking her husband. A local family sponsored another immigrating former prisoner, hiring him to work in their quarry. Nellie also remembered the lone permanent building used as the camp PX where guards and prisoners could purchase items.[11]

Donald Reinke. Bonduel, WI -
"I experienced a generous taste of anxiety and apprehension while transporting bus loads of German prisoners. . . . Especially alarming was when the one and only American guard would enter the bus, toss his rifle to a prisoner to hold, and then sit up in front and visit with me during the trip." As his father's substitute bus driver, 17-year-old Donald Reinke sometimes transported the PW's from Hortonville to the Flanagan Kraut Factory in Bear Creek. Reinke decided that gun so readily tossed about in his bus must have been unloaded.[12]

John Groat. New London, WI -
Eventually, the military conceded and allowed Edward Craig to keep his six man prisoner crew for a week at a time. At first, Craig picked up the work crew each morning and returned them again that night. However, the roads were so poor between Camp Hortonville and his Royalton farm that too much time was consumed in traveling to make the trip practical. Craig and the military settled on a weekly schedule. Returning he week's crew on Friday, he picked up the next group and took them home. On Saturday, he and the prisoners got to know each other as they toured the farm. On Sunday, a no-work rule was strictly enforced, so Edward would take his PW crew to their preferred church; St. Mary's Catholic, the Congregational Church of Royalton, or the Lutheran Church in Manawa. Craig had converted a garage into a sleeping barracks. His wife received additional ration stamps to feed the prisoners who ate with the family and other hired help. As Craig told it, many of these prisoners came from Bavaria where the terrain and climate are similar to this part of Wisconsin. A hired hand as well as many neighbors spoke fluent German, so some camaraderie between the prisoners and neighbors grew. From John Groat's conversations with Edward Craig, his father-in-law, Groat understood that the prisoners might even casually walk into town (Royalton) for a beer in the evening.[13]

Ralph Melchert. Seymour, WI -

The guard with the gun slung over his shoulder always frightened young Ralph Melchert. Ralph confronted this guard whenever
he rode with his father to the Seymour canning factory to pick up
a prisoner to help on the farm. "The PW's were not scary at all.
They were just ordinary looking men and didn't have any guns." It
was not always the same prisoner who came out to help. But one
came more often than the others. This prisoner would try to "wait
for the man in the black car," hoping to work for Ralph's German
speaking father, Ray. At the Melchert farm, the PW would always be
brought into the kitchen to eat with the family at noon and share
friendly conversation as well.[14]

Marion Root Books. Hortonville, WI -

While using his horse drawn hay mower, side delivery rack, and
hay loader, Elmer Root became a special attraction to the PW's that
lined the common fence to watch. This method of harvesting must
have been a real curiosity to the prisoners because they pointed
and talked among each other as they watched Elmer work. Living
on the adjoining farm, Marion (Root) Books recalled no sense of
danger felt by her family or others in the area. She also repeated a
story her father heard from guards at camp. The first load of coal
delivered to the camp disappeared overnight. A little puzzled, the
military delivered another load, but by morning that coal had also
disappeared. Upon investigation the guards found the prisoners
had taken all the coal and buried it beneath their tents, hoarding
it for expected future winter shortages.[15]

Bernita Rynders. Hortonville, WI -

Labor was so short that Bernita Rynders of Hortonville recalled
her husband hiring off-duty camp guards to work mixing concrete
in their Rynders Gravel and Block Concrete Company. During the
camp's existence several different guards worked for him, happy
to make a few extra dollars. While Rynders paid the going wages,
he rewarded two outstanding workers with a trip to a Green Bay
Packer game. Bernita recalled these guards being unafraid of their
prisoners believing they would not even try to escape, content to
be well fed and out of the fighting. She also remembered the daily
rumble of open military vehicles driving past their house transporting PW's from the camp to the cannery in town.[16]

Peter Olke. Land O' Lakes, WI -

"My Aunt Alma Olke never married and worked as a postmistress at the Hortonville Post Office during World War II. She often told us kids about the nice German boys fresh from the war who would walk down to the post office to mail letters home. Aunt Alma grew up speaking both English and German. She also told us that many of the town folk took picnic lunches to the prisoners when they worked in the fields. A few of the residents even found some of the prisoners somehow related to them. Alma could not remember one escape attempt."[17]

Name Withheld. Black Creek, WI -

"When I got to the viner and the prisoners saw me, boy, did they start buzzing. I couldn't understand what was being said, but my father could. As a 16-year-old, I had lipstick on when I arrived with Daddy's lunch at the pea viner. Evidently, in Germany at the time, only ladies of the night wore lipstick. Daddy got to know the men as he supervised them day after day. When he told mother he had

Illustration of PW's rolling barrels of kraut, drawn by PW J. Geisler in 1946. Photo courtesy of Willie Rau, used by permission of the U.S. Army, Fort McCoy.

given his father's gold watch to one of the PW's to be fixed, she was angry, sure he would never see that watch again. But several days later, the watch returned in good working order. The folks corresponded with one PW for some time after the war. In later years, mother regretted not continuing the correspondence."[18]

Lois Melchert Coomer. Fond du Lac, WI -
After the war and during the Berlin Airlift, the Melchert family sent flour, sugar, coffee, soap, toothbrushes and paste, and other hard to get items to the Willi Kurschinski family in West Berlin. In return, Lois and Janet, the Melchert daughters, played with a lovely doll tea set sent from Germany. When Lois graduated from college, she and three friends took a European tour. Staying at the Kurschinski home several days, they were shown the famous Berlin Wall. In 1978, Ellen Kurschinski, daughter of Willi, returned the visit. A life-long friendship had developed while Willi, a PW, worked on the Melchert family farm.[19]

Camp Janesville 1944 & 1945

An ambush awaited the PW's when they arrived in Janesville. Five young boys were prepared to take on these German enemy soldiers. Three even had their bows and arrows strung. These youngsters were also in the right location. While many other disappointed area residents had gone to the depot anticipating getting a look at these captives as they got off the train, the boys and a few lucky local residents waited at the Western Avenue railroad crossing. It was June 21, 1944, when the first 240 prisoners and guards arrived in New York Central cars on the Chicago North Western line. At the Western Avenue crossing six rail cars were uncoupled from the train and the Janesville prisoners got off. The remaining cars of prisoners proceeded to the Jefferson area. Their ambush ready, the boys were in an open door of a box car near the passenger train but were noticed and warned by the police.[1] As the train halted, an Army officer contacted John, a former German top sergeant, with orders to have prisoners unload. Fluent in English, John acted as the camp "*lagerfuhrer*" or prisoner spokesman. In German, John then gave the orders, and the prisoners filed out of the railroad cars and formed up, five abreast, on the roadway leading to the camp.[2] After a quick review and head count they marched, singing, the five or so blocks to their camp at the top of the hill. Once in camp, they pitched their two-man tents, getting ready for work the following day.

A cookhouse, shower and bath buildings, a dining tent and about 125 tents for sleeping all surrounded by a snow fence and barb wire made up Camp Janesville. A second row of fencing was in place the first year. Observation towers at opposite corners allowed the guards to keep an eye on the area between the fences.[3] This encampment was located on the southwestern edge of the city at the corner of Crosby and Western Avenues. Before the arrival of the PW's, the city ran a water pipeline for shower and sanitary facilities and arranged for the connection of electricity for floodlighting the ten acre camp. Meals were prepared in the cookhouse and served in a large mess tent set up for eating. The guards as well as prisoners slept in the tents.[4] Most food served at camp was trucked in from the Truax base in Madison. Often the prisoners ate their lunch at the local cafe nearest their canning plant. From this camp trucks took the prison labor force to canneries in Whitewater, Evansville, Walworth, Stoughton, Fort Atkinson, Lake Geneva and Elkhorn. During the short intervals between the harvest of different crops for canning, they also worked for area farmers.[5]

The camp stood on one side of the road and the mobile home housing the 1944 camp commander, Captain Hugh Lee and his wife, Mary, stood on the opposite side. The soccer field behind their trailer bordered a cornfield. Although there was little trouble among the approximately 240 prisoners in the camp, one escape attempt did occur. Two prisoners hid in the cornfield during a soccer match, but the guards quickly rounded them up without trouble. As a psychological deterrent to further escape attempts, Captain Lee chose this time to demonstrate his expert marksmanship with a pistol by going around camp shooting rats. (Fearing the plague, the Germans hated rats and now respected Captain Lee's pistol as well.) No additional escape attempts occurred. However, the guards sometimes had difficulty keeping the local young girls away from the camp. After the 1944 canning season, these German prisoners were shipped to Nebraska to work in the potato fields.[6]

The 1945 encampment commanded by Captain Witenhall held a much larger detachment of men. During the pea pack approximately 350 prisoners occupied the camp, and that number grew to nearly 600 for the corn pack. On June 21, 1945, the first of these prisoners arrived from Billy Mitchell Field with tentage and supplies to set up camp. This contingent and the others arriving later worked from June 22 to October 22 putting in 87,540 man-hours of work. The last of the prisoners packed up the remaining tents and left October 29, some headed to Billy Mitchell Field, the others to Hines, Illinois.[7]

In a two vehicle accident, nineteen German PW's were injured, seven seriously enough to be hospitalized. Attempting to avoid an oncoming truck the vehicle transporting the prisoners skidded and overturned on County Highway A near Johnstown the morning of August 13, 1945. The incident happened as the prisoners headed to a work site on a farm near Delavan. The only military personnel on board was the driver, T/5 Jack Ary who was uninjured.[8]

Two local men had a good deal of individual contact with the

Johnstown Center viner crew, July 1945. Photo courtesy of Arthur Pratt.

camp. Dr. Erland Otterholt served as the "contract surgeon" during the summer of 1945. His duties required him to visit the camp three times a week to take care of any minor injuries or illnesses. Father Joseph Strange was Associate Pastor at St. Patrick's Church in Janesville. Additionally, he regularly held Sunday mass at the camp. Usually, between twenty five and thirty prisoners attended his services. Both Otterholt and Strange believed the prisoners to be well disciplined and of little threat to the community. The prisoners seemed to be biding their time, waiting to be sent home.[9]

In August, when told of the Japanese surrender, the German prisoners made no show of emotion, but their spokesman said, "We are glad — we are glad. Many lives will be saved." Captain Witenhall believed the men were hoping they would soon be sent home because the war finally ended on all fronts.[10]

The PW's stationed at Camp Janesville put in a tremendous effort helping harvest and process the local vegetables. A local news article suggested, "It is doubtful that this food could have been saved without PW help."[11] The article also included the monetary value of their work as reported by Fort Sheridan. In a press release quoted, the military presented figures showing the PW earnings paid by private companies to the military in 1945 from Janesville totaled $45,940.

RECOLLECTIONS
Mary Lee. Eau Claire, WI -
One of very few women to live in a PW camp, Mrs. Mary Lee,

wife of Captain Lee, had several recollections of her summer at Janesville. Accompanying her husband on inspection runs, she occasionally ate at the local cafes with the prisoners. She was surprised to find that apple pie (an unknown item in Germany) quickly became the favorite dessert of the prisoners. Two of the restaurants the PW's frequented included the Villa Restaurant in Elkhorn[12] and College Grill in Whitewater.[13] At camp, Mary also noted some strange food habits. It seemed the prisoners preferred chopped onions in lard on their bread instead of butter. Once the PW spokesman came to the trailer asking permission of the captain to give a cake to his wife. The prisoners had made several for a birthday celebration. Mary remembered the cake to be more of a torte than a cake. About six to eight inches across and sliced in thin layers, the cake had marmalade between the layers. Frosted with a rich powdered sugar and butter frosting the cake decorated by the prisoners had corn flakes around the edge and pineapple arranged like flowers on the top. Although a female living in an American PW camp during the war, Mary Lee was never afraid of any prisoners in Janesville. She noted that during stays at other camps, she was uncomfortable with two prisoners, both of whom were eventually identified as SS men. When she and her husband were transferred from a PW camp at Sidnaw, Michigan, they decided to send their accumulated furnishings back to her parents in Eau Claire, Wisconsin. With prisoners Rudy and Willi, who had also been with them at Janesville, driving a truck full of their belongings, they followed in their car. All four stayed the night with her parents, the Everett Joneses in Eau Claire, returning to Michigan the following day. Mary recalled John Ziegler as the most memorable PW at the Janesville camp. Prior to the war, he had a violin factory in Leipzig and traveled from Milwaukee to Minneapolis and around the Midwest selling his violins. Fluent in English, familiar with the Midwest, it was natural for him to become the camp "*lagersprecher*," representative. Because of Ziegler's position, the Lees had more association with him than any other individual prisoner. In 1949, the Lees were stationed in Oberammergau, Germany for a two year period. While in Germany, they made contact with John Ziegler and several other former prisoners and maintained correspondence with several of these men after returning to the States. A few years later John Ziegler requested that Mary sponsor and host his daughter who wanted to immigrate to America. But she was unable to do so at the time.[14]

Donald Roedl. Janesville, WI -

Donald Roedl, Janesville canning company foreman, remembered that the first year the prisoners worked there, they demanded treatment according to the Geneva Treaty rules, refusing to work more than twelve hours. He said they simply quit working and walked away from their jobs after twelve hours. However, the second year "They would work twenty hours a day without complaining." While usually bussed from camp to the factory, sometimes they marched under guard to and from work. During their marches Roedl and many other neighbors recalled their robust singing along the way.[15]

Dorothy Wyss. Janesville, WI -

"I never hear 'Lili Marlene' without thinking of those men," Dorothy Wyss said. She lived near the camp at the time and heard them as they marched to and from work as well as on many Sundays when they marched to Monterey Stadium for calisthenics.[16]

Doris Waters. Janesville, WI -

Only a teen at the time, Doris Waters lived just down the road from the camp. Her mother often made coffee for the guards. Listening to their conversations, Doris realized the biggest problem facing the guards involved the girls who frequently visited the camp. A guard once told how he prevented a determined girl from crawling under a prisoner's tent.[17]

Robert Voss. Walworth, WI -

"I hid in the cornfield to watch them," said Robert Voss. He watched the PW's load hemp onto a flatbed truck on the Myrl Nash farm next door. The loaded hemp went to a plant in Darien to be made into rope. Though they looked like ordinary men, Voss saw the PW on their clothing, understood them to be enemy soldiers, and feared them.[18]

Mary L Jensen. Darien, WI -

"As a child in Elkhorn, I remember chasing after trucks carrying German prisoners to the pea cannery there. We would run behind the open trucks shouting 'Hi-Ho, Hitler' at them, and I remember they would laugh and shout back to us."[19]

Hildegard Hoefler. Whitewater, WI -

"When we said grace before meals, the three PW's folded

their hands and bowed their heads. We had a small farm and for extra cash my husband worked on the Hugh Miller farm's milk trucks. When two of Miller's trucks broke down, Hugh needed my husband's services immediately, but we had grain to shock and corn to husk. So, Miller made a deal. He would send over three PW's that worked for him in trade for the mechanical labor. Miller asked me to be responsible for feeding them, which I did. We had a nice dinner at noon and a lunch around 5:00 p.m. Usually, my husband returned them to the Miller place between 7:00 and 7:30 each evening. But one time he was busy, so we had our daughter Rose drive them the seven or so miles. Rose and I laugh now because she was only 9 at the time and remembers passing a state patrolman on the way. We never had any fear about her being alone with those men."[20]

Edward Witcpalek. Ashland, WI -

A group of five to ten PW's with a couple of guards went to the local dime store to use their funny money (scrip) to purchase incidentals. Edward Witcpalek understood the business owner redeemed the scrip for cash at camp. Witcpalek assumed these prisoners were being rewarded for good behavior for these special opportunities. He did not recall seeing them ever going to a restaurant or bar. However, he did recall shouting matches between some of the local teenage boys and these prisoners. As Witcpalek recalled witnessing these activities, he also remembered the knee-high boots on those prisoners and their distinct fatigue uniforms.[21]

Leigh Morris. Naperville, IL -

The only time my father, Staff Sergeant Eugene Morris, knew he actually hit an enemy soldier was when he fired while escorting a PW transfer from Kansas to Wisconsin. When the train stopped, a German officer managed to make a break. My father spotted him and ordered the prisoner to halt in both English and in German. When the German prisoner ignored the order, my father fired a single shot from his service pistol, hitting the PW in the leg and brought him down. Leigh Morris remembered being fairly young when he first heard the story and remembered asking his father if he felt good when he shot the Nazi. "My dad looked at me and, in words I'll never forget said, 'Son, I did what I had to and I would do it again, but it never feels good to shoot a man. His blood was as red as our blood, and he hurt just as much as we would. I pray you will never have to fire a shot at an enemy soldier.' I sure didn't appreciate what he said back then, but I grew to understand his sentiments." Staff Sergeant Morris guarded PW's at Camp Janesville and in Door County. [22]

Arthur Pratt. Beloit, WI -

Once Arthur Pratt came home from work toting a Nazi hat emblem with the eagle on it. On other days, he returned with epaulets, stripes, and German coins. As a 15-year-old, Art worked as a checker, weighing the shelled peas at the Johnstown Center viner on County Trunk A. Young Pratt would trade half pound packages of Ploughboy or Summertime tobacco from his father's local country store for these German trinkets. The second shift, working from 3:00 p.m. to 9:00 p.m. or 10:00 p.m., caused some trouble and had to be split up. They repeatedly put huge loads of peas into the viner, shearing the pin as the load hit the cutters. Moving the tractor, untangling the vines and replacing the pin all took time. After the PW's ignored repeated warnings, the boss considered their actions intentional sabotage and reported them. That group of prisoners did not return. The day crew, however, was a friendly bunch, pleasant and willing to work. Arthur learned that one had been a pilot, one an aircraft gunner, one on a submarine, another a paratrooper and the other four infantrymen. One noon break, PW Richard Stanilaus borrowed Arthur's bike for a little ride, but he didn't come back as expected. Arthur began to fear he had lost his bike as the PW made his escape. However, the prisoner returned all excited about the black cows he had seen about a mile and a half down the road. Frank Zellnow, the viner boss, stuffed the whole crew in his car and took them down to the neighbors to see their first black Angus cattle. Pratt remembered August, the artist among the crew who asked for pens or anything that he could paint and draw with. "Auggie" decorated the big canvas drop sheets between the viners with mountain scenes. He also made the hats he and many of the crew wore. He used cardboard and covered them with the cheesecloth Zellnow bought for him. Once in a while Werner, the Messerschmit pilot, would do Arthur's figuring for him, but he used the European seven. Pratt often reminded him not to put the slash across the sevens or the boss would know he wasn't doing his own job.[23]

Camp Jefferson
1944

It had been a long ride when the train finally pulled into the Janesville depot. The prisoners looked forward to getting off and stretching their legs after riding straight through from Michigan. But these Germans were ordered to stay in their seats. Instead, six rear passenger cars of prisoners were uncoupled at that brief stop. And for this group of PW's their journey continued on to Jefferson. Many local curiosity seekers there expressed disappointment at the spectacle. "Are these Hitler's supermen?" one surprised lady demanded. She and about 100 other spectators watched the arrival of 180 PW's at the Jefferson station, June 23, 1944. The crowd noticed that most of the prisoners wore African campaign ribbons and at least two wore the narrow blue sleeve band of the crack Hermann Goering division. One German youth proudly wore the Iron Cross and a few others wore other unidentified decorations. With eighteen guards and two officers, they sang cadence as they marched to the Jefferson County Fairgrounds where they would be quartered for the season.[1] *The Fort Daily News* reported the guards accompanying the prisoners were all equipped with tommy guns. This group had come from Camp Custer in Michigan and had been in Colorado prior to their Michigan assignment.

The canning factories of Watertown, Lake Mills, Fort Atkinson and Waterloo paid the cost of improvements to the fairgrounds for housing the prisoners. They also paid the cost of returning the buildings to conditions for fair use at the end of the encampment.[2] The American officers immediately set up headquarters in the dance hall, and the educational building was arranged as a mess hall.[3] Cots were placed in other buildings on the grounds and tents were erected to provide sleeping space. Located between the race track and the east boundary of the fairgrounds, the camp was surrounded by a fence with two strands of wire. Under orders of their commander, Captain Graff, military guards patrolled the enclosure constantly.[4]

Stalag Wisconsin

A week later, the June 29, 1944, *Jefferson Banner* ran two articles about the camp. The first included a request by Col. Wm. H. Mc-Carthy, the Commander of the Wisconsin-Upper Michigan District, that civilians stay away from the camp. Quoted were his standard phrases about the "short-lived nature of this work . . . (and) the war prisoners (should) be allowed to devote their entire efforts to the projects without being distracted by interested on-lookers." In the second article, Commander Captain Graff called on parents to keep children away from the camp fences. It seemed many boys and girls and their bikes were on the road near the fence, creating a safety concern for the Army trucks transporting prisoners to and from job sites.[5] Local children and adults viewed the PW's regularly marching the two blocks from the fairgrounds to the Rock River for a swim. Though stationed at Jefferson, the PW's were employed at Libby canneries outside the community. Transported by truck back and forth daily, thirty worked at Watertown, ninety at Lake Mills, thirty went to Waterloo and another forty were employed at the Fort Atkinson plant.[6] A few others remained at camp as cooks and maintenance personnel. These prisoners and their guards stayed in Jefferson only for the pea pack. They left as scheduled, in plenty of time to prepare the grounds for the Jefferson County Fair held each August. The local press mentioned their departure July 25th expressing relief that there had been no escapes from this camp, unlike many other camps around the state and country.[7]

RECOLLECTIONS
Name Withheld. Jefferson, WI -
Though Reverend August Bergmann was retired he occasionally still held special "German Services" in the old pioneer Christberg Church outside of town. Having been orphaned and coming to the U.S. from Germany, he had maintained fluency in his native language. So Camp Jefferson called on the retired reverend to regularly hold services in German for the prisoners at the local camp. Grandpa Bergmann had fond memories of that experience as he related them to his grandchildren.[8]

Thomas Tiller. Greendale, WI -
"As a 14-year-old, I visited the residence of the soon to be U.S. Congressman Robert K. Henry. He was a banker at the time and lived in a stately house. Beyond his large back yard was a cornfield and next to that was a large barracks housing German PW's. The Henrys had a maid whose job included feeding the family pet, a

**PW's head to sheds for coffee and treats during a break on
the Creydt farm near Lebannon in June 1944. Photo courtesy
of Glenn Schwock.**

Dachshund named Schatze. Sometimes the maid had to call Schatze for dinner as he ran into the cornfield. She went to the edge of
the field and called 'Schatze' several times. The prisoners would
come to the wire fence and hoot and holler back at the maid who
never understood why. I don't believe anyone ever told her that
'*Schatze*' in German means 'sweetheart'."[9]

Faith Blaese Madzar. Natick, MA -
"My family lived just two blocks from the local (Watertown)
canning factory. During the pea canning season our interest was
piqued as we loved the sweet raw peas. On several occasions we
went to the factory fence and implored the German PW's to toss
some vines over the fence to us. This effort was not exactly fraught
with danger, but it was surely an out of the ordinary adventure for
a 9-year-old and her friends. And they DID toss over the peas!"[10]

Alma Haubenschild. Jefferson, WI -
The Germans marched right past our house on North High Street
both coming from the depot to the fairgrounds and then returning
at the end of their stay. They were the first men I had ever seen
wearing shorts. At times they also marched from the fairgrounds
across a cow pasture to the Rock River for a swim. They were always guarded by soldiers with sub machine guns. And while they
were swimming, the bridge across the river as well as the river

bank were also guarded. At camp, the PW's often sang at night, and neighbors walked down toward the fairgrounds to listen from a distance. Many of us spoke German and could understand the words as well as enjoy their music. They could really sang beautifully, but they were still the enemy! When they left, the buildings had to be whitewashed again to cover the swastikas marked on the walls.[11]

Betty Buelow. Goddard, WI -
Betty Buelow didn't get out of work until 10:00 p.m. each night. She worked as a switchboard operator for Wisconsin Bell located above Burge's Grocery Store. While taking numbers for the old cord board, she often got comments like, "You have a nice sweet voice. I'd like to take you out." In the brief conversations she learned these callers were guards at Camp Jefferson. The voices made it known they knew where the phone company was located and often asked when she got off work, suggesting they would wait for her. She quickly learned to tell such callers she got off work at midnight and would very cautiously slip out to walk home alone at the end of her 10 p.m. shift. Though Betty never heard any stories about these guards attacking any local gals, she was uncomfortable with her own situation. Don Buelow, her fiancee at the time, was also a little put out, being sent off to Europe while other GI's were back home attempting to invade his territory.[12]

Barbara Whally Suetzholz. Racine, WI -
"Mother sternly warned: 'Don't look at them, they are German prisoners.' But as a small child I didn't understand. To me they were just men working on the nearby farm. They were friendly and would always smile at me."[13]

Lake Keesus 1944

When 250 Nazis checked into the Lake Keesus Resort Hotel, they entered perhaps the most posh PW camp in the nation. Prior to the war, this resort offered guests luxury and many amenities including the best swimming in the area. The large bathhouse had separate male and female changing rooms and a basket area for securing personal belongings. Not only those staying at the resort used the facility but area residents had also been welcome. The beach area had a nice dock with a diving board on the pier providing a unique form of recreation. The resort also boasted a large beautiful hardwood dance hall with stage. But these facilities were no longer available to civilians. In mid-June, 1944, German prisoners and their guards took over the establishment. These prisoners helped in the Merton, Sussex, Oconomowoc and Hartford canneries.[1] Earl Fieldhack, the owner of the hotel, moved his bar to a nearby summer cottage. This move allowed him to keep his liquor license while the prisoners took over his hotel that season. The relocation did not hurt business as the cottage now became a regular watering hole for the guards as well as continuing to serve the local patrons. Another cottage became camp headquarters. The Lake Keesus Hotel bar became the kitchen and mess while the dance hall easily transformed into sleeping quarters with the addition of rows of bunk beds stacked four high. The hotel above the dance hall housed the American officers and guards. A snow fence surrounded the compound. The military also put up a second fence of rope about two feet outside the snow fence, behind which local spectators were to stay. Across the road from the resort the ball diamond and large open field became available for the PW's to play soccer.[2]

Some of the prisoners rode trucks to work in neighboring community canneries. But each morning many of the prisoners marched the mile or so down the road into the village of Merton to their jobs at that canning factory. Housewives often lined the sidewalks clutching their offspring as they watched this recurring parade. Other area residents traveled out to the resort to get a peek at these prisoners. On weekends, German people from Milwaukee came to visit with the prisoners over the fences.[3]

In late June panic set in. Breaking the quiet of the downtown street in Merton, loud-speakers blared out the warnings: "War prisoners have escaped! Stay under cover! We will shoot to kill!." These orders were shouted by two guards as they searched for two missing prisoners. Since the escapees were enemy war prisoners, they must be murderous villains. Terror stricken, many people closed their windows and curtains, barred their doors, and feared for their lives. Within an hour the two German soldiers were found walking along a country road keeping their dates with two local girls.[4] On July 21, 1944, the camp internal security office reported the return of four other German prisoners of war who had escaped. In truth, these PW's had not even left the compound but were celebrating their anticipated upcoming move to another camp. (Bill Fieldhack, son of the resort owner, believed that about fourteen prisoners escaped in total, but each was rounded up and returned to camp fairly quickly.) Camp Keesus closed the last week in July, most of its prisoners moving on to Camp Rockfield and Camp Hartford.[5]

Perhaps it was his wife's missing chickens or maybe the terrific damage the military boots did to the dance floor, but for whatever reason, Earl Fieldhack did not lease the property to the military again the following year. Elated area residents got their swimming hole back. However, prisoners would still be in the area. Transported in from other camps, they continued to fill the labor shortage in the Merton cannery in 1945.

RECOLLECTIONS
Robert Weber. Merton, WI -

"Dibble Dabble" was a water game played by the prisoners and a few guests at the Lake Keesus Hotel swimming hole. One swimmer would take a matchstick down as deep as he could and release it. Those swimmers on top would then fight to be the one to get the matchstick as it rose and earn a point. Bob Weber, who often swam with the prisoners, recalled a lot of rough housing and even pushing each other off the pier to get the stick. Prior to the war the hotel swimming beach and large bath house was a local favorite. The lake had a rock bottom that dropped off quickly, so the pier and two diving boards were well used. According to Bob, the Germans were good swimmers. Weber recalls that when the prisoners first came, the swimming hole and bathhouse became

A watercolor painting of the Lake Keesus Resort from the water by Helen Johnson, summer 1944. Photo courtesy of Helen Johnson.

off limits to all civilians, but it wasn't too long before the guards realized that the local boys/men that worked with the PW's were not going to cause any trouble and were allowed to use the facility again. Not only did Bob and several others swim with the prisoners but also enjoyed the evening campfires and sing-alongs that occurred on the hotel lawn that sloped down to the lake. After his regular evening milking chores on his parents' farm, Bob Weber would go to the hotel and pick up a load of prisoners on a 1932 stake platform truck taking the men to the Merton Canning factory for the second shift. There they would work until that day's harvest was packed, somewhere between 11:00 p.m. and 3:00 a.m. A rapport quickly developed between Bob and the prisoners as they shared not only the work but also the laughter and song back at the resort. The lake also provided good fishing for the guards as well as the locals, according to Bob.[6]

Helen Schiek Johnson. Oconomowoc, WI -

Hauling the piano outside for accompaniment, the PW's would sing, entertaining themselves as well as the spectators outside the fence. For those that could not understand German, their voices and harmony were still very enjoyable.[7]

Betty Fieldhack Dost. Ogema, WI -
Betty Fieldhack Dost recalled that the PW's found their old wind-up Victrola and would also haul that outside and play it to death. It played the big '78' records.[8]

Richard R. Figlesthaler. Greendale, WI -
"I was 15 and had a scrapbook full of newspaper announcements of our servicemen who were killed or missing in action, and I knew my oldest brother was going through hell in the South Pacific. We spent most of the summer of 1944 at Lake Keesus, not far from the hotel that housed the PW's. While they worked during the day, in the evening the PW's were allowed to sit around outside and swim and sing and play music. Well, my brothers and I resented that, knowing our boys were treated like animals in their PW camps. So we would row our boat past them in the dark and shoot our BB guns and slingshots at them. It was our way of exacting a little revenge for what they had done."[9]

William Fieldhack. Merton, WI -
The chickens were gone!! Snitching them from the chicken coop, the prisoners had butchered and eaten every one of Mabel Fieldhack's chickens. Bill Fieldhack remembered his mother being so furious. Meat was a precious and rationed commodity at that time. Bill's dad, Earl Fieldhack, did not lease the resort out to the military the following year. Perhaps his wife's wrath over her missing chickens was a factor in that decision.[10]

John Eimermann. Merton, WI -
As a tow-headed 6-year-old, he was "adopted" by two of the Texan guards that summer. John Eimermann was spending his summer at the family cottage on the lake. His Uncle Bill's black and white dog, Mitzy, was over at the camp so often it became the camp mascot and left with the prisoners. As the camp was about to close, six or seven prisoners tried to make their escape. They stole a family rowboat and got only about five hundred yards. The boat was probably very overloaded. After ditching the boat, they headed inland and were recaptured along the nearby railroad tracks.[11]

Owen W. Van Pietersom. Menomonee Falls, WI -
"In our Wisconsin State Guard uniforms we were early for our

meeting at the Richards Street Armory in Milwaukee. So we decided to tour the nearby Granville canning factory on the way. The guard had no objection and let us in. As soon as the PW's saw us, everything stopped. They came over to see what kind of uniforms we were wearing and what our patches signified. They couldn't believe we were reserve units. One PW told us that our big cities like New York and Washington, D.C. were all flattened and even showed us picture postcards of them. About this time the guard told us to move along."[12]

Betty Fieldhack Dost. Ogema, WI -

"It took us a couple years to get the building (Lake Keesus Hotel) straightened out. They (PW's) were very greasy cooks." The dance hall had a beautiful wooden floor the size of a regulation basketball court with a stage built up on one side. "Their walking traffic wore the floor plenty bad." Betty Fieldhack Dost also remembered cottage number one being used as camp headquarters and the bar being moved into cottage number three. The cottages didn't need the extensive restoration that the main building required. Eventually, the resort did cater to civilian guests again.[13]

Dr. Michael Wheeler. Merton, WI -

On a 1988 trip to Europe, Dr. Michael Wheeler was traveling by train from Milan, Italy, to Innsbruck, Austria. Since the train was crowded, he was seated at a dining table with an elderly gentleman. Attempting to practice their respective foreign languages, the conversation developed and inquiries were made as to where each man came from. The elderly gent came from Germany and was surprised to find his young, fellow traveler from Wisconsin. Had the Wisconsin fellow ever heard of the small town of Merton? Of course, since he now owned Essential Industries, a manufacturing company housed in the old Merton Canning factory. That was the same factory that the German once worked in as a PW during the war. Wheeler's fears of an unpleasant meal were quickly allayed as the German spoke of his good treatment there at the hands of German speaking folks. This former prisoner who had been captured by the Americans on his way to the Russian front was more than satisfied with his PW experienced. As a thank-you to the people of Merton, the former prisoner insisted on paying for Wheeler's breakfast.[14]

Camp Lodi
1944 & 1945

In May of 1944, the military informed the Lodi Fair Association that the Army planned to lay concrete flooring under the grandstand, and in the fine arts hall, the agriculture building, the office and the chicken building. The military also planned several roof repairs. As the work concluded, the well fenced fairgrounds of Lodi became home to 250 German prisoners in 1944 and 233 PW's in 1945. Two new guard towers added extra security to the compound called Camp Lodi. The original plan called for all of the guards and most of the prisoners to live in the buildings with the overflow sleeping in tents. The Fair Association installed a large steam heating system for showers and cooking. Upon arrival, the prisoners did not use the fairground buildings for sleeping quarters. Instead, they lived in a tent city. Lodi expected the 100 Germans arriving on June 2, 1944, to be supplemented with 250 additional prisoners to arrive shortly before the pea pack started.[1] Due to an extreme heat wave, the pea crop shriveled and was about 30 percent below normal. As a result of the poor crop, the labor force needed in the area canning factories was also reduced. Therefore, the second group consisted of a much smaller number of prisoners than originally expected, the majority of that work battalion was permanently transferred to other camps where labor shortages did exist. Only eighteen prisoners worked at the Lodi Canning Company during the pea pack, and the city cannery even reduced the call for local employees. With the fairgrounds on the northeast side of the town and the Lodi canning factory on the southwest side, the small unit of prisoners marched to and from work each day. With a guard in front and another in back of the group, they often sang as they marched. Seven nearby canneries including those in Poynette, Arlington and Fall River hired the remaining prisoners.

The prisoners vacated Camp Lodi after the pea pack at the end of July, then returned for the corn pack. While Captain Thompson commanded both groups, a different company of German prisoners made up the 160 who arrived by special train Monday afternoon August 14, 1944. From the depot the prisoners marched to the camp. This group of men worked in the Lodi cannery and also rode trucks to canneries in Reedsburg, North Freedom, Baraboo, Pardeville, Poynette, Arlington, Sauk City and Waunakee.[2] The 1944 canning season ended on a bright note, the canners happy with the production level and work of their special employees. As this work battalion departed, *The Lodi Enterprise* reported the PW's as "a gang of downright 'good guys' (who) left Lodi last Monday . . . (on their way) to Janesville and to Sturtevant." And as they left, Captain Thompson agreed with the departing soldiers, noting the hospitality shown the guards was "splendid indeed."[3]

Early the following June, 1945, an advance Army work party set up the camp again at the Lodi Fairgrounds. This year farmers experienced a bumper crop of peas and expected about 450 prisoners to take up residence during the pea pack.[4] To the disappointment of local farmers, the camp opened with only 233 prisoners and their thirty guards plus two officers. Captain Otto A. Gast ran the camp that year. Prodded by Captain Gast and other area camp commanders, Columbia County Sheriff William Orth issued a statement of concern regarding fraternization between civilians and the 2,240 prisoners scattered in camps around Columbia county. He threatened that "Sentimental people or those of questionable loyalty will get into trouble if they make any effort to extend favors to German prisoners. They will be called upon to answer to federal or local statutes applying to their actions."[5] Orth's statement also reminded citizens that aiding and abetting the enemy were treasonous crimes, while loitering, trespassing and refusing to obey a legitimate order violated local ordinances.

At the end of the record pea pack, the prisoners remained to assist farmers rather than be shipped to Door County as expected. Joe Racek alone hired 150 Germans on his big cucumber farm at Mazomanie. Before the final harvest started, Dr. T. E Goeres, head of the Lodi Canning Company, issued an interesting and unique announcement. His company had decided to charge the farmers the expense of the improvements to the fairgrounds. He announced that farmers contracting these prisoners would pay 62 1/2 cents an hour. Sixty cents went to the government and the other 2 1/2 cents would pay for camp maintenance.[6]

A near fatal accident involving PW's occurred August 9, 1945. Returning from the Sparks Pickle Co. at Mazomanie, a company truck transporting twenty-five prisoners and one guard rolled over twice, throwing the men onto the blacktop. One German PW suffered a possible skull fracture while the others were not seriously hurt. The accident happened on County Trunk J about six miles from the camp. The investigation resulted in mixed testimony. Was a prisoner driving the truck against military rules? Initially, the military believed it was a prisoner driving an unfamiliar road who may have been going too fast for the curve. However, Fort Sheridan later released a statement saying that the brakes on the truck had failed. The military withdrew all prisoner help from the Sparks Food Corp. pending an investigation of both the poor brakes and the driver.[7] Injuries from the accident were more serious than first reported. The injured included twelve prisoners and guard Pfc. John W. Jewell from Antigo. All were hospitalized at Truax Field for the better part of the week.[8]

Prisoners stayed in the area through the corn pack. Unlike the record pea crop, the corn crop was very sporadic and later than usual. The military discussed several options before it finally agreed to remove all the prisoners during the October 5-7 Lodi Fair. However, housing the guards that remained caused a space problem. The weather became wet and cold so the army requested that the guards be housed in the vegetable and fine arts buildings. The military then brought in tents but not enough to replace the exhibit areas usurped by the Army personnel.[9] After the fair the

PW's enjoy cigarettes after lunch at the Kopan farm, August 1945. Photo courtesy of Robert Kopan.

PW's returned, working until November when they vacated Camp Lodi. Since local canning factories paid higher wages than most factories around the state, the difference was quickly reflected in Fort Sheridan's September press release. According to that release, Camp Lodi prisoners had already earned $61,142 for the government.The monetary value of the final six weeks of wages would later add to that figure.[10]

RECOLLECTIONS
Herbert Noltemeyer. DeForest, WI -

"The 1944 -1945 seasons brought severe labor shortages, bringing about the intervention of the U.S. Government. In our area, PW camps were established at the fairgrounds in Lodi, nine miles away and one at Columbus, twenty miles away. Arrangements for use of these prisoners were made through the State Employment Service and the U.S. Government. At the California Packing Corporation in Arlington where I was the payroll timekeeper, we hired twenty-five to thirty for each day and night shift from the Lodi camp and occasionally from Columbus. We transported them on a local farmer's cattle truck. Two guards accompanied the PW's and brought meals for themselves and prisoners. We used those speaking English as interpreters. They were very good workers and in only one case did we send one of them back to camp, for what reason I do not remember. The government billed us for their labor, we paid the government, and understood that the military paid the prisoners. In addition to the prisoners, we employed Jamaicans, Mexican nationals, Mexicans from Texas, and Truax Field soldiers and had no conflicts with any groups. Many local females joined the work force to operate machines as well work on the sorting tables. We also hired part time workers from the Badger Ordnance Plant and other area industries."[11]

Hazel Buchannan. Lodi, WI -

Hazel Buchannan, whose yard adjoined the fairgrounds fence, recalled, "they never bothered us, we never bothered them." But she did remember watching the guards go up the ladder, rifle in hand, to the guard towers. She also recalled seeing the prisoners doing calisthenics and other exercises together and playing ball in the camp. Her family watched them march down the street to various churches on Sunday mornings. Often the prisoners sang their own German hymns on their way. Hazel did not recall any fear of the prisoners or hard feelings toward them in the town. In fact, she recalled several prisoners returning to the Lodi area to live after the war. Kurt Pechmann and George Hall were among the PW's who returned to the area.[12]

Hazel's neighbor, Alma Paulson, added to her family income by doing laundry for the guards. Army shirts and trousers regularly hung on her clotheslines. These items did have to be pressed very precisely for which she may have charged as much as twenty-five cents each to launder. Hazel also knew Alma to bake cakes and other treats for the guards.[13]

Violet (Chick) Godfrey. Lodi, WI -
Another neighbor got in trouble with the guards one day. Violet (Chick) Godfrey also lived with the camp fence in her backyard. So when her little dog "Boots" went under that fence and into the compound, Violet climbed over the fence topped by a single string of barbed wire to retrieve the dog. (In many camps, at least part of the "fence" system was nothing more than snow fence. Note Camp Rockfield photo.) Of course, she was immediately stopped by a guard, rifle in hand. While she was allowed to call the dog back, she was sent home through the main gate after being admonished not to climb the fence again. Violet also remembered the prisoners always smoking cigarettes and a beer truck regularly stopping at the camp on Saturday nights. She and her family heard the PW's singing in the evenings. Reports circulated that one prisoner refused to work, claiming to be an opera star. He had long hair and a big build, but Violet could not recall his name. Another common story repeated by Violet was that certain local girls would climb the fence at night, chasing something other than dogs.[14]

Ann Hanneman Munz. Baraboo, WI -
"My two younger brothers, Lester and Charles, and their friends had a real scare while playing in a nearby grain field. The grain was standing in shocks and the boys were ducking behind them playing cops and robbers with their wooden rubber guns. All of a sudden Army jeeps and trucks came rolling into the field. Armed soldiers jumped out of the vehicles, expecting to find escaping prisoners, not little boys playing as they had for years. The field adjoined our lot and the camp was another lot away in the opposite direction. As we shouted back and forth over the fence with the prisoners, one in particular took a liking to me and called me his "little sister." We children had lots of other attention, too. Mother would often invite guards to Sunday dinner. "Pops" was the older

PW's take a break on a Kopan farm tractor, August 1945. Photo courtesy of Robert Kopan.

guard who had children about our age at home and took us under his wing. The prisoners sang so beautifully in the evenings and as they marched to St. Patrick's Catholic Church on Sundays."[15]

Al Haller. Fort Atkinson, WI -

Field supervisor Al Haller often gave agricultural lessons during lunch break as he answered questions from interested prisoners about various farming methods. The PW's were especially interested in dairy farming and how we handled, milked and fed so many cows. Raising beef cattle also intrigued them because it was not done in Germany. Since the tractors in their homeland were mostly diesel and smaller than ours, the PW's competed to drive our tractors, especially when pulling a huge, four-bottom plow. WOW!! Haller spoke fluent German and interviewed newcomers trying to find out if they had a farm background, what skills and experience they had, and which jobs they liked to do best. He attempted to use the prisoners as efficiently as possible. He asked the guards to send the "farm boys" to him, keeping the others for work around the canning factory itself. Though never having any real serious trouble out of the couple hundred PW's he dealt with, Haller did have some problems with a couple of his prisoner crew members. One lunch break, a Nazi-type prisoner tried to re-indocrinate his comrades. He encouraged them to slow down their work efforts and not aid the enemy. Al complained about the Nazi attempting to disrupt the work effort when he took the group back to the canning plant at Wanakee and never saw that PW again. The second problem arose at the end of the harvest banquet. Between forty and fifty prisoners were seated on long benches awaiting a thank you meal put on by the Waunakee plant. When a platter of sweet corn came by, one disgruntled prisoner dumped the platter yelling "swine fodder"! His comrades at the table immediately rose to their feet and the four nearest him quickly ushered him out the door to the awaiting guards. The others sat back down and enjoyed the meal. Al always found it amazing that some of those prisoners still believed the German propaganda claiming that all the Americans of German ancestry would immediately rise up and join the German army. As first generation born in America to German immigrants, he understood that most Germans left their native land because they did not like it there and were very much better off here in this country.[16]

Camp Markesan 1945

Was there a murder in Markesan in 1945? According to La Verne Pomplun, one Nazi prisoner killed another and stabbed a guard at Camp Markesan. Reports of that incident spread throughout the Grand River Canning Company where Pomplun worked with prisoners.[1] The local papers never reported the incident, but such a killing inside the compound would have been an "internal" matter and the military would have minimized any publicity. Furthermore, *The Markesan Herald* cooperated fully with the Army, keeping its reports of the camp and prisoners to an absolute minimum. Certainly a mix of attitudes existed among the PW's brought to Markesan. Goose-stepping, arrogant, Nazi types, blended with conscripts caught up in the times.

We know German PW's were in Markesan. In 1944, they came by truck or bus to the area canning factories from Camp Green Lake. But in 1945, the Germans camped right in town. As many as 637 started arriving by train in June for the canning season which ran into October. Authorities distributed them daily to the Grand River, Markesan, Fairwater and Fall River canning factories and some to area farms that contracted crops to those canneries.

Quartered on the Grand River Canning Company property, the grounds soon came to be known as Camp Markesan. They bivouacked in a tent city enclosed with a stockade fence. In *The Markesan Herald*, September 11, 1986, Harold Schreiber remembered large tents, about 30x80 feet each, with trenches dug out around them so the floors wouldn't get wet.[2] The company grounds also contained a quonset hut that served several purposes: a meeting room, a theater, a chapel and a dayroom where prisoners relaxed on their days off work.[3]

As with the other camps scattered around the state, local residents had mixed emotions about bringing the prisoners into their community. But reports from the area canning factories suggest that the PW's were good workers, completing their tasks as

Top, this rose-carved frame presented to Clarence Krause included the photo of carver PW Willi Pioch. Below left, a plaque carved from a pine crate and inscribed by PW Wilhelm Seeger of Bez Gremen, Germany, while interned at Camp Markesan. Below right, an elephant carving from a pine crate inscribed "PW Camp Markesan, Markesan, Wis." and presented to Clarence Krause in 1945. All three photos courtesy of a private collection.

assigned. Area resident and company foreman, Clarence Krause, recalled that while "guards took them to their work stations, the guards did not stay around while we worked. Once in a while a guard might come down to look in, but I never had any standing around where we were." Krause spoke German and quickly established a good rapport with the PW's. "They knew I was their boss," he recalled.[4] Clarence also remembered certain prisoners were designated as "trustees" and allowed to leave the compound without guards, some even known to walk uptown to drink a beer or two[5] or perhaps go to a movie. In October, the PW's vacated the camp and boarded a train to Montana for several weeks of work there before being sent back to Germany.[6] According to a September press release from Fort Sheridan, the PW's earned well over $49,000 for the military during their five month stay in Markesan.[7]

Camp Markesan played another unique role in the community the summer of 1945. The guards organized their own baseball team that regularly participated in the local league. Camp commander, Captain Klein, played right field on that team.[8]

RECOLLECTIONS
La Verne Pomplun. Wautoma, WI

"When I was a fourteen year old girl, I was hired to do a man's job. I worked side by side with the German prisoners for the Grand River Canning Company. Since I could speak and understand both "high" and "low" German, I was the interpreter for them and the American guards. It was a very interesting experience. The youngest prisoner was a sixteen year old. He seemed sincerely interested in coming to the U.S. to live after the war. The oldest man I worked with was sixty-three. When his ship was sunk, he swam through the burning oil floating on the water. Severely burned, he had no

A quonset hut was turned into a meeting and entertainment room with a movie screen at the front at Camp Markesan, 1945. Photo courtesy of William Slate.

PW's from Grand River Canning Company in Markesan, 1945. Rose frame carver Willi Pioch is at top right. Photo courtesy of William Slate.

hair, ears or nose. He had also lost his dentures and hoped to earn enough money working at the canning factory to buy new teeth. A very nice man, he was very lonesome for his family. At the end of the pea season things changed. The new group of prisoners to arrive were entirely different from the previous group. The first night in Markesan, they killed another German prisoner and stabbed an American guard. I was terrified! Tall, stately, good looking men, these prisoners had a mean, steely look in their eyes. They walked with a goose-step and looked like they enjoyed killing. I was very happy when told to leave. I hated being anywhere near them."[9]

Nancy Sexton. Appleton, WI
As a youngster, Nancy Sexton remembered the prisoners making lots of noise with their boots as they entered the Markesan Theater on Sunday evenings to watch the latest movie. They came together and sat as a group.[10]

Clarence Krause. Markesan, WI
The Grand River Canning Company plant foreman, Clarence

Krause, got along with the prisoners well enough to be the recipient of hand-carved gifts. Krause received an elephant and a rose plaque, both carved from the white pine crates used in the factories. At the same time another PW carved a beautifully detailed Indian head plaque for a co-worker. Krause often wondered to himself what the prisoners carved these gifts with, since he thought they were not allowed knives.[11]

Kay Schulz. Markesan, WI

Kay Schulz of Markesan remembered that as a child "I went

Camp Markesan entertainment corner includes a record player, radio, movie projector, movies, records, apple peeler. Photo courtesy of William Slate.

down to the river that runs right near the present Friday Canning Company . . . with my cousins. The others were five to seven years older than me, so they could cross the river without any problem on the stepping stones. But, being only 4 or 5 years old, well, it was a real challenge for me and I just couldn't get across. You know how kids are — they just take off and forget about the little kid left behind. Well, I must have been looking very lost and confused and probably crying. These men (PW's) were working on the other side of the river for the factory and one of them must have heard me and came across to help me. As I recall, he picked me up in his arms, carried me across and set me down. He said that I reminded him of his little girl at home. That was it. It was just a part of the day to me and I just accepted it and thought that he was nice."[12]

Roger Burlingame. Ripon, WI

"Some of the prisoners that came to our farm were older with gray hair. However, the majority were probably in their twenties and thirties. Most wore that wool German cap with flaps that came around the front and button under the chin. Sometime they sang as they worked in the field, probably to pass the time. In the hot sun, many took off their shirts exposing various scars. As a youngster, I was not too shy to ask about the hole in the upper arm of one. He indicated it was a bullet wound. At the time, I suppose I thought that was neat."[13]

Leona Kelm. Markesan, WI

In order to finance the war, the U.S. government encouraged civilians to purchase savings bonds. To generate interest in the bonds, military authorities transported the Japanese mini-sub captured in the Pearl Harbor attack around the country. The sub toured Wisconsin including the Markesan and Kingston area during the summer of 1944. Windows cut through the sides of the submarine allowed people to peer inside. Quite a unique site, it attracted much attention. With all the promotional publicity, the whole story remained untold as there was no mention of the sub's commander, Ensign Kazua Sakamaki, being held a PW in Camp McCoy most of the war.[14]

John Scharschmidt.   Markesan, WI

"My father, Felix Scharschmidt Sr., told us he wanted to take them outside, line them all up and shoot them. He hired six PW's to turn over the hemp in our small field, but he made a terrible mistake by inviting them inside to the big noon meal mother had fixed. Dad spoke German and as he visited with the prisoners during lunch, he got into a big argument with them. They were real Nazis and so arrogant! We had prisoners both years, so I can not say if this crew came from Markesan or Green Lake. I also recall that the PW's working at the nearby viner were very nice men."[15]

Lorraine Menke Laybourn. Markesan, WI

Another group of PW's became a constant irritation at the viner near the Menke farm. Frank Menke and his son Harvey hauled their peas to that viner between Fairwater and Markesan. The PW's there often disrupted the work by throwing stuff into the viner to slow up the process or actually jam the viner. Somehow the boxes of shelled peas often tipped over as well, a problem that did not occur before or after the PW's worked there.[16]

Camp Marshfield
1945

"**P**risoner of war labor cost more than free labor because of the necessity of the secure camp and additional sanitation measures required." Rudolph Binzel, manager of the local cannery, told that story in a news interview. He noted those expenses as he publicly announced his regret in the necessity of bringing in war prisoners. Binzel probably felt very uncomfortable at the time. The migrant workers imported the previous year provided some unique labor problems. He was troubled by what might happen with this group of workers. In 1944, Marshfield canning factory utilized men from Barbados who had access to the city during their free hours. In the interview Binzel did not mention various problems these imported, black workers encountered in the local community during that 1944 experiment. As Marshfield experienced its first exposure to racial diversity, many local bars and restaurants refused the Barbadians service.[1]

Local residents first learned of the plan to use PW's in a *Marshfield News Herald* story: "German War Prisoners to Work For Central State Pea Canners." On May 26, 1945, the story revealed that Marshfield had been selected as a site for a PW camp. The number of prisoners to come would be determined later based on results of local employment recruiting. The military planned a tent city on Marshfield Canning Company grounds, where the Army would control and feed the prisoners. The article assured local readers that prisoners would be well screened before being shipped to a work station such as this. Furthermore, the Germans would be well-guarded, remain in their compound when not working, and segregated from civilian employees as much as possible when on the job. The announcement noted these prisoners would supply labor for the Marshfield plant and the cannery at Stratford. (Actually, some worked at Loyal instead of Stratford.) Finally, in the story authorities asked area readers to stay away from the camp, reminding them of the "no fraternizing" rule and that "the curious only get in the way."[2] In a later announcement, the military explained that 50 percent of the Marshfield cannery output was consigned to the armed forces and that supply must continue. The U.S. government contracted the prisoners at a standard wage of fifty-five cents an hour for those employed at Marshfield and fifty cents an hour for those working at Loyal. The canners paid this money to the military, which in turn paid the prisoners their eighty cents per day in canteen scrip. Captain Detmars, the military spokesman, reported that the Army spent about thirty-five cents a day to feed a prisoner of war as compared to an average of fifty-eight cents a day for a member of the American military. Detmars also addressed reader concerns when he noted the food served the prisoners required only about 50 percent of the red and blue ration points allotted to civilians. The meat for the prisoners generally included less desirable cuts such as sausage, carp, pickled herring, hearts and livers. Prisoners received no butter and were allotted only four pounds of sugar per 100 men per day.[3]

Under camp commander Captain Kopps, an advance party of forty prisoners and guards set up the six acre camp. First, they used snow fence and barbed wire to enclose the Golden State property at the rear of the local canning company. Then, two guardhouses, one sentry house, showers and latrines went up. Tents provided shelter for mess and sleeping. Mostly young English speaking members of the Afrika Korps comprised this advance group of PW's. On July 8, the rest of the Germans arrived in ten army trucks. More than 243 prisoners guarded by Captain Jack Lyle and thirty-nine guards pitched additional tents and moved in. Captain Lyle reported that 125 of these men worked at the local cannery, another 100 at Loyal, and 18 maintained the camp doing the cooking, laundry and other chores.[4]

The following day a military convoy picked up the extra prisoners and headed toward Milwaukee. But along Highway 13 on the south edge of town, a car driven by 20-year-old Elmer E. Kumm from Pittsville struck the truck. The truck careened into the nearby ditch, rolling on it's side. Four prisoners remained hospitalized at St. Joseph's Hospital in Marshfield, one with serious chest injuries. Six others from the overturned truck returned to camp after being checked and released. Also checked and released, the passengers in the car, twins Ila and Ina Hartnett, sustained only minor injuries. Uninjured himself, Kumm was cited for failing to stop.[5]

With an abundant crop, new equipment, a new system of air

dusting the pea fields, and plenty of workers, the pea pack set a local and state record. As the bean pack neared completion, all but fifty PW's moved out to unnamed locations the second week of September. Captain Thomas Ryan, the new camp commander, and the remaining PW's stayed to help finish the bean crop and warehouse work.

This last contingent of PW's and their guards left after disbanding the camp October 1, 1945.[6] As the last of the PW's moved out, plant manager Rudolph Benzel felt very satisfied. There had been no unpleasant incidents involving these prisoner employees in the area. Very pleased with the work and behavior of the Germans, he and the other plant managers noted that the PW's had helped harvest and process the record pea crop and helped with the beans as well.[7] In putting forth that effort, the PW's housed at Camp Marshfield earned $32,649 in wages paid to the military, according to the September, 1945, report from Fort Sheridan.[8]

RECOLLECTIONS
John Smrecek. Marshfield, WI -
John Smrecek remembered his father taking his pickup to Loyal to hire as many as a dozen prisoners. Dad returned the prisoners back to Loyal after the day's picking. No guards accompanied the PW's to their day job. The cannery expected each prisoner to pick a quota of 120 pounds of beans per prisoner per day. After the healthier or more ambitious PW's picked their quotas they would often help out their fellow captives. The Smreceks had orders to feed them but give them no dessert or special treatment. But John's mother baked a cake anyway, allowing the PW's to share it with her large family. The Smrecek farm had a contract to provide beans to the canning company that year. The harvest was successful enough to buy a new Farmall tractor at the end of the season. John recalled that beans fetched three cents a pound and the steel wheeled tractor cost about $870.[9]

Florence Smrecek. Marshfield, WI -
Fearing the loss of her job, 16-year-old Florence Smrecek never talked to the PW's that worked with her in the Marshfield canning factory. Guards stood around also, increasing her apprehension. Perhaps believed at the time, Florence and the other girls in the cannery often repeated the rumored story that the PW's were fed the beans that dropped on the floor.[10]

Vern Volrath. Janesville, WI -

"Back in Germany that would never be allowed!" remarked a surprised PW as he watched the peas washed down the drain. The peas had spilled on the floor when a sealing machine jammed. Vern Volrath worked on one of the machines while the PW's loaded the sealed cans into baskets headed for the cookers. He spoke enough German to get the gist of the conversation among the PW's. From their exchange, Vern noted even the older ladies working in the Loyal Canning Plant looked pretty good to these female-starved, young prisoners. The same guard always accompanied the PW's in the stake-truck they arrived in from Marshfield each day but often seemed to vanish. Rumor had it the guard went uptown to a local bar.[11]

Barbara See Spencer, WI -

Fluent in German, Barbara See's mother learned from conversations with them that the PW's ranged in age from 14 to 20. As she visited with them she learned some had been in the Hitler Youth since age 10 or 11 and had no idea if their families were still alive or not. Barbara's brother, Philip, had been killed in April fighting Germany. These prisoners were surprised to learn that Germans were fighting Germany and they didn't seem to know what Germany was fighting for. The PW's also marveled at the size of the farm and number of buildings all belonging to one family. The See family hired several PW's to pitch peas for four days. A canning factory truck dropped off the prisoners for the day's work about 9 a.m. and picked them up again about 5 p.m. No guard accompanied them. Finding shade by the barn for noon break, the prisoners ate their sack lunch. Barbara's mother brought them water and visited with them.[12]

Leatrice Seefluth Meier. Wisconsin Rapids, WI -

My mother, Emma Seefluth, and I ran the Loyal Cafe at the time and had been hired to feed the PW's their noon meal. The prisoners worked nearby at the Loyal Canning plant. At the designated time, they came to the back door where we handed out their lunches. Never allowed in, they always ate outside.[13]

Delmer Capelle. Loyal, WI -

Perhaps he came from the grape growing area of Germany because one PW who worked on our farm outside Loyal took great interest in our grapes. Phillip Capelle and that PW had a very extensive conversation about raising grapes in this climate.[14]

Herman Albrecht. Arpin, WI -
Before leaving, the truck driver gave my father, Herman Albrecht, Sr., strict orders not to associate with the PW's and to leave them alone at lunch time. But Herman had already told his wife to fix a nice meal for noon since they were having company. When the driver went to town, probably for his own lunch, Herman invited the PW's inside to eat. Sent up on the roof, son Herman Jr. watched for the returning driver in order to warn the PW's to get back outside. After the war, the Albrecht family maintained correspondence with a couple of the PW's. Herman shared the reoccurring situation his sister experienced as she visited with the former prisoner, Paul Schley, in Germany. If the German family and their American guests went out to a club, the group would be made to feel unwelcome. But the host would simply go to the rest room and visit with the local men in there explaining the reason for the friendship. Then the entire group would be "in solid." Schley and his wife, Millie, returned to the U.S. touring central Wisconsin for five weeks in 1983, and spent some time with the Albrechts.[15]

Roger Liebzeit. Greenwood, WI -
A ride in an Army Jeep thrilled young Roger Liebzeit whose folks had eight or nine prisoners on their farm loading the peas. The MP sergeant guarding them from his Jeep gave young Liebzeit a ride one day. Roger remembered that a truck with large, metal containers of food came out each day to serve the prisoners lunch. "My family was German and still spoke the language. Mother usually brought out cake or some other treat in the evening to the men who generally worked until dark. At the end of the harvest, the sergeant allowed the PW's to go into the barn to see the twenty-five or so milk cows and the four horses. The prisoners looked closely at the cows, then petted the horses and checked out the harnesses and other equipment."[16]

Camp Milltown
1944 & 1945

The military was probably ecstatic about the lack of press coverage of Camp Milltown. It received absolutely no press coverage in 1944. The area press kept secret the fact that 180 Nazi prisoners of war bivouacked there and worked in area agriculture.[1] With as little fanfare as when they arrived, the military very quietly transferred the prisoners to Sidnaw, Michigan, for a pulpwood cutting detail at the end of August, 1944.[2] Milltown itself had no newspaper, the nearest being the *Polk County Ledger* in Balsam Lake, which ignored the camp completely that first year. In the following year, the *Polk County Ledger* only mentioned the coming of the Germans in July and published one additional article about them as they left.

During the first season the PW's utilized barracks on the Stokely property and tents across Highway 35 from the factory in Milltown for sleeping quarters. The cook shack on the property grounds became their mess as well. From this location, they walked across the road to the Milltown plant or were transported to work sites in nearby canning factories and farms as needed.[3] In 1945, the numbers of PW's in Milltown almost doubled that of the previous year. The canning industry listed 325 PW's deployed to Milltown in 1945.[4] This number of prisoners would suggest that about forty guards and officers also came to the community to supervise the prisoners. To house this larger group, the military relocated the camp and erected a tent city at the east end of the Milltown Park near the ball field.[5] By mid-October, 1945, the prison camp at Milltown closed for the last time. The prisoners tore down their tent city and moved out. They had completed their local work harvesting and packing area crops.

On October 25, the *Polk Country Ledger* summarized the press release from Fort Sheridan pertaining to the work efforts of the PW's stationed at Milltown. Their work was not as insignificant as the press coverage had been. The Germans at Camp Milltown had earned a total of $88,970 for the U.S. government, according to the Fort Sheridan report. Those wages came from combined work for the Friday Canning Company of New Richmond, the Stokely Foods, Inc. at Frederic and Milltown, the Lakeside Packing Company at Amery and the Hy-Dry Food Products, Inc. plant in Centuria.[6]

RECOLLECTIONS

Harriet Sund Anderson. Eau Claire, WI -

Harriet Sund Anderson recalled that "at harvest time a crew of six PW's with a guard was brought to the family farm to pick the peas my father (Alex Sund) had grown. When noon rolled around, it was time for a big country-style dinner. In the dining room, the German prisoners feasted on Mom's good wholesome food, topped off by her homemade pies. It was hard to picture these hungry young men as the enemy. We could tell by their smiles they really appreciated the meal." Harriet helped to cook and serve this meal. She also worked at the Stokely Brothers Canning factory in Milltown. Working with her on the platform were PW's without guards. She remembered one handsome young prisoner who motioned to her, trying to coax her to a secluded corner. Thinking he wanted a kiss, with a big smile Harriet said "I was too shy to go."[7]

Phyllis Larsen Beaulieu. Milltown, WI -

A tall, handsome blond-haired, blue-eyed young prisoner caught the eye of Phyllis Larsen when she was a girl on her father's farm four miles south of Milltown. Her father had requested some prisoners to help with the pea harvest. Four prisoners and two guards came to pitch the peas onto the pea loader. At lunch time, the prisoners were invited into the dining room to eat with the family. There the PW's also shared the "stew" that had been sent out with them for lunch that day. If the prisoners had returned with their rations, the food sent with them on the next farm assignment would be reduced. The young handsome one spoke good English and was the spokesman for the group. He seemed well educated and not pro-Nazi. For the first time Phyllis saw gold or silver work on (his) teeth. Pleased with their work, her father, Carl Larsen, requested the same group the following day. Mother Ella told the guards that she would feed them and the following day they returned without food from the camp. But in late August, a different crew of prisoners came to pick corn. They were less friendly and guards with rifles walked along the rows with this group of prisoners. In the apple orchard they ate what they brought for lunch. Later in the season, another crew of PW's worked along the roadside, digging holes for the electric poles that would soon bring electricity to the neighborhood. Concerned for their safety, Carl put the bull away in the barn as the PW's were digging in his area.[8]

Darwin Wosepka. Haugen, WI -
At Milltown, a prisoner went over the fence. Actually the guard spotted him and shot at him as he returned. However, since there was no bullet in the chamber of the guard's rifle, the prisoner was uninjured. Upon further inquiry, the guard learned that the prisoner had just left for a minute to mail a letter.[9]

Stuart Olson. Taylors Falls, MN -
Grabbed and carried up the ladder to the top of the stack of pea silage by a tall husky German prisoner, 6-year-old Stuart Olson was terrified. He struggled to get free. For what seemed like forever to the boy, the PW squatted down, holding Stuart tight as he rubbed his head. Eventually, the PW started to cry. A conversation in German took place between the PW holding the boy and others still on the ground. One prisoner spoke enough English to make Stuart and his horrified older friends, Lowell and Dale Fradeen, understand the situation. Stuart reminded the PW of his own little boy left behind several years ago, and the man just could not resist hugging this small child. The incident occurred a short distance from Stuart Olson's home at the Ubet pea vinery owned by Lakeside Canning Company of Amery. As curious youngsters, Stuart and his friends continued to wander down to watch the six to ten prisoners pitching peas or perhaps marching the short distance to the Route Country Store, where Mrs. Ruth Route fed them. However, they never got so close to the prisoners again.[10]

James Route. St. Croix Falls, WI -
For both the 1944 and 1945 harvest seasons, the table was set twice a day for hungry prisoners on Ruth Route's all-weather porch. The canning factory hired her to feed them as they worked the two shifts at the pea viner just down the road from her family's Route Country Store on F at Ubet. The prisoners appreciated her tasty home cooked hot meals as her husband attempted to converse with them in his limited German. A youngster at the time, Jim Route remembered his mother's guests well and remembered they sometimes purchased small items like candy in the store before heading back to work at the viner. The guard always seemed unconcerned,

dozing in the pickup or leaning his gun against his vehicle as he joined the PW's on the porch for dinner, too.[11]

Esther Anderson. Milltown, WI -

When the prisoners moved out, they left behind hand made wooden tables, stools and chairs. The cleanup crew allowed those interested to take these pieces. Esther Anderson remembered her boys dragging several items home and using them in their room for several years.[12]

Camp Oakfield
1945

A real Wisconsin blizzard ended the Oakfield sugar beet harvest. The blizzard came so unexpectedly and Camp Oakfield had only two shovels at the time.[1] Camp Oakfield quickly ordered more shovels as it became one of only six in the state to remain open into December of 1945. In the middle of June, a construction unit of German PW's set up Camp Oakfield on the northern edge of the village. Today, the local VFW post sits where the main gate to the camp was located. The prisoners staked and fenced the grounds, piped water onto the premises and erected poles for lighting facilities. They also made tables and benches to accommodate the sixty-eight or so "guests" they were expecting in their tent city.[2] Camp Oakfield supplied prisoner labor for the Star Canning Co. at Lomira; the Brownsville Canning Co. at Brownsville; and the Mammoth Springs Canning Co. in Oakfield, Eden and Sussex.[3] Because of the labor needs of these canneries, the camp quickly grew beyond all expectations. At the end of July, the canneries employed 238 Oakfield prisoners daily. The PW's quickly went to work putting in 46,340 man hours of labor by September.[4] In the middle of that month, a Fort Sheridan press release credited the Oakfield camp with total earnings of $40,132.[5] The PW's continued earning their keep through most of the sugar beet harvest. An early cold snap and that major snowfall put an end to their beet season, but only after they could no longer even chip the precious sugar beets out of the ground.

The local community became involved with the camp in several ways. The pastor of St. Luke's Lutheran Church was a German immigrant, Reverend John Dowidat. For that reason, he not only ministered to his own congregation but went out to the camp and ministered to the prisoners.[6]

The Oakfield ladies took seriously the request by the local camp commander to provide social outlets for the GI's serving at the camp. The camp reciprocated with a special event held at

Liberty Hall on August 31. Mrs. C. P Herr, Mrs. C. Walker and Mrs. H Castiano, wives of service men at the camp, helped T/4 Harry E. Michails and Sergant Wayne Petty with the decorations as the

Camp Oakfield officers and enlisted men held an informal dance party there. A seven piece orchestra furnished the music. Camp mess sergeant, Elderigo Eramo, supervised and helped serve a buffet lunch that completed the evening. Guests included village officials, representatives of the canning company and friends.[7]

RECOLLECTIONS
Maynard Chadwick Jr. Oakfield, WI -

Using the only two shovels in camp, two PWs make a path after an early blizzard. Photo courtesy of R.T. Heldt.

"The first men I ever saw wearing shorts were the PW's in the canning factory at Oakfield," said Maynard Chadwick Jr. His father reported the lax attitude of the guards while working at the Better Farms Inc. sugar beet harvest. One day the weather turned cold and a light snow

Camp Oakfield, 1945. Photo courtesy of R.T. Heldt.

fell. The southern born MP's found the temperatures very uncomfortable. They took every opportunity to ride in the trucks with the sugar beets to the railroad siding, often leaving the prisoners unguarded in the fields. One guard who had left his gun at the far end of the row sent one of the PW's back to get it. Both Chadwicks had limited respect for the guards who left their Jeeps and trucks regularly parked at the local bars.[8]

Clifford Gelhar. Oshkosh, WI -

"Willi Lindner begged me to take him to visit his sister in Milwaukee," Cliff Gelhar recalled. "But, of course, I couldn't do that — I didn't want to get into trouble. Willi was a PW working for me at the Mammoth Spring Canning Company Dehydrating Plant in Oakfield. I talked to the Red Cross in Fond du Lac and they made the contact for him. His sister came up to visit Willi. While the Red Cross kept me out of trouble, one of my civilian crew was not so lucky. He admired the high boots most of those German prisoners wore and bought a pair from one of them. Unfortunately, it was against the rules to give the PW's money. When the MP's discovered the sale, they demanded the boots and money be returned. My employee refused to give up the boots, so it took several days to work things out with the military." Gelhar's last recollections are the most amusing. "Stacks of alfalfa being dried attracted many mice, so we had a cat at the plant to keep the rodents down. The PW's took one young cat and then later a couple more kittens back to camp as pets. The PW's then caught mice at the plant, to take back to camp to feed their pets. Transporting the PW's between camp and the plant, we went past a bowling alley every day. *'Keggling'* is what the PW's called both drinking and bowling, and they often suggested we all go *'keggling'* together. The night before the PW's moved out, a couple at a time, six prisoners walked the half mile from their camp to my house to say goodbye. (They had permission from the commander.) Of course, I had been good to them as they were good workers for me. One prisoner loved mechanical work and would stay late to work on the company tractors. In the shop I kept a box full of 1776 tobacco with the understanding that the PW's could help themselves and roll their own. I would also bring down a *Fond du Lac Commonwealth Reporter* each day for the prisoners. They seemed to believe what they were reading. All in all, it was an interesting experience."[9]

Robert Heldt, right, and a fellow MP in front of their Camp Oakfield quarters, 1945. Photo courtesy of R.T. Heldt.

Robert. T. Heldt. Chicago, IL - At Camp Oakfield, prisoners and guards alike all lived in tents. The camp lacked proper sanitary conditions and guard Robert Heldt got impetigo. Heldt recalled his suffering got worse. A surprise blizzard brought a significant snow fall to the camp and surrounding area which complicated both living conditions and the sugar beet harvest. The only two shovels at camp quickly went into action digging paths between the tents, latrines and mess tent. Heldt remembered other, more pleasant, aspects of camp life as well. He and the other guards always looked for M-1 rifles to replace the "grease guns," their submachine guns, that they were issued. In order to lighten these heavy guns the guards often put only enough bullets in the clip to keep it from falling out of the gun rather than filling the clip completely. Neither guards nor officers ever worried about prisoners escaping. Bob spent a couple of days in Fond du Lac, when a truck tipped over sending several prisoners to the hospital there, where Bob guarded them. Several times Heldt drove a truck to Fort Sheridan, the primary purpose to pick up food and boxes of frozen meat, usually livers. Sometimes his cargo included mattress covers full of bread. Often he transported a sick prisoner and/or brought a recovered PW back to camp as well. In his free time, He'd set bowling pins at a local alley for a nickel a line.[10]

Bonnie J. Gilbert. Eau Claire, WI -
"What a summer to remember!! At the age of 9, I had my first train ride, acquired my first pair of slacks and first purse, attended my first Catholic high Mass wedding, ate lots of ice cream cones, watched German PW's play soccer, and saw my Grandma for the

last time. From the Chippewa Falls depot, my Grandmother, Augustus Scheuer, and I took a train to Lomira. There Aunt Bertie met us and took us to the apartment where she and Uncle John Conrad lived. Aunt Bertie worked in an ice cream parlor past the cannery and Grandma took a job at Star Canning Company. I quickly made friends with another girl my age. She and I frequently rode our bikes to get some of Aunt Bertie's ice cream. Often we would stop at the factory's big high fence and watch the PW's. We watched, fascinated, as they kicked the ball and then bounced it off their heads. Sometimes they tried to talk to us, but we could never understand what they said. We never went too close to that fence, fearing they might somehow grab us and pull us through it. But Grandma said, 'Honey Girl, they won't hurt you. They're just men who have families back home.' My parents drove down to pick me up before school started. But Grandma stayed on. We never saw her again. She had a massive heart attack and actually died on the line at the canning factory in October of that year."[11]

Camp Plymouth 1944 & 1945

German prisoners made a grand entrance into Plymouth, singing as they marched through the city from the train depot to the fairgrounds. Under the command of First Lieutenant John J. Pavlick and Second Lieutenant Harry A. Johnson, 180 PW's had been sent from Fort Sheridan to work for local canning factories.[1] In preparation for their arrival, a ten foot high barbed-wire fence had been completed and showers, hot water and heating equipment installed. The military contracted for the use of several fairgrounds buildings including the Woman's building, the Merchant and Manufacturers' building, the 4-H Club building and the office. While the grounds around these buildings also became part of the compound, the rest of the fair area remained available to the community.[2]

Within the camp the prisoners led a simple life. They worked in shifts, alternating rest periods in the fair buildings converted to barracks. Though at separate tables both the enlisted men and the prisoners ate in one large mess tent. Along with the regular Army cooking unit, this camp kitchen acquired two huge bratwurst roasters used for broiling food and for cooking in huge Army frying pans. Camp Plymouth had both a canteen and its own library. This camp also contained a unique piece of fire-fighting equipment that was an old-fashioned hose-cart that originally would have been drawn by horses. Though antiquated, once cleaned and polished, it still operated efficiently. Restored, it became a safety feature for these all wooden structures. While fistball and soccer seemed the favorite pastimes of the prisoners, many also took up the American game of horseshoes.[3]

These PW's worked at the Stokely Plant in Plymouth as well as the Elkhart Lake Canning Company and the Waldo Canning Factory. As with other camps, some area farmers contracted a few prisoners to help with their harvests.

During the three month season the camp was open, there was

so much traffic past the fairgrounds and so many curious residents hanging on the fence that the street adjacent to the fairgrounds had to be closed.[4] A sharp editorial in the July 24, 1944, *Sheboygan Press* did little to dissuade continued gestures of kindness and friendship shown to the PW's. That editorial shamed an elderly woman for attempting to slip into the camp a basket full of doughnuts freshly baked for the prisoners. The column also referred readers to an article in a recent issue of *Time* magazine. In that article, *Time* reported details of a woman visiting her ailing mother in a German hospital. While there, she also offered a wounded Canadian airman an orange and some flowers. For her kindness, the German woman was given one year at hard labor and a suspension of her civil rights for three years. While the *Press* editorial did not advocate such harsh penalties for Plymouth citizens, it reminded readers that the PW's were enemy soldiers. The article went on to suggest that since the German captives were healthy, well-treated, and well-fed, additional offerings from the local citizenry might actually be secretly regarded by the PW's themselves as foolish acts of treason — giving aid and comfort to enemies.

Observable for nearly a week, trucks moved camp equipment and baggage from the fairgrounds to the depot. The prisoners then marched down the street and sang on their way back to the railroad station. Some locals criticized authorities for allowing them to sing, noting that the Nazi's probably would not treat our boys as well. Other residents enjoyed the harmony. Local onlookers jammed the Plymouth depot platform as the Germans departed August 4, 1944. This entire work brigade headed for a new assignment at Sodus, Michigan.[5]

Expecting another 170 prisoners to arrive in 1945, Sheriff Theodore Mosch attempted to gain the upper hand on the would-be onlookers. He cautioned civilians to stay away from the camp and warned that the area would be patrolled. Traffic problems and reports of cakes and other treats given to the prisoners the previous year prompted his tough stand.[6]

This second year, it was Captain L. L. Kettering who commanded the camp. He encouraged the Plymouth residents to show the same hospitality that they had displayed to the American MP's the year before. He suggested invitations phoned to headquarters inviting two or three for dinner would likely be well received. "Even if you did not serve meat or butter but had second helpings of hospitality the boys would enjoy it."[7]

With the aid of Fort Sheridan's public relations officer, Captain

Fred H. Dettmar, Captain Kettering gave a tour of the camp to selected visitors. This year the public received an inside look at what went on at Camp Plymouth. Impressed with the order, and cleanliness of the camp, the guests credited the well-supervised management. To satisfy the visitors' interest in the separate menus for the guards and the prisoners, the tour guides displayed the Army's monthly master menu that was followed as close as local supplies allowed. The prisoners menu provided 3,400 calories, but the GI's menu provided 4,500 calories. A government medical team observed the prisoners and their work requirements and on occasion ordered increases in the caloric diet to suit additional heavy labor assignments. One medical officer, Lieutenant Richard. W. Gwartney, looked after the health needs of prisoners at Chilton, Sheboygan, and Plymouth. The guests observed separate canteens for prisoners and guards with a larger variety of items available for the MP's. Finally, Captain. Kettering explained arrangements made for Lutheran and Catholic services held regularly during the week for those prisoners who wished to attend.[8]

Again this second season, the Germans stayed in the area only a short time. The last of the prisoners transferred elsewhere the first week of August. Split into two groups, the PW's went to Appleton or Sheboygan to help with the corn harvest in those locations. Stokely's sought more help from local women for their beet canning which was about to begin in Plymouth.[9]

RECOLLECTIONS
Muriel Neerhof Storm. Waldo, WI -
Muriel Storm remembered prisoners working on her father, Albert's, farm. His Dutch background allowed him some communication with the PW's and he found them satisfactory workers. However, her 9-year-old brother, Ralph, became upset because the prisoners were being paid and he wasn't. One of the prisoners who spoke some English once asked Ralph how old his sister was. In the Waldo Canning Factory, the 15-year-old Muriel worked next to PW's who would bring up the boxes of cans as others packed cans into boxes. PW's worked both the pea and corn packs at Waldo.[10]

Voleria Mauk. Elkhart Lake, WI -
Prior to becoming Principle of Elkhart Lake High School, Ronald Mauk taught German. So he easily communicated with the PW's he transported during the summers of 1944 and 1945 for the Elkhart Lake Canning Factory. During his conversations with the prison-

PW's get off a train and walk to trucks they'll take to camp. Photo by W.C. Schroeder.

ers, he had a difficult time convincing them that the Empire State Building had not been damaged by Nazi planes as they had been told. Another common topic of prisoner discussion included the various automobiles seen in the area. Ronald never had a fear of the PW's but was concerned about a guard who regularly got drunk during the day and fell asleep on the bus back to the Plymouth Fairgrounds.[11]

Robert Koepsel. Chippewa Falls, WI -
German prisoners worked on the farm of Robert Koepsel's father, Elmer, seven miles north of Plymouth. Two PW's in the group still stand out in Robert's mind. Inside an older prisoner's large jacket, eleven American insignia buttons were neatly sewn in a row. The family thought the PW might have worn them as a record, similar to "notches on his gun." The other PW's seemed a little afraid of him. With paper and pencil in hand, the second memorable prisoner followed Elmer all around. The PW continually asked questions about farming, the size of the silo, the type of fertilizer used, and when he planted crops, taking extensive notes.

Finally Koepsel asked his purpose. The PW replied that the war would not last forever and he hoped someday to return and farm here. The family does not know if the repartiated prisoner ever did immigrate back to Wisconsin.[12]

Camp Reedsburg
1945

The arrival of PW's in Reedsburg seemed to polarize this community and surrounding area. Area residents included a sizable number of residents of German descent, most of whom approved of this influx of prisoners. However, many other neighbors vehemently opposed their arrival and the good treatment these enemy soldiers received. When many local residents went to the camp to listen to the music or visit with the prisoners over the fence, still more animosity grew between the opposing viewpoints. The strong opposition to having enemy prisoners here at all was expressed in several letters to the editor. The *Reedsburg Times-Press,* July 12, 1945, edition printed perhaps the most scathing letter in which an unidentified reader opened with the question, "Is Nazi POW labor preferred over local labor?" The writer reminded readers of stories of "members of our Army riding coast to coast in day coaches, while Nazis POW's ride in Pullmans," and a "GI gets a prison sentence and dishonorable discharge for slapping a Nazis POW." He continued to ask, "Are not these POW's the same Nazis that have violated every law of God or man? Are they not the same Nazis that murdered our boys in cold blood after they had been disarmed? Are they not the same ones that burned and buried alive civilian men, women and children?" He went on to challenge the patriotism and loyalty of the employers and city officials that brought these Nazis into the community.[1] (Fifty years later, the author still found great reluctance among community members to talk about this specific segment of their local history.) Perhaps as a result of this letter, the prisoners were never mentioned again in the local press, not even as they left. Nevertheless, even after Police Chief Frank Camp asked the Reedsburg citizens to open their homes to the guards but to stay away from the camp, the visits to the compound continued by many area residents.

The Reedsburg Foods Corp. contracted with the military for 137 PW's to help with the pea pack in 1945. Some of these prisoners also worked at the St. Mary's plant at North Freedom and at the Herfort Canning Company in Baraboo.[2]

Located on the north end of Webb Avenue along the Baraboo River, the PW camp was near Brewery Hill. The military erected a few portable buildings seen scattered within the tent city. To ease the fears of a few little old ladies, a token fence surrounded the compound. Two officers and twenty guards, mostly veterans of the South Pacific, supervised the camp. The local folks often watched the PW's march the six blocks between the camp and canning factory every day. Covered trucks transported the PW's to outlying work assignments and to job sites within the city in inclement weather. While most of these PW's worked in the canneries, some also worked for area farms doing field work. A few did some cement work as well. Farmers reported the guards accompanying the PW's sometimes set their guns down and asked farmer and PW's to give warning if they saw any military vehicle approach. The guards then pitched in with the farm work.

The public relations officer, Captain Fred Dittmar, stated that the prisoners received no cigarettes, candy or beer while working in the state. He also noted that their daily food ration was set at thirty-five cents per man, the menu consisting largely of carp and pickled herring, beef hearts and livers. With some margarine, sugar and fresh vegetables, their food in red point value would be fifty percent of what civilians were allowed.[3]

This small company of prisoners stationed at Camp Reedsburg stayed only from June 29 to late August, so they earned limited wages. Fort Sheridan reported the Reedsburg PW earnings paid by private companies to the military in 1945 totaled only $9,987.[4]

RECOLLECTIONS
Dr. James Pawlisch. Reedsburg, WI -
Small red and white flags with the swastika in the center were on the lower corner of several of the railroad car windows when the PW train pulled into the Reedsburg depot. On their bikes, young Jim Pawlisch and a couple of friends went to the depot to check out this invasion. "We waved," said Pawlisch, "at the men in the window. Some waved back, but none smiled. They looked pretty glum and hostile." Later in the season, while fishing in a boat on the Baraboo River above the Woolen Mill Dam, he and another friend saw PW's along the bank below their compound fishing. "We tried to communicate and one of them spoke very broken English. He told us where in Germany he had come from and where he had

been captured. He even showed us his Iron Cross. At least this group was friendlier than those we saw on the train the day they arrived," remarked Pawlisch.[5]

Eber Janzen. Reedsburg, WI -

"The smell in the camp kitchen was enough to make you sick," according to Eber Janzen, who delivered milk to the PW's that summer. He and his partner drove through the camp to the kitchen and put the milk in the ice boxes in the kitchen tent. All the steam from the cooking rising up into the canvas ceiling and the hot sun beating down on that canvas, created a terrible odor. Eber said, "I always wondered if the smell got into the food." The Janzen family lived across a field, about a block away from the camp. From their back porch they would often sit and listen to the religious services, especially the German hymns being sung on Sunday mornings. Then in the afternoon, they were fascinated watching the soccer games. Spectators always seemed to be available to toss a wayward ball back inside the snow fence perimeter of the field. [6]

Philipp Schweke. La Crosse, WI -

As a young German speaking boy, Philip Schweke regularly went to the Baraboo River to fish. That summer he met some prisoners who taught him to tie the proper knots, put the cork on and to use old beef for fishing turtles. (Philip could sell his turtles to a German family in town.) Schweke remembered the PW's roaming outside the fence during their free time, but understood they had to be in by roll call.[7]

Marty Koenecke. Reedsburg, WI -

Lunch break often meant a sing-a-long at the Koenecke farm. Martin and Della hired several PW's to help with the shocking of oats that August. The Koeneckes treated these prisoners like any other hired help, inviting them in for the noon meal. After lunch, one very tall, lean, blond prisoner would play the family upright piano. About thirty years old, the piano player was perhaps the oldest of the bunch. The prisoners and family alike listened and/or sang along to popular German tunes.[8]

Shirley Mahr Burmeste. Reedsburg, WI -

"On my way home from the night shift at the canning factory, a guard followed me. I got scared and started to run and he ran after me. Fearing I would be raped or something, I cut across the school yard, taking several jogs in direction, hoping to throw him off. I was a fast running 19 year old and made it home. Dad took me down to the police station to report him, as I knew who he was. My father would not let me return to work at the cannery either. I worked full-time as a dental assistant during the day. My job at the canning factory was only part-time, to help fill the labor shortage during the busy season. Strange to say, I was never afraid of the PW's who worked with me. They were always so polite, especially to us women in the factory. Unlike the male civilian employees, the PW's would insist we go to the head of the line for water, stand back and let us pass first. They were good workers, too."[9]

Camp Rhinelander
1945

If you didn't hire them, you didn't know that German prisoners of war were in the area. The farms near Rhinelander were far apart with lots of woodland between them. Back into the woods an abandoned CCC camp hid and housed the 190 PW's that arrived in Oneida County. In a federal nursery two miles west of Rhinelander near Highway 8, the U.S. Forest Service LobLolly Pine Tree Lab stood adjacent to the PW Camp. The abandoned camp needed only a good cleaning to prepare it for new occupants. The largest building became sleeping quarters for the PW's. German speaking camp Commander Captain Kunze and his forty or so guards slept in another dormitory type building. This work battalion found the old CCC mess and bathing facilities still usable. While some food arrived from Fort Sheridan, most of the food was purchased from a local A & P in downtown Rhinelander. Captain Kunze negotiated a deal with the A&P to buy quality beef and call it "bologna." This gesture proved well worth the money. The PW's appreciated the "bologna sausage" and responded with excellent cooperation throughout their stay. With no cleared level area large enough for soccer, there was little recreation available here, other than cards, reading and letter writing. The local Dr. Van Komaszynski contracted with the camp to provide medical services and tended the PW's and guards as needed. At Camp Rhinelander security was minimal, with neither a fence, guard station or tower. Dispatched each morning in Jeeps, U.S. Army MP's stationed with the PW's accompanied the prisoner work details to the area farms. Always visible for show, the guns were not loaded, as the guards never worried for their own safety or about escapes.[1]

The PW's came to Rhinelander in two waves, the first ninety arrived on August 29, 1945, with the additional 100 trucked in on September 4th. The Oneida County Farm Labor Association Co-operative had arrangements with the government for their assistance to pick beans and harvest potatoes at the going wage of fifty-five cents per hour.[2] Thirty-five U.S. Army MP's accompanied the first contingent of prisoners when they arrived with their gear in twenty-four trucks and two jeeps. Major Elmer A. Ward, assisted by German speaking Captain A. I. Kunze, was in charge of this company of PW's.[3] School buses and trucks used to pick up and deliver the PW's to their work sites each morning, returned them to camp again in the evening. Even with the additional 100 prisoners that did arrive later, the potato growers still had a serious labor shortage and put a plea for help in the October 11, 1945, edition of *The New North.*[4] The farmers recruited high school teens for Saturday work to help save the crop. Camp Rhinelander closed at the end of October as the potato harvest ended.[5]

RECOLLECTIONS

Lynn Bell. Milwaukee, WI -

"They started giving us rides in the wheelbarrows around the area. They were laughing and so were we. These men had uniforms on with real big PW on the back of their fatigue type shirts. My siblings and I didn't know anything about prisoners of war. We were just snooping around the big warehouse just a stone's throw from our house three miles east of Rhinelander. Farmers stored their potatoes there at the time. We never saw the men again."[6]

PW's from Camp Rhinelander pick up rocks from a field, 1945. Photo courtesy of W.C. Schroeder.

DeLore Deau. Rhinelander, WI -

DeLore Deau recalled about fifty PW's being fed sack lunches in Browns' Park near the old Chicago North Western depot. About 16 years old at the time, he was surprised to see that these enemy soldiers were mere kids rather than the terrible "Huns" American media had told him about.[7]

Deau also recalled a young German woman who came to town in the mid 1990s. She inquired about the camp and prisoners. She was attempting to trace her father's tour of Wisconsin when he was held as a PW during the war.[8]

Sgt. Anthony E Beres. Dunedin, FL -

Tony Beres offered several stories about his time spent as a guard at Camp Rhinelander. Private Kay Kettner, one of Tony's fellow MP's was an unhappy man, although a native of Rhinelander. Recently rescued from a German PW camp he returned to the states until his enlistment was up. One can only imagine his thoughts about our treatment of the German PW's stationed in Camp Rhinelander. One day his emotions erupted and he burned the entire PW payroll. Since the payroll was military scrip, it was not too difficult to replace, but did take some time to get more. "I was one of three military personnel who knew about this incident and covered for him," recalled Tony.[9]

Sgt. Anthony Beres at Camp Rhinelander, 1945. Photo courtesy of Anthony Beres.

According to Tony, the MP's here had a unique pastime. They went bull-head fishing, which is best done after dark. With a lantern in hand, a local woman, Ms. Dorothy Yurich, led the way to Pine Lake about a half mile from camp. Fishing was often very good and the men sometimes brought back up to 100 fish. They would then rouse the cooks out of bed to do the honors. "Who would care about breakfast, after a meal of catfish?," asked Beres. After the feed, "Ms. Yurich would be escorted home by a soldier we all could trust our sisters with." Dorothy also served as local intelligence, telling the guards where they could and could not go in Rhinelander.[10]

In consortium with the University of Wisconsin, Leleah Starke raised seed potatoes, insuring quality and quantity for the state potato growers. Tony remembered that Ms. Starke spoke mostly German, so she quickly bonded with the PW's hired on her 100-acre farm. Her good German home cooking also helped the relationship between her and the prisoners she hired.[11]

Tony Beres mentioned that Captain Kunze recognized the artistic talents of one young PW. As a result, he kept this prisoner back at camp to protect his hands. The commander brought small photos of his family and the artist enlarged them in oils.[12]

Assigned to help the company clerk, Sergeant Beres recorded the work of the PW's during their stay. Two heel-clicking Germans among the prisoners surprisingly regarded the American soldiers as true gentlemen. These two and most of the others in the detachment of PW's at Rhinelander had been captured in Africa. Told the German Luftwaffe had leveled New York, they had been very surprised to see the Statue of Liberty greeting them as they came through the Port of New York. The fact that the German leadership had misinformed them became immediately obvious to them, and they quickly opened to information provided by their captors. Tony had no fear of the prisoners. Without even a side-arm he would take an English speaking prisoner with him on his biweekly runs to Fort Sheridan for supplies. Of the four different PW camps to which Tony was assigned, he found Camp Rhinelander to be the most lax about security. But he also remembered, the prisoners had no place to go, terrorized by the sound of wolves howling in the woods each night.[13]

Juanita Spafford Kichefski. Rhinelander, WI -
Three PW's loaded and stacked the gunny sacks of potatoes onto the back of trucks, hauled them to the Spafford warehouse and restacked them inside. Juanita Kichefsk said that at the end of each day they reported the number of sacks they had stacked and at the end of the season they told her dad the total of number of sacks of potatoes in his warehouse. Their record keeping was actually unnecessary because a ticket system that allowed the pickers to be paid by the number of sacks they filled also gave the count. But Juanita still recalled how impressed her father, Joe Spafford, was with the accuracy of the prisoners and especially how they maintained the accumulating count in their heads over the entire season.[14]

Betty Kuczmarski. Rhinelander, WI -

It didn't happen too often, but a couple of times the PW's worked an extra hour or so before heading back to Camp Rhinelander. Fearing a predicted frost during the night, the prisoners worked until done picking the potatoes in the field. Their assigned school bus waited to take them back to camp. Betty Kuczmarski doesn't remember the PW's complaining about the overtime. Perhaps it was because her husband, Emil, had said, "If you want a horse to work you have to feed it and treat it right." According to Betty, that was his philosophy in dealing with the prisoners as well.[15]

Marvin Spafford. Eagle River, WI -

Handshakes went all round when the season was over. The three PW's seemed a little saddened about moving on. During their work in our potato fields, Dad had treated them to Lucky Strike cigarettes and mother had supplemented their sack lunches with whatever we had on the table. Marvin Spafford recalled that one of the three PW's could speak a little English and his mother could speak a little German. The prisoners expressed surprise at the size of this country and our industry and seemed to understand the futility of the war. Mother received a letter from one after he was repatriated.[16]

Camp Ripon
1945

The tables quickly turned for three of the guards stationed at Camp Ripon. Just months earlier, they themselves had been prisoners of the Germans. Captured during the Battle of the Bulge, they were held captive for 103 days. Treatment at the hands of the Nazis can only be imagined as each of the three had lost more than forty pounds during their captivity. Since rescue, they had fully recovered, at least physically. Included in this trio was one Wisconsin soldier, Sergeant Frank Kaplan from Armstrong Creek, Wisconsin. Another guard now stationed at Ripon could hardly be happier and still be in the Army. Originally from Ripon, Staff Sergeant Walter Zweiger served in the Pacific before being returned stateside and assigned duty in his home town. His parents, Mr. and Mrs. Herman Zweiger still lived in the city.[1]

The largest in the area this year, Camp Ripon housed nearly 600 German prisoners of war. While twenty remained in camp, assigned to various camp details, the others took daily bus rides to their work assignments. From the camp, 200 PW's worked at the local canning plants, 215 went to Rosendale and 120 rode to Pickett each day. A contingent of nearly sixty American soldiers and officers guarded the internees in camp and on their work details.[2]

Located on a site south of the Central Wisconsin Canning Company plant on the east side of Douglas Street, Camp Ripon was secured with a newly installed fence and floodlight system.[3] The prisoners and their guards lived in nearly one hundred regulation army tents. Set up in orderly rows, each tent contained army cots, mattresses, and blankets. Temporary frame buildings sheltered the camp kitchen, supply room and showers. Visible from the fence, a large steam boiler provided the hot water for the camp. In another tent erected for the purpose, the Reverend E. E. Schieler of the First Evangelical Lutheran Church officiated at the first church service June 24, 1945.[4]

In a news report, Brigadier General H. M. Bryan Jr. mentioned

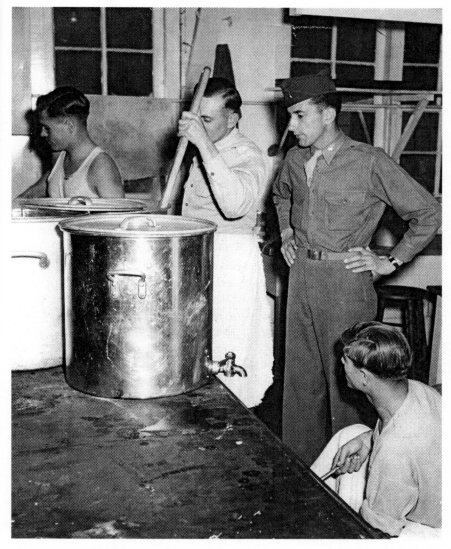

A guard supervises PW cooks, 1945. Photo courtesy of W.C. Schroeder.

camp menus and noted the PW's received little beef and pork and then only the less desirable cuts. "Meat from beef," he said, "is limited to shanks, flanks, skirts, liver, hearts, kidneys, ox tails, tripe and brains. In the pig line, they are fed hearts, livers, kidneys, tails, neck bones, fat backs, salt pork, dry salt bellies and oily pork not acceptable under existing specifications for Army feedings. They get no butter." The general further noted that PW's doing hard work

received 3,400 calories of food per day, moderate work earned 3,
000 calories, and those not working received 2,500 calories per
day.[5] Food for all was prepared in the same kitchen, but separate
menus provided better food for the guards. Because the prisoners
did the cooking, they prepared the food European style. Saving and
accumulating the small amounts of sugar issued to the prisoners,
the cooks occasionally provided German desserts. In this camp,
canners provided the noon lunch at their respective factories.

In an early press tour of the camp, commanding officer First
Lieutenant Karol A. Lula reported the local prisoners had already
completed $2,400 worth of needed labor. Edward Mathwig, manager
of the Ripon canning plant nearest the camp, labeled the work of
the prisoners as very satisfactory and stated he had no trouble
supervising them. These prisoners ranged in age from 18 to 61 and
represented practically every corps of Hitler's army.[6] During that
same tour, the journalist from the *Ripon Commonwealth Reporter*
noted that these prisoners lacked the cockiness and arrogance
of the group housed at Green Lake the previous year. Captured in
recent campaigns in France and Germany, the PW's interned this
year knew the Allies had the upper hand in the war.

As usual, when a camp opened, Captain Dettmar the military's
public relations man, encouraged residents to extend friendship
and courtesies to the guards, most of whom were combat veterans. However, he warned against fraternization between the local
residents and PW's. Emphasizing his special concern, Dettmar
continued, "and tell the mothers of your daughters that it would
be wise to instruct them not to loiter anywhere near the camp."[7]

Camp Commander Captain Edward Rand spoke at the local
Kiwanis meeting Tuesday July 5. There he denied the rumored escape of two prisoners, saying that such rumors commonly spread
in localities around PW camps. On behalf of the sixty guards, he
expressed appreciation for the courtesies extended to them by
local citizens. As he spoke he did note the recurring problem of
civilian fraternization with inmates of the prison compound. He
also discouraged any loitering in the vicinity.[8]

Judged in violation of Army rules, the Garden City Pickle Company lost its use of PW labor. Ottmar Rendemann, head of the
Ripon company, had an agreement with the military to provide
mid-day lunches for his two to four prisoner employees. Having
no facilities at the pickle factory, he ordered noon meals for them.
He took them to the Gem Restaurant nearby. His expressed regret
in violating the rules was not sufficient to allow him continued

use of prisoners.[9] This charge of an infraction of the rules seemed curious, since in many locations, the MP's themselves escorted prisoners to nearby restaurants for meals.

After the pea pack, the Ripon camp numbers decreased to 143 prisoners. These remaining prisoners helped area farmers harvest, thresh and complete general farm work. Those prisoners that left, joined many others from nearby camps, traveled to Michigan for a time and expected to return to Wisconsin for the corn pack.[10] In fact, local corn canners requested 790 prisoners to fill jobs. The new camp commander, Lieutenant Karol Lula, said only 650 would be available. The additional numbers arrived the second week in September.[11] These prisoners worked the corn harvest and pack at Silver Creek, Rosendale, Berlin and Pickett as well as in the Ripon plants. Though hoping for more prisoners to fill their labor shortages, the area canners appreciated the help they had received. The significance of the efforts of the prisoners became obvious with the release of the final earnings figures. When Camp Ripon closed October 11, 1945, its PW's had earned the substantial total of $130,000 for the U.S. government.[12]

RECOLLECTIONS
Leander Wagner. Pickett, WI -
The canning factory wanted Leander Wagner for a crew boss because he spoke German. However, there was a problem. He spoke "Low" German and the PW's spoke "High" German. As a result of this difference in dialect, very little communication actually occurred in the sweet corn fields around Pickett.[13]

Peter Amend. Ripon, WI-
Returning to camp one evening, Dave Dolske, a bus driver, became aware that a prisoner was missing. Turning the bus around, he found the prisoner running along the road trying to catch the bus.[14]

Glen Sasada. Ripon, WI -
"One young very blond prisoner was a carpenter by trade and asked me if he could look at our barn. He wanted to see its structure. I gave him permission to go inside and take a peek. The PW's worked at our place during the pea and corn harvest. My dad, Albert, drove a truck for the cannery hauling the peas from the viner to the canning factory. He had the same PW riding, loading and unloading with him most of the season. The two became friendly,

and Dad even shared his cigarettes with the grateful prisoner. That prisoner once commented to Dad, '*America ist shine!*' (American is beautiful!) and '*Deutschland ist kaput!*' (Germany is finished!)"[15]

Dwain Werch. Ripon, WI -
"A truckload of PW's with three armed guards came to our place just out of Ripon to pick sweet corn. My father, Amil Werch, hired them through the canning factory. As a kid, I was impressed with the MP's and their rifles. One would stand guard on each end of the field and another would ride on top of the pick-up cab as the PW's snapped the corn and tossed it into the truck. We would all share a picnic lunch my mother brought out to the field. The prisoners teased me and gave me several German coins."[16]

Dr. John Steinbring. Ripon, WI -
"What does a bored 16-year-old do all day when his job is to watch a gauge that measures the salt in the brine as the peas are canned in the Ripon plant? I brought my leather thong and practiced snapping it like a whip. I learned to fling it out and jerk it just the right way. I got so proficient with it, I could actually hit a stray pea and make it fly. That was until one PW complained to his guard that I had hit him in the eye with a pea. I didn't think I had hit him. The guard and my supervisor recognized this prisoner to be an agitator and told me not to use my 'whip' when the PW's were around. We civilians put in much longer days than the Germans. They were being treated 'humanely' we were told."[17]

Camp Rockfield
1944 & 1945

By storing up potatoes and beets and shipping in additional potatoes, the area canning factories continued operation through the fall of 1944 and into February of 1945, not long before spring harvest started over again.[1] Using those supply strategies, Camp Rockfield became one of two PW camps in Wisconsin operating continuously from its opening in July 1944, until permanently closed. Rockfield also became one of only five branch camps in the state to stay open into 1946, closing in January of that year.

Planned as a future warehouse, the new building was hastily erected to house the incoming enlisted men near the Herbert A. Niemann Canning Co. Rows of tents housed the prisoners. Snow fencing soon surrounded the camp which had guardhouses at each corner. A post exchange/canteen offered sundry items to both PW's and their guards. On a rudimentary athletic field established within the compound, soccer became the favorite amusement during off hours. In their day room, the PW's also had a ping pong table and reading materials available.[2]

When it opened during the first week in July 1944, Camp Rockfield held 257 German prisoners. Transported to various canning plants in Washington and Ozaukee counties, these PW's worked in the pea pack. Although limited to an eight hour work day, the prisoners could be away from camp up to twelve hours maximum. This unpaid time extension allowed for transportation to and from the work sites. Typically, some prisoners remained at camp to do the cooking and maintenance.

In an effort to maintain a friendly and open atmosphere between the camp and community, camp commander Lt. C. L. Thompson spoke to the Cedarburg Woman's Club in October. He noted that the numbers of prisoners in Camp Rockfield had quickly risen to 531. The numbers of guards now stationed there had also increased to seventy. He explained that church services were provided each

Sunday using a prayer book and hymnal, both printed in German. In answer to a question about the "Hitler Service" in which the word Hitler is substituted for God, he emphatically stated, ". . . German prisoners are not allowed to practice this service in our camps." While the first group of prisoners came from the Afrika Korps and tended to be pro-Nazi, the commander indicated those captured later at Cherbourg weren't so cocky. The audience heard surprising answers to other questions. They learned that prisoners were allowed two pints of beer a day and that Fort Sheridan censored their mail and opened packages before distribution to prisoners. In addition, visitors, mostly Milwaukee relatives, were allowed visitation on Sundays, and marriages by proxy regularly occurred with the necessary paperwork forwarded to Germany.[3]

Although Lt. Thompson referred to the die-hard Nazis among his first group of PW's, he never mentioned the friction within the camp between the Nazi and anti-Nazi factions. Local citizenry learned of that problem by word of mouth. German speaking Henry Beuscher, the maintenance supervisor, worked with the PW's in the local plant. The PW's told him that anti-Nazi PW's "stood their own watches to make sure none of them got smothered with a pillow during the night" — something they heard had occurred in other camps.[4]

By January 1945 the camp command had changed hands when Capt. Harold A. Christiansen took charge. With the camp population remaining at well over 400, new employment opportunities became available that year. While continuing the common canning factory jobs, the PW's at Camp Rockfield found themselves working at several dissimilar tasks as well. Some worked for the Pick Manufacturing Company loading lumber.[5] Still others were transported daily to the Neimann Brothers Fox Farm for a wide variety of assignments. A few of the jobs there included digging irrigation ditches, butchering horses for feed, feeding and watering the foxes and cleaning the pens. Area employers kept the PW's busy. During July 1945 the 454 prisoners amassed a total of 76,222 man hours of labor for 5 work contracts and earned for the U.S. Treasury $40,086.[6] By September, their 1945 wages totaled $226,668.[7] Although the prisoners worked into January 1946, their additional earnings are unknown because the military released no such figures to the public.

RECOLLECTIONS

Walter Hauser. Germantown, WI -

The first group of PW's transported to Rockfield had to be sent back to Fort Sheridan or their prior camp. Walter Hauser recalled that those young, most under twenty, PW's refused to work or even report for work. Perhaps they were homesick or just hard core Nazis. A second group of cooperative, hard working PW's quickly replaced that recalcitrant brigade. A fond memory Hauser had of the second group concerned their reaction to American sweet corn. During the canning season, Hauser and fellow workers filled a gunny-sack with ears of corn and put it on top of a large canning cooker. When the cooker was done, the steam from the cooker had also steamed the sack of corn. At first the PW's refused the treat, saying, "*Das ist fir schwien!*" But once they tasted it, they couldn't get enough.[8]

John Fromm. Mequon, WI -

From Camp Rockfield two trucks, each with one guard and about twenty PW's, traveled daily to the Herbert A. Neimann Fox Farm just out of Mequon. The huge fox farm offered the prisoners a wide variety of tasks. Butchering became the assignment of the four PW's with previous butchering training or experience. Feeding

The front entrance of Camp Rockfield, 1945. Photo courtesy of Jean Johnson and Helen Beuscher.

Camp Rockfield guard post and fencing, 1945. Photo courtesy of Jean Johnson.

25,000 foxes required meat from 20-25 horses each day. Coming out of the west, many of these animals were good clean horses, unlike the dead or downed cattle procured locally for feed . With little meat on their camp menu, the PW butchers happily took the "prime" cuts of horse meat and cooked them for their own enjoyment on a small stove provided by co-workers. Manager John Fromm remembered them eating their specialty on the spot, not sharing with the other prisoners. John also remembered several PW's being taken to a field across the road to dig irrigation ditches. There, five feet down in the ditch where no one could see them, some of the civilian employees fed the PW's sausages and other treats. The owners and many local employees had German backgrounds and many spoke German. According to Fromm, these PW's were only boys perhaps none older than 20, and many seemed very homesick. One of the PW's was an artist who drew from photos very exceptional pictures of John's two daughters.[9]

John Fromm's aunt Emogene Plumb, who taught German at Milton College, often communicated with the PW's. To celebrate her birthday, she held a picnic for the PW's in the warehouse, adding candies and other treats to their regular soup ration sent out from Camp Rockfield. In return, the PW's presented the family with a pamphlet compiled by the camp artist that included the names of each PW and a lovely poem.[10]

Henry Beuscher. Rockfield, WI -
"Sneaking up on a sleeping guard, PW's grabbed and hid the rifle of the MP. When he awoke, the guard was very upset, while the prisoners had a good laugh," recalled Beuscher, who worked for the canning factory for more than thirty years. One of the prisoners presented the Beuschers with a lovely painting of a Swiss mountain scene as a wedding gift. The PW made it out of common materials using a rectangle of composition board from the boxes as backing and a scrap of brown shoestring for the hanger. Evidently the artist had requested wood for the frame, but where the oils came from was a mystery to the family.[11]

Jerome Rinzel. Muskego, WI -
"My dad said there were two kinds of PW's — the vast majority regular people, easy to speak to and get along with; and a small group of die-hard Nazis who continually upbraided him for being so unwilling to help the great German Fatherland in its worldwide struggle. I was fascinated with my father's ability to speak German to the PW's we saw going through the camp. The government contracted my dad, Arthur Z. Rinzel, to construct barracks next to the Rockfield Canning Company."[12]

Rockfield PW's relax after hand-picking the corn on the truck behind them. Truck owner Herbert Kruepke delivered this produce to the Jackson Canning Factory, 1945. Photo courtesy of Donna Kruepke Spaeth.

Tent city of Camp Rockfield. Photo courtesy of Helen Beuscher.

Helen Beuscher. Germantown, WI -
"The guards with their guns just sat and watched and would not be happy if you talked with a PW for long. The prisoners lined up and marched to and from their camp to the canning factory every day. They worked both the day and night shifts. I worked the night shift with them. Lots of music, including a male chorus, and soccer were the common recreational activities back at their camp. Rumor had it that the PW's made alcohol back at camp, too, probably using extra sugar snitched from the cannery. On Sundays, lots of traffic came through town to see this strange sight, but no one was allowed into the camp to my knowledge."[13]

Dan Sennott. Whitefish Bay, WI -
" I was a king at West Bend High School in 1944 because I had chewing gum, something not readily available to my classmates. At the time, I worked at the Texaco filling station, the only one in Germantown or Rockfield, so the military trucks filled up there. I got friendly with a couple of the regular drivers who would often make the run to Fort Sheridan, usually transporting sick PW's or picking others up. Several of the guards had private autos but no gas. So occasionally I would trade gas (charged to one of

the military trucks) for chewing gum. Heading to Fort Sheridan, one of my truck driver friends came to the double railroad track crossing in Rockfield. He stopped for the train traveling down the track, but when that train passed, he pulled out without thinking or looking and was struck by a second train coming from the other direction. The driver and his several PW passengers all perished as the truck was rolled from one side of the ditch to the other for some distance down the line"[14]

Ulrich Huber. Rockfield, WI -
"When the prisoners finished harvesting my corn, one of the guards asked me if his water-boy could have some water from my pump for the crew. When I told him he could, the MP was very thankful. I said 'you act like this is a privilege.' He replied, 'Some farmers my PW's work for won't let them take any water.' Some neighbors chose to look at the PW's as the bad guys. Others like me felt that they were just unlucky fellows who got drafted into the Germany army."[15]

John S. Peters. West Bend, WI -
"No Beer for Veterans," "West Bend Asshole Town," and "Wonderbread and Water" were graffiti phrases on the Pick Manufacturing men's room walls. The PW's who worked the night shift there refurbishing brake linings and oil filters were not happy. They hated the soft white bread and did not get their beer ration.[16]

Camp Sheboygan
1945

"All the windows were broken and inside were mattresses piled high and covered with spider webs."[1] That described what the advance party found as they arrived to get Camp Sheboygan ready for prisoners. The old abandoned Sheboygan County Asylum had been selected to house the PW's. Along with the report of seventeen military trucks of equipment arrived to make ready for Camp Sheboygan came the notice that absolutely no visitors would be allowed at the Sheboygan County Asylum once the prisoners moved in. While the old asylum could easily accommodate the expected 550 prisoners, the maximum number housed in the three-story brick building never exceeded 450.[2] This number was significant enough for the Army to staff both a full time chaplain and medic on the premises. The first contingent of Germans to come included only 200 prisoners and their guards.[3] While inspecting the buildings, Camp Commander Captain Carl R. Birkholz noted the complex was ideal and would need few changes for its new purpose. While the prisoners were accommodated in the asylum itself, the American soldiers stayed in three officers tents and eight other smaller tents for the enlisted men. The advance team had put up a secure fence around the perimeter with these tents and the camp headquarters set up at the entrance to the asylum grounds. Residents passing by also saw the four guard towers equipped with searchlights capable of covering every inch of the grounds. From Camp Sheboygan six area plants would be served by prison labor. Included were Lakeside Packing Co. of Sheboygan, Cleveland Canning Co., Calumet-Dutch Packing Co. at Cedar Grove, Oostburg Canning Co., Geidel Canning Co. at Adell and the Waldo Canning Co.[4]

Camp Sheboygan remained open into December. These prisoners kept busy both in the fields and the canning factories, helping first with the pea harvest, then through the red beets, carrots, sweet corn, and ending with the late sugar beet harvest in November.[5] With three more months of work ahead, the mid-September Fort Sheridan news release reported the total earnings for the Sheboygan prisoners from July through September 1 as $37,916.[6] The final earnings figure was never made public.

RECOLLECTIONS

Name withheld. Sheboygan, WI

"All the windows were broken and inside were mattresses piled high and covered with spider webs." That was what one of the advance party found as they were sent to get the old asylum ready for the POWs. The group came in a couple of Jeeps and several trucks filled with fencing and other materials for fixing the place. They

Pencil drawing of Camp Sheboygan commander Capt. Carl R. Birkholz. Photo courtesy of Carl R.F. Birkholz.

were also given some cash to cover hotel and food bills until Camp Sheboygan would open.[7]

Carl Birkholz. Elkhart Lake, WI -

According to Carl, the biggest trouble his father, camp commander Captain Carl R. Birkholz, had was with local teenage girls. They regularly tried to sneak into the prisoner area sometimes even having sex with the Germans. If the guards caught them, they immediately turned them over to the Sheboygan police. Carl remembered this happening regularly. Another special memory of Carl's included a rather common arrowhead. While hoeing sweet corn near Howards Grove, a prisoner found an Indian arrowhead. He picked it up and brought it back to camp. He presented it to Captain Birkholz, wanting to know what it was and where he had to turn it in. In his fluent German the captain explained that Native Americans had made it for hunting and it was his to keep to show his children. The PW was as delighted as if the captain had given him a thousand dollar bill. In Germany, such things belonged to the state. Another recollection involved a surprised, older prisoner who missed the bus back to camp from the farm his group was working at. Evidently he lingered too long in the outhouse. When he came out, he found the bus, other prisoners and guards all gone. So he went knocking on the farmhouse door. Luckily the farmer spoke German and called the camp to report the problem. At the command post Carl heard his father ask one of the guards to take a Jeep and pick up the tardy prisoner. Happy to have an opportunity to drive a Jeep, the GI quickly took off with his just delivered package from home. When the Jeep arrived to pick up the prisoner, not only was the prisoner not shot as the German feared might happen, the guard didn't even have a weapon. All the GI had were the home-made cookies he offered to share with the PW on the trip back to Camp Sheboygan.[8]

Wilfrid Turba. Elkhart Lake, WI-
"What were we thinking? We actually handed each enemy POW a large knife that certainly could do great damage if used as a weapon. The special sugar beet machetes with their hook on the front to pick up the beets and the sharp blade to whack off the tops were issued to each POW helping with the harvest on our farm outside Sheboygan. Because all they brought were skimpy brown bag lunches, my mother would bring out a pot of chili or other soup which she served on the wind free side of the house. We had been forbidden to allow them into the house. I also worked in the local pea cannery and often acted as interpreter between the supervisors and the PW's because I spoke German quite well. I remember one day the German headman questioned exactly what they were to do. They were told to load a railroad freight car with cases of canned peas. 'How long do we have to do this?' the headman queried. The factory foreman said, 'three hours.' 'And

The asylum before it was converted to a PW camp. Photo courtesy of Sheboygan County Historical Research Center.

A pull toy made by a PW for co-worker Herbert Prange's daughter. Photo courtesy Sharon Prange Claerbaut.

if we finish sooner do we get a rest period till three hours have elapsed?' 'Yes,' was the foreman's response. The prisoners all got into a long line and passed the cases of peas down the line with no one moving other than to pass the forty pound pea cases along. At age 16 that was the hardest I had ever worked and I was totally exhausted by the time we had the freight car loaded. The POW's did the job in about two hours, so their spokesman announced, 'Jetzt knen mir rauchen!' or 'Now we can smoke,' I do believe every POW lit up a cigarette."[9]

Martin Bangert. Sheboygan, WI -
"My father, Martin J. Bangert, was a Lutheran parochial teacher and musician and over the years often spoke of this unique season. That fall father often accompanied our pastor as they conducted services in German for the POWs. The Reverend Victor Mennicke Sr. and my father even took a choir with them on occasion. They would use a pickup choir of older people. These choral singers came from their own church choir at St. Paul Lutheran Church as well as from The Lutheran Chorus of Sheboygan — an all city Lutheran group from all LCMS parishes. The pick-up nature of the choir was necessary since younger members did not know German, while the older ones spoke it as a second or sometimes first language. Proof of that is my parents used German whenever they wanted to hide something from me. I had to learn my German the hard way, in school! The Missouri Synod church that also participated

in ministering to the camp at the time would have been Trinity Lutheran Church with Reverend Schulz and his organist/pianist Mr. Rommelmann. The prisoners enjoyed the worship and singing because it was part of their whole understanding of life."[10]

Chuck Rieck. Middleton, WI -
During an unannounced inspection of PW quarters, Chuck Rieck and fellow guards seized an interesting photo. It showed several happy PW's drinking Schlitz beer. Upon investigation, camp authorities determined that the farmer had supplied the beverages to his work crew. The farmer was reprimanded for his action, and Chuck also recalled suggesting to the prisoners not to post such things on such a visible bulletin board.[11]

Sharon Prange Claerbaut. Oostburg, WI -
"I want to make something for the *kline mite* (little one)," a PW told Herbert Prange as they worked together at the Oostburg Canning Co. Prange was a year round employee of the company, and his wife occasionally brought their toddler, Sharon, down to visit her father. Herbert worked with the PW's in the cannery as well as in the field. The PW carved a motion toy and hung it up in the steam room to dry, but it fell apart. After showing Herbert the damaged piece, he set out to carve another, this time requesting paint to finish the toy. Daughter Sharon Claerbaut still has that toy, and when the string is pulled the arms still go up and down like a man doing jumping jacks.[12]

Mary Howard Hawkins. Eau Claire, WI -
Teenager Mary Howard and several other girl friends enjoyed horseback riding. Next to the asylum, then Camp Sheboygan, stood a riding stable they frequented. The bridle path actually circled the old building just outside the fence. As they rode every other week or so they often saw five or six PW's sitting on the steps just on the other side of that fence. The girls often waved to these young prisoners who didn't seem much older than they were. The PW's would smile and wave back, but never approached the fence.[13]

Robert Lawrenz. Sheboygan, WI -
"Seated at the family dinning table for Sunday dinner, we saw a couple of strange men walking up the neighbor's driveway. They wore long trenchcoats and when one turned we could read PW

on the back. Then they came to our door. My father answered, recognized one of the men as his brother and invited them inside. Because the conversation was in German, we three kids couldn't understand. But it all seemed to be very pleasant. Eventually another knock on the door came announcing an officer and two MP's. Dad had mother quickly hide his brother and friend in the basement, then answered the door. When the officer inquired about a couple of prisoners, my father hemmed and hawed, denying he had seen them. The officer was puzzled since the prisoners had permission to go visit a relative and wondered where they had actually gone. Then dad admitted the PW's were there. The visit with the military men and prisoners didn't last much longer before all these unexpected guests left, heading back to camp. My father, Walter Lawrenz, had immigrated from Germany through Canada and left his past behind. I never heard him speak of his family, and this uncle was his only relative I ever met. I do not even recall this uncle's name. Though my mother had also immigrated from Germany, the folks never spoke German in the house. I do not remember if my father ever visited his brother at the camp. If he did, it didn't register in my 12-year-old mind. I do remember clearly, however, that my friends and I would often go to visit with the guards there."[14]

Camp Sturgeon Bay 1945

With over 2,000 Nazi soldiers on the peninsula, local folks could be frightened very easily. No prisoners or guards were killed in the area, though rumors about a riot circulated wildly. One of the rumors told of a gang of prisoners seizing guns from guards resulting in the death of two guards and five prisoners. The spreading tales differed in numbers involved and even in which camp the supposed incident took place. Door County Agricultural Agent, G. I. Mullendore, stated definitively that no such trouble occurred.[1] The agent reminded the residents that the war in Europe had ended and these prisoners were being very cooperative as they awaited their orders to return home. Though quickly squashed, a work stoppage had occurred, perhaps sparking these rumors. Camp authorities immediately presented to the striking prisoners a "No Work, No Eat" ultimatum and they decided they would rather eat. After that incident the production rose from eleven pails of cherries picked per man to twenty pails per man for each day of labor, according to figures reported August 3 by Brigadier Gen. John T. Pierce, commander of Fort Sheridan. Area orchard owners, farmers and canning factory managers were all pleased with the work of the PW's.[2]

Unique among the branch camps in Wisconsin, Camp Sturgeon Bay included seven scattered camps with a population second only to Billy Mitchell Field. All under one command, the combined peak total of prisoners housed in Door County grew to about 2,100 PW's. Prisoners renovated the camp and built additional barracks in the fairgrounds at Sturgeon Bay where the largest group stayed. The camp commander, Captain Lester G. Carpenter, and his administration overseeing all of the Door County operations headquartered there as well. The other prisoners bivouacked at the various orchards usually in the sleeping barracks commonly used by migrant workers or civilian pickers that came each season.

Hostility surrounded the mid-May arrival of the first eighty-one

PWs register at Martin Orchards. Photo by W.C. Schroeder.

PW's at Camp Sturgeon Bay, housed at the Martin Orchard. As the war in Europe ended, the numbers of local war dead grew to fifty.[3] The horrors of the Nazi concentration camps, and the mistreatment of our own men held prisoner also became public information. Adding to these frustrations, a variety of rumors spread including the unfortunate and incorrect story that these German prisoners would be paid a full 50 cents an hour. The *Door County Advocate* printed a retraction explaining that the U.S. government received forty cents per hour for prisoner labor and allowed the PW's themselves to keep only eighty cents per day in canteen coupons for their nine hours of work. On May 25, 1945, the *Door County Advocate* then printed a photo essay of the prisoner camp life. To ease tensions further, a quickly arranged press tour of the camp took place. Captain Fred H. Dettmar of the Fort Sheridan public relations office and Camp Sturgeon Bay commander Carpenter showed the press and local dignitaries the living conditions of the PW's. The visitors saw menus, rules of behavior and the cast-off clothing supplied to the prisoners. Being a very temporary camp, no arrangement for leisure activities had been made. Though PW's generally had some with them, the reporters didn't even spot any playing cards during their tour. Again the military pointed out to them that these prisoners were just biding their time waiting to be sent home and posed no danger to the local citizenry. In fact, these prisoners earned money for Uncle Sam while helping to feed our troops still in Europe and those engaged in the war still raging in the Pacific.

Traveling a special, nonstop twelve-car train from the Nebraska sugar beet fields, 500 additional PW's arrived in Sturgeon Bay on Tuesday, July 10, 1945. Expected the following Monday, another 1,125 arrived from various locations. More PW's continued to trickle into Door County increasing the total to about 2,100 Germans. These PW's worked with the 1,100 Jamaican and Mexican migrant workers to pick quickly ripening cherries. About 500 stayed at Door County Fairgrounds, 350 at the Martin Orchard, another 250 billeted at the Reynolds Bros. Orchard, 300 slept at the M. W. Miller place, 200 at the Goldman Orchard near Little Harbor, 250 in Camp Witte at Fish Creek and the Friedlund Orchard at Ellison Bay took 290.[4] Even with this huge number of imported laborers, the orchards and canneries continued advertising for help for its month long harvest. Expected a week or two earlier, many of these prisoners had been delayed by the record pea harvest. Although most of their labor would be in the cherry orchards, many PW's also helped harvest area potatoes and apples. Additionally, their

PW "tree grubbing" in a Door County orchard. Photo by W.C. Schroeder.

labor was used processing the fruit in the area canning factories including the Door County Canning Company, Thomas H. Smith and Son, Jennings Packing Company and Reynolds Brothers Canning Company.

Martin Orchard provided typical living arrangements similar to the other orchard camps. The PW's stayed in existing barracks, the "North Dorm" at Martin's. In this two story building, the prisoners slept upstairs with cooking, eating, and commons areas on first floor. A separate building next to the dorm contained shower facilities. A new high fence surrounded and separated the PW dorm area from the rest of the complex. The PW's received packed lunches in the orchard at lunch time. In the field, tankers regularly filled large barrels of water for the work crews. Those prisoners transported to other smaller orchards in the area always had a guard accompanying them.[5]

While picking cherries in the orchards, the price of twenty cents per pail earned by civilian pickers also went to the Army as wages for the prisoners.[6] Throughout the Door County orchards, German war prisoners picked 508,020 pails of cherries earning $101,604 for the U.S. government that season.[7] Some PW's stayed to pick the apples that ripened later. Those prisoners that remained kept busy in the interim picking potatoes and rocks and doing some orchard maintenance .

RECOLLECTIONS
Joyce Johnson Janeshek. Kingsford, MI -
Pails of cherries were checked and boxed at stations around the orchard. Joyce Janeshek manned one of the stations both years, checking in the cherries the prisoners picked. She remembered a low level of fear or apprehension but an armed guard was always nearby while another walked around the orchard. As a precaution, authorities required the girls to wear slacks rather than shorts and ordered them to stay near their cabins at night. Joyce, her mother and sister, like most of the workers all stayed at the orchard for the harvest season. Joyce remembered that when the end of the war was announced to the German prisoners, they tossed their cherry buckets in the air and jumped with glee. She believed the prisoners anticipated going home soon. Joyce also remembered listening to the prisoners sing at night, surprised that they sang *"Lili Marlene"* in English. Mouth organs were the only instrument she recalled them having. On Sundays, many PW's played ball in their little yard area, always with a guard present.[8]

An MP oversees PW's picking rocks. Photo by W.C. Schroeder.

James Robertson. Sturgeon Bay, WI -
"The biggest surprise for a youngster seeing the prisoners for the first time was that they were not monocled Nazis sprouting horns. Except for the big PW painted on their jacket and the seat of their pants, they looked every bit like the boy next door," Jim Robertson reported. He was home on leave while his ship underwent a conversion in a New York shipyard. The PW's worked the neighboring orchard of his uncle, Chris Trodahl. Jim remembered the prisoners chatting and smiling more as they became comfortable with the place. His favorite recollection came the day his leave ended. "Before, the prisoners had seen me only in my work clothes and had assumed I was a farm boy helping in the harvest. Now, they saw me for the first time in my Navy uniform as I walked into the orchard to bid goodbye to my dad. The orchard suddenly became strangely quiet. I was no longer the farm boy but a member of the powerful U.S. Navy that had helped to destroy their illusion of a master race."[9]

Gladys Schultz. Sturgeon Bay, WI -
Gladys Schultz has a beautiful hand carved box made by a prisoner her father befriended at Goldman Orchard. Her father,

Louis Anschutz, worked for Goldmans and since he spoke German fluently he oversaw several prisoners. At lunch break, all the pickers would head back to the shop. There Anschutz would sit with his team, sometimes bringing extra cookies for his men. At other times, Mrs. Goldman came out with a big kettle of soup to augment the sandwiches carried from camp by the prisoners. Anschutz became especially fond of one prisoner with whom he corresponded after the war. The Anschutz family sent several boxes with clothing, coffee and other items in short supply to Germany and received the hand carved box as a thank you. Eventually, the former PW requested that Louis sponsor him to return to the U.S. Though saddened he could not help, Louis felt he could not take on the added responsibility for the two years required of such sponsors.[10]

Connie Nebel Brick. Sturgeon Bay, WI -
   "Despite the tremendous Coast Guard presence on Lake Michigan, some of the true believers among the PW's were certain that their bombers would fly over the Great Lakes and cut the U.S. in half. During the summers, including the war years, we worked in my

PW's on break in a Door County orchard. Photo by W.C. Schroeder.

Uncle Leo Schlise's orchard. To help as additional cherry pickers, PW's marched from the fairgrounds and back with a guard in front and another in back of the group. Since the sack lunch each PW carried contained only a black bread and lard sandwich, Uncle Leo brought sausage or cheese to add to the sandwiches. My youngest sister attended the Catholic German Girls School in Milwaukee and often came to talk to the prisoners. One PW kept asking me for a "pattern" which I finally understood to mean a map. Whether he hoped to escape or just wanted to know where he was I'll never know. After the war my family sent "care packages" to the Dieter Helcouir family, one of the PW's who worked for us."[11]

Robert Bjorke. Sturgeon Bay, WI -
"Guards with .30-caliber carbines came with the PW's picking in the orchards. One day, I saw the PW's jumping up on the 2 1/2 ton truck on their way back to camp. Without any thought or concern the guard handed his gun to a PW while another helped lift him up into the truck."[12]

Lucille Eckert Stadler. Cottage Grove, WI -
The high fence of Camp Witte at Fish Creek came right up to

A hand-carved gift box from a PW to Louis Anschutz. Photo courtesy of Gladys Anschutz Schultz.

the road at the bottom of a steep hill. As teens, we often rushed down that hill on our bikes picking up speed all the way. The ride was exhilarating! With big smiles for us, the PW's there would stop talking and singing to watch us as we sped down toward them. Guards standing in the short towers usually turned around toward us with their rifles in hand, to check what the PW's were looking at. We were never afraid of the prisoners, but a little concerned about the rifles the guards held. Those guards and rifles also came to the orchard with the PW's where they picked cherries just a couple of rows over from us. Once, we kids got confused and ended up in the same area as the PW's who came and tried to talk to us. They

laughed and pointed at us until a guard with a gun arrived and shooed us over to our designated row of trees. The old barn that had been converted into a barracks for the Fish Creek PW's that summer was torn down after they left. But the silo of that barn is used today as an exclusive three story summer rental.[13]

Werner Krauskopf. Remscheid, Germany -

One final jump over the Fried-lund Orchard camp fence and two PW's were on the loose and headed to Lake Michigan. Knowing they were about to be sent

Girl on a pedestal carved and presented by a PW to Donald Brauer. Photo courtesy of Kenneth A. Smith.

home, Werner Krauskopf and a fellow PW decided they couldn't leave without a swim in this great lake. Returning in 1990, to visit the areas where he spent much of WWII, Werner recalled that, like other tourists, the duo found the lake to be "much cooler and much rockier than we ever expected."[14]

Camp Sturtevant 1944 & 1945

Singing Hitler's "Youth Song" and goose-stepping, the 250 German prisoners marched from the troop train to Camp Sturtevant. A thunderstorm broke and drenched the men as they marched. Changing into shorts, they hung their rain-soaked blue denims on the two-strand barbed wire fence that surrounded their four acre camp. At 8:00 p.m. that evening the prisoners marched in line to be issued regulation Army blankets, which were also dampened by the rain. Mother Nature hit the camp again three nights later. On Friday, June 16, 1944, a small tornado whirled through the area ripping apart the recently erected Army tents in the internment camp.

Along Highway 11 between 7th and 8th streets, the county owned thirty-four lots, part of which the village used as a baseball field at the time.[1] The military leased the area and put up fifty tents to house the PW's while sentries patrolled the perimeter at 60-yard distances. Floodlights burned throughout the night.[2] Once refrigerators had been brought in and water lines piped from the village mains to provide water to the area, Camp Sturtevant became operational.

However, the cooking facilities had not arrived when the prisoners reached Sturtevant. So camp commander Capt. Richard Brooks called on the Racine County American Red Cross to send a mobile canteen to the camp. Utilizing its mobile unit, the Red Cross fed the guards and prisoners. The Red Cross ladies provided sauerkraut and wieners, doughnuts, pie and coffee for the men. Later the Racine Chapter of the Red Cross also furnished a day room in one of the eighteen foot by eighteen foot tents. There, they provided chairs, card tables, games, a radio, books and magazines for the use of the internees.[3] Until after the war, the local residents remained unaware that these captives had been part of Field Marshal Rommel's elite Afrika Korps. Even without this information, curiosity ran high the following day, Sunday. Sightseers went looking at the tornado damage and the camp. The sheriff's deputies kept automobiles moving as hundreds of cars circled the baseball field for a glimpse of Camp Sturtevant.

The Racine-Kenosha County Truck Growers Association had contracted with the military for these PW's. They intended to employ the men weeding, hoeing, and picking vegetables, shocking and threshing grain and harvesting corn. Farmers agreed to pay the government the prevailing wage of $5 a day for each man working.[4] The day after their arrival the PW's were sent to work. Many trucks from large farms in the area arrived at camp by 7:30 a.m. to take the denim-garbed prisoners to their fields for weeding. Because the thunderstorm soaked many fields, the demand for workers did not require all the prisoners that first day.[5] With the sunshine came more than enough work for the PW's. The following month, July, an additional 100 German captives arrived, bringing the total number in Camp Sturtevant to its 1944 peak of 350 prisoners.

Rumors circulating about Camp Sturtevant were running wild. So Mrs. Bennett Whirl, executive secretary of the USO, and William Johnson, chairman of the Memorial Hall Commission, asked the aid of the *Journal-Times* to stop the rumors. First, the dance issue needed clarification. The dance planned by the USO at Memorial Hall was only for the guards stationed at the camp. No prisoners would be allowed to attend. Evidently people had been telephoning USO officials day and night protesting against the dance for war prisoners. The news article clarifying the situation also denied and labeled as rumor the allegation that prisoners used the city beaches in Racine. Army officials forcefully stated that prisoners left camp only under guard and only to go to work stations.[6] After the news article explanations, most of the community uproar settled down.

In May of the following year, Camp Sturtevant reopened under a new commander, Capt. Edward R. Kiel. An initial 150 prisoners arrived by truck from Billy Mitchell Field to open the camp. Additional prisoners transferred in later. The electrical and water facilities remained from the previous year so little preparation was needed.[7] The entire operation proceeded much like it had in 1944. Again the wage rate paid by farmers to the government remained at 50 cents an hour. Kiel said rules of non-fraternization would be enforced as well as the requirement for GI style haircuts and daily shaves.[8] Lunches for the prisoners went to the fields in vacuum containers. But, as all over the country, the reduced food ration for the PW's this season contained less meat and more potatoes and bread.[9]

Some county residents became "too friendly" with the prisoners, giving them cartons of cigarettes, candy and even pocket knives shortly after their arrival. These actions seriously concerned Capt. Kiel when such gifts were discovered during a routine but unannounced inspection. By that time the camp housed 323 Germans, and this fraternization created serious military discipline problems.[10] The commander demanded such fraternization stop immediately.

In August, Major Gen. Henry S. Aurand, Commanding Officer of the Sixth Service Command, selected Camp Sturtevant as one of seven camps in the state he would personally inspect. After his tour, he pronounced Sturtevant one of the finest camps in the country. Without naming the other locations, the general said that of the seven he visited in the state he found three to be under excellent supervision by the contractors, three good and one only fair.[11]

Unlike most camps in the state, Camp Sturtevant continued to operate through the fall and into December, 1945.[12] In September Fort Sheridan announced that private companies paid to the military $50,730 for work done in 1945 by the PW's at Sturtevant.[13] But another three months earnings had yet to be collected. The military never released the final figures.

RECOLLECTIONS
John Batikis. Racine, WI -
When soldier John Batikis came home to Racine on leave, a neighbor took him out to the camp where he was surprised to

Camp Sturtevant, 1945. Photo courtesy of Ruth Moon.

see a lack of security and only four-foot high snow fencing as the perimeter. John quickly lost his concern when he came to understand the prisoners had the choice of staying or returning to live under Hitler. Who wouldn't choose to stay?[14]

Unidentified Racine Journal Times *Reporter. Racine, WI -*
From a nearby airfield, airplanes circled over the camp. The prisoners thought the planes were guarding them from the air. When told that the planes were just trainers from a nearby airport teaching civilians to fly, one of them snorted, "Propaganda!"[15]

Fred Zimbars. Racine, WI -
"When I was 5 or 6 years old, I was playing in the silo on the area farm where we lived. A German SS officer in charge of a small group of men brought them in to clean the silo for grain storage. Startled, I took off screaming toward our house as they scared the heck out of me. The neighbor who was overseeing their work ran after me, but he didn't catch up to me until I got into the kitchen. He tried to assure my mother and me that everything was OK and these men weren't after me." Fred still has a clear image of the high leather boots, uniform and hat of that officer in charge.[16]

Emery &Virginia Creuziger. Sturtevant, WI -
The 780-acre Creuziger farm hired nine PW's to work mostly with cabbage and potatoes. Emery recalled the PW's helping crate cabbage in the shed and the disbelief among the prisoners when they heard that the Siegfried line had fallen. The prisoners thought it was just propaganda but later came to recognize the truth. Sometimes when no guard came with the prisoners, his father, Charles Creuziger, would drive the prisoners out to the field in his used green 1941 Cadillac. "The PW's loved that car almost as much as Dad did," according to Emery. The camp brought lunch out to the prisoners. And for a while friends from Kenosha brought sweet rolls from their bakery as a treat about once a week. The baked goods abruptly stopped when some of these prisoners were beaten up back at camp for getting favored treatment. Emery's new bride, Virginia, also worked in the potato fields with the prisoners without any fear or concern for her safety. The family maintained correspondence with several of the prisoners after their repatriation. Charles Creuziger eventually sponsored former prisoner Rudolf Kaden, helping him to immigrate back to Wisconsin after the war. Kaden still resides in Milwaukee.[17]

Jeremiah Dustin. Crivitz, WI -

For the summer season both years, we hired five PW's per day to help on our 120 acre vegetable farm. What a difference between the 1944 group and those that came in 1945! The first group included older men, well disciplined and hard working, while the 1945 cadre contained very young captives. A couple of 17-year-old prisoners were particularly unruly and recalcitrant workers. Even with the help of the PW's, we couldn't harvest all the vegetables ripening and had no one to pick tomatoes. So the Jewish produce fellows from Milwaukee came to pick the tomatoes themselves to take back to the city. I ordered the two unruly PW's to help the Jews. Boy, they didn't like that and shaped up pretty good. We got more work out of our prisoners than the neighbors: but I worked in the field with them while the neighbor didn't. We also gave them treats every day, usually cigarettes, occasionally a beer or swig of whiskey. During the first year, the Army delivered meals, but the next year, the PW's came with sack lunches. My wife, Dorothy, thought they needed more and cooked extra chili or spaghetti or something to feed them on the porch at lunch, too. Our property was on the north edge of Racine, right on Lake Michigan, so on their lunch break they often went down to the lake, skinny-dipping to cool off. As I drove them back to camp at the end of the day, we sometimes stopped in my brother's tavern. They put the money I gave them in the juke box and my brother gave them a free beer. On the whole, they were good workers, even drove the car and the tractor.[18]

Pauline Mertz Hoye. Mentor, OH -

We would laugh at the PW's when they fell flat to the ground every time a low flying plane passed over. Since the farm was not too far from the Racine, Kenosha or Milwaukee airports, lots of planes flew over. We tried to convince them the planes wouldn't shoot them. My sister and I were the only civilians working with the PW's at that time on a farm on County Line Road in Kenosha County. Both she and I could speak German fluently, so we conversed with the prisoners often. I will say the guards were professional, very alert and kept good watch, at the same time treating the prisoners as human beings. We never saw any prisoners get out of line or be disrespectful to the guards. The PW's arrived at the fields each morning in big trucks, and another truck came later to bring

Virginia Creuziger and PW crew in a potato field, 1945. Photo courtesy of Emery and Virginia Creuziger.

their lunches. We sisters did envy them — they had good meals, usually a soup or stew with bread. They would sit outside in the shade and eat, as did we from our lunch bags. Never allowed to mingle at any time during the lunches, we exchanged comments while in the fields as we worked up and down the rows of produce. We all could talk as long as we kept working. My father had been a prisoner of war in Germany during WWI. He was captured as a wounded Russian soldier and at that time was well treated. I now know that our prisoners were badly treated in Japan and Germany.

But our country can be proud of the humane treatment we gave the soldiers we captured.[19]

Charles Moelter. Lake Geneva, WI -
Local folks, my family included, would go to the camp fence to listen to the regular outdoor concert the PW's put on. They had a nice band, but where they got the instruments I do not know. As special treats the men performed a few plays. Again, most of us sat outside the fence to enjoy them, but some civilians were invited inside. The soccer matches also drew some spectators to the fence.[20]

Lee Wood. Racine, WI -
The Army stake-truck of prisoners with their armed guard stopped and picked us boys up at the street corner on the edge of Racine. We youngsters walked or rode our bikes to that pickup location and got a ride out to the fields where we all, prisoners and boys alike, picked potatoes or onions. I often worked the row between Karl and Herman, my PW buddies. I tried to teach them a little English as we worked. Since they were probably in their early 20s and I only 12, they could pick faster. Often they would toss potatoes or onions into my bushel basket to help me out. We got a chip for each bushel we filled and at the end of the day (civilians) were paid ten cents for each one. Eight to ten trucks of men might stop at one farm and clean up the entire field in one day.[21]

Eric Riesselmann. Kenosha, WI -
My grandparents, George and Ethel Lichter, had a farm on Sheridan Road on the south side of Kenosha. During busier times an armed guard from Sturtevant brought twelve to fifteen men over at 6 a.m. or 7 a.m. and stayed with them until 6 or 7 at night. The prisoners always brought a sandwich for lunch. The very first day they came, Grandma fixed a big meal and served them at noon. After working the rest of the day, Grandpa announced, "You work hard, you get a meal like you had before. If you don't, you eat what you brought." Thereafter there were only one or two lazy men whom Grandpa had to tell to get working.[22]

Camp Waterloo 1945

In mid-June, a construction crew of forty prisoners and guards took over the Balmer building and property on Highway 19 to set up Camp Waterloo. The camp officially opened June 28, housing 310 working German prisoners, 40 guards and 2 officers. The Army contracted this prison labor out to the following five companies: Waterloo Canning Association, Watertown Canning Company, Oconomowoc Canning company at Sun Prairie, Libby, McNeil and Libby Company at Lake Mills and the Reeseville canning plant. Between working the pea and corn packs, these PW's picked cherries and filled other labor shortages. Rations similar to prisoners in other camps were provided. To aid in enforcing the non-fraternization rules, local law authorities requested people stay at least fifteen feet from the camp fence. The military also directed employers to segregate prisoners from civilians as much as possible on the job. Noting the only entertainment available to the guards would be the social opportunities provided by the community, authorities encouraged local families to show an interest in the American servicemen. Many combat veterans, recently returned from the European Theater, served in the cadre of guards. These men expected to be replaced as American soldiers held by the Germans were released and returned to this country. Encouraging the Nazis to see what our democracy offered, the military placed no restrictions on magazines or newspapers available to the PW's and allowed uncensored radio listening as well.[1]

During the canning season, one young high school graduate and one of the prisoners found themselves under investigation by the MP's. *The Milwaukee Journal* reported that the PW was put in the camp "hoosegow" for fraternizing with the young lady. The girl's locket turned up on the German.[2]

According to Fort Sheridan, the German prisoners quartered at Camp Waterloo earned over $43,279 for the government through September 1. After the release of the Fort Sheridan wage figures, these prisoners continued to earn an additional but unreported sum of money as they worked in Waterloo at the Waterloo Canning Assn., in Sun Prairie at the Oconomowoc Canning Co. and the W. P. Renk and Son, in Lake Mills at Libby, McNeil and Libby and in Watertown at the Watertown Canning Co. Without any further announcements, the military vacated the camp as soon as the food packing finished at the end of the month.[3]

RECOLLECTIONS
Earl Weichmann. Sun Prairie, WI -
An older but very muscular Nazi refused to get on Earl's truck to leave for the fields. The prison guard pulled out his pistol and demanded that the Nazi get on the truck. A younger German talked him into boarding the truck. When Earl got to the field, that same Nazi then refused to leave the truck. Earl told the younger Germans to convince him to leave the truck, promising that he wouldn't work the prisoners like animals, offering them breaks and time to relax. The older Nazi finally got off the truck and through the interpreter later expressed his appreciation for Earl's treatment of the prisoners. Over the season Earl had found the older PW's to be tougher to handle, with the younger prisoners more cooperative and probably less indoctrinated into Hitler's philosophy.[4]

While at work, one of the prisoners at the Oconomowoc Canning Co. at Sun Prairie received a letter notifying him his entire family had been killed in the war. The German went "crazy" and started to run away from the factory along the railroad tracks. A guard fired at least two shots into the air before the prisoner stopped.[5]

The same guard later went into the pea-sorting floor of the Sun Prairie cannery. He thought the Germans were not working hard enough and started yelling at them. In charge of the work crew, Pete Hart told the guard to leave. The guard then pulled his gun on Pete. As soon as the MP left, Pete reported the incident to John Mount, the manager of the plant. Mount immediately applied pressure on camp authorities to have that MP removed. That guard never return to the plant. Although Pete Hart had heart problems, he seemed to have no side effects from the ordeal.[6]

Camp Waupun 1945

Waupun boasted two prisons in the summer of 1945. Added to the Wisconsin state prison that had been there for years, Camp Waupun opened as a prison camp for captured German soldiers. Inside the state prison, the convicts worked on various jobs related to the war effort. Across town 350 German prisoners of war spent the canning season helping to feed our Army as well as our civilians.

The PW's lived in a tent city on the field south of Doty Street, next to the Waupun Canning Company property. A large mess tent and a wooden shack had been constructed to house the cooking stoves and other equipment. Designed more to outline the camp boundaries rather than to prevent escape, a snow fence surrounded the area. However, four guard posts offered some security. The forty enlisted men guarding the prisoners were billeted across the street in their own tent city between Maxon and Morse Streets. Not only did the military take special efforts to segregate the prisoners and guards, but the employers also made similar provisions to separate their civilian and prisoner employees. In Waupun, the prevailing wage was sixty cents per hour, which the canning companies paid to the government for the prisoner labor. From Camp Waupun, 150 Germans were employed at the Waupun Canning Company, 80 went to the Canned Foods, Inc., and 100 worked for the Stokely Foods Corporation at Brandon. About twenty-five prisoners remained in camp to do the KP, canteen work, laundry and other maintanence tasks. During their stay, Chief of Police W. L. Tetzlaff threatened disorderly conduct citations to any citizens not cooperating with the order to stay away from the camp. At the same time, the local residents were encouraged to extend their hospitality to the forty-two soldiers and officers guarding the camp.[1] Throughout the season, the canners experienced no trouble with the prisoners of war they utilized.[2] While some of the PW's were shipped out after the pea pack, many remained until the last of the corn pack was finished in Brandon about mid-October.[3] Their efforts paid off. Fort Sheridan reported that private companies in the area paid $40,374 to the military for the Camp Waupun PW labor in 1945. [4]

RECOLLECTIONS
Waupun Leader-News, *September 20, 1945, p. 1.* -
"ADULTERY" headlines quickly spread from Waupun across the state. One PW was involved in an adultery charge that cost the local lady her reputation and the PW serious punishment. The incident almost cost the camp commander, Capt. John A. Knowles, his position as well. Horst Wirst, one of the prisoner interpreters, began exchanging notes with Mrs. Albert Wilderman, who lived next door to the camp. The note exchanges quickly grew to his evening visits to her house, until neighbors started to raise questions. Wirst wore a raincoat turned inside out so the PW letters did not show. For some time, the neighbors thought Mrs. Wilderman, whose husband was on active duty in the Pacific, was entertaining one of the guards. The police investigated after several complaints and discovered that the visitor was actually a German prisoner. After admitting his guilt, Wirst was immediately returned to Fort Sheridan, IL. There he suffered the maximum punishment allowed,

Camp Waupun tent city, 1945. Photo courtesy of James Laird.

A view of Camp Waupun from atop the Waupun Canning Company, 1945. Photo courtesy of James Laird.

bread and water for 14 days followed by hard labor for an additional 16 days. Mrs. Wilderman admitted a two month relationship with the prisoner and was bound over to circuit court for her trial.[5] Declining to have an attorney represent her, Mrs. Wilderman pleaded guilty and received a sentence of one year on probation.[6] First, news reports stated that Capt. Knowles would be relieved of his duties there, but later that was retracted. During the investigation, Col. Cushman, in charge of all camps in the area, found that there wasn't the breach of security as he first thought. As the prisoner spokesman, Wirst had the authority to leave the compound, supposedly to go to the office across the street.[7] Knowles ordered security tightened by doubling the number of guards posted from two to four per night shift.

Theresa Dreikosen. Waupun, WI -
Theresa Dreikosen and husband farmed nearby and found hired help hard to get. Over the season, they hired two different prisoners. Theresa has special recollections of each of them. One PW, Alouis Guggemous, sang as he drove their tractor. During a lunch break, he noted that the Germans had diesel tractors while Dreikosens did not. During threshing, PW Frederick Stratzman remarked each time he was invited inside to eat lunch that it was a *Hochzeitsfest*, a wedding feast (with so much to eat). Theresa's neighbor also hired PW's to work on his pea viner. He took beer out to the men for a treat. After the war, the Dreikosens received several letters from Europe in which Frederick thanked them for

their hospitality and requested help. He also thanked them with a gift box made of inlaid woods which he had carved with a pen knife. Theresa has kept stamps in the box ever since.[8]

Edward Ucker. Waupun, WI -
The front pew at the Alto Dutch Reform Church was reserved for PW's during the canning season of 1945. A light guard escorted those PW's who chose to attend the services each week.[9]

Eugene Buchholz. Waupun, WI -
"He did the best he could, but I thought he was slacking for a while. I supervised a group of PW's in the Waupun Canning factory as they picked the sealed cans of peas off the end of the line and put them into baskets headed for the cookers. All the men wore gloves and commonly grabbed four cans at a time in each hand. But this one chubby PW would take only three at a time. When I approached him on the matter, he pulled off his gloves to show two missing fingers."[10]

Chester Possin. Big Green Lake, WI -
Back from the European Theater, Chester Possin was in Chicago on his way to the Pacific when the atomic bomb was dropped on Japan. Thankfully, his orders quickly changed. He had only to report to Camp McCoy before heading home. He arrived back on the family farm south of Waupun still in uniform. There he found three German PW's helping his folks with the work. That situation provided Chester with several stories he fondly remembered. When the PW's first saw him in uniform, one said to the others (in German), "Air Force." Coming from a German speaking household, Chester didn't let them know he understood what they said. (A short while later, his knowledge of the language would be exposed.) His father thought the Germans were mixing the concrete too thick and told his son to go tell them to thin it up a bit, so Chester approached them and spoke in German. They certainly were surprised and probably wondered what else they had said in his presence. The same three men helped around the farm for a week. Chester's father drove to town to pick them up each morning and to return them in the evening. His mother made a big noon meal for all. Chester had lots of cheap cigarettes from the military but didn't smoke, so he shared them with the prisoners.The PW named Carl had his eye on Chester's younger sister. After Carl was repatriated, he sent her a letter, but she never responded. Chester also told of their

pastor, Otto Mueller, from Pella Lutheran Church who went out to the camp and conducted services. Chester thought their minister only went twice a month, perhaps some other minister or priest preached at the camp on the other Sundays.[11]

Camp Wisconsin Rapids 1945

Quietly the military signed a lease with Tri-City Airways Inc. for use of the airport facilities to house PW's from May 1 to December 1, 1945. In this contract, the military agreed to pay the "maximum allowed by the War Department." (This figure was based on the appraised value of the property or at the rate of 5¢ per prisoner per day — whichever figure was determined to be lower.)[1] The military requested that the press not mention the camp until the prisoners had arrived, according to the *Wisconsin Rapids Daily Tribune,* May 7, 1945. Capt. Thomas R. Ryan took command of the German prisoners as they arrived on Sunday, May 6th, establishing Tri-City Airport as Camp Wisconsin Rapids. Much of the subsequent *Daily Tribune* article reviewed the area labor shortage problem and the subsequent need for these PW's. The U.S. Employment Service spokesman, Mr. Nelson, called the prisoners a "Godsend."[2]

Wisconsin State Cranberry Growers Association contracted these prisoners to work in the cranberry marshes. Some were also employed by other businesses including the Sampson Canning Company , Pittsville Canning Company and Griffith State Nursery. The Nekoosa Papers Inc. hired PW's to cut pulp wood and work in their nursery a couple of miles from the airport. Eventually area farmers hired prisoners between their other work assignments.

The guards were generally veterans of foreign combat, many recovered from wounds, others still suffering from malaria and other ailments. These prisoners had been captured not only in North Africa but also in Normandy, Belgium and Germany itself as late as March 25th.[3] Their *"lagerfuehrer"* was a young 17-year-old captive, very fluent in English. When camp officials read the war department proclamation announcing the official surrender of Germany, many of the prisoners shouted *"gut,"* meaning good.

The local Red Cross quickly became actively involved with this camp. In a phone call to its commander, Capt. Thomas R. Ryan,

Illustration of PW's in the woods by PW W. Hoernchen, 1946. Photo courtesy of Willi Rau with permission from the U.S. Army, Fort McCoy.

the volunteers inquired about the needs of the camp. Resulting from that phone call, a canteen project was soon developed as Mrs. Arthur Treutel chaired a group attempting to assist the American servicemen guarding the camp. First, the ladies solicited donations to furnish a day room for the MP's. Then they encouraged local residents to involve these men in family dinners, fishing trips and other social outings. With an outpouring of community response both objectives were quickly met. The day room received a variety of furniture, a ping pong table, phonograph and records and radios, as well as books and magazines. Individual guards were invited and welcomed into local homes. Rooms were made available for visiting wives and guests of these GI's.[4]

Two weeks after the arrival of the PW's, the area press enthusiastically participated in a tour of the camp and reported their findings. Sanitary conveniences, water and electric supply had been improved at the expense of the Cranberry Growers Association. Utilizing suitable buildings on the property, cots were set up in an old hangar to sleep the 100-200 prisoners housed there. The abandoned Army Air Force Navigation Training School housed the thirty or so guards. Another barracks served as mess hall and a solitary-confinement hut was built. The compound also included a concrete well house and shower room. A high fence surrounded the property with wooden guard towers built at strategic points along the fence to secure the camp.[5]

Included in that press tour, a trip to a cranberry marsh allowed the reporters to watch the prisoners as they weeded one bog and ditched another. Both jobs were back breaking work without machinery.

Later in the season, two prisoners suffered injury in separate accidents as a result of catching legs in grass cutters. Transported to Riverview Hospital from the Potter and Son Marsh, Erick Kroha, a 20-year-old PW, received treatment for a lacerated and fractured right leg.[6] A month later, 23-year-old prisoner Siegfried Imbuelten was transported to the hospital at Camp McCoy where medics amputated his big toe. His his left foot had gotten caught and mangled in another grass cutter. This accident happened in the A.E. Bennett and Son Cranberry Marsh.[7]

The military usually fed the larger work crews on the cranberry marshes a hot meal, transported from camp in marite (insulated) cans. Often it contained a pasty of sorts, a dough ball full of kidney stew, or the stew itself with plain bread. On the smaller jobs sandwiches sent with the prisoners in the morning had to suffice for lunch.

At the end of the season, Fort Sheridan, IL. reported that PW earnings paid by private companies to the military in 1945 from Camp Wisconsin Rapids totaled $54,506.[8] This figure included earnings only into September and the PW's continued working out of Camp Wisconsin Rapids and earning money into November, 1945.

RECOLLECTIONS

Dave Rucinski. Wisconsin Rapids, WI -
If Dave Rucinski knew then what he knows now, he might not have shared the prisoner lunches brought out to the field from the camp. The dough balls were filled with kidney stew. As a 15-year-old, Dave worked with the prisoners at the Griffith State Nursery weeding the tree beds. He also did the yard work for the house a guard was renting. On weekends, he sometimes ate with the guards or prisoners in their separate messes back at camp. Of Polish ancestry, Dave spoke no German, but says he could communicate with the few words shared and plenty of gestures. He also felt the PW's had no intention of escape and was sure the military felt the same. Dave and a couple of buddies often played at the back of the camp where two creeks converge. The boys noted that during the camp days the military never repaired the old south fence, which had holes big enough for a man to easily go through.[9]

Joan Staub Haasl. Wisconsin Rapids, WI -
Unlike her two friends, Joan Staub Haasl, didn't get that summer job as an aide in Riverview Hospital the summer of 1945. She had admitted she was not going into nurses training after high school. As a result, Joan missed more than medical lessons. Her friends, Nona and Grace, had the unique experience of dealing with Erick Kroha, the PW who had his leg broken in a cranberry marsh accident. At first, they thought he was cute as well as young enough, but they quickly found him to be very unpleasant. Shouting "Heil Hitler" and saluting from his bed, the girls believed him to be a true Nazi. Kroha still believed Germany would win the war and let everyone in the hospital know it. Perhaps he thought news of the German surrender was just more propaganda.[10]

Larry Truchinski. Wisconsin Rapids, WI -
Larry Truchinski also worked in the cranberry marshes with the

Germans. Although the rules required non-fraternization, this was a loosely run camp. During one lunch break, Larry wrestled a big PW. Just as in the war, the American won and quickly received congratulations from his co-workers and boss, Hank Westfall, foreman at the Potter and Son Marsh. Truchinski also remembered the PW's making themselves sick. They had saved the residual sugar from the corners of the canning factory sugar sacks and mixed it with mashed cranberries. Then, at one sitting they ate all of their concoction raw.[11]

Walter S. Schalla. Bridger, MT -
Birthday cake for all was the treat at lunch if one of the thirty or so PW's or the two local young men overseeing them were celebrating their day. Mrs. Hank Westfall, wife of the boss, would bring out the cake at the noon break. Walter Schalla worked on the Roy Potter Marsh and recalled the cakes as well as the big kettles of stew or soup brought from Camp Rapids to the PW's at lunch time. Schalla also recalled that the guards never stayed at the marsh, instead making a drive though check of the PW's each mid morning and mid afternoon. Potter also had a small mink raising operation on an island on his property with four PW's assigned to the care of that livestock. Those prisoners mixed the feed, watered the mink

PW's on break at Potters' cranberry marsh. Two still are wearing waders. Photo courtesy of Larry Truchinski.

and cleaned the pens. Most of the prisoners working at this marsh had been captured during or shortly after the Normandy invasion. One final recollection of Walter still irritated him. The PW's usually had tailor made cigarettes while cigarettes were very difficult to get for civilians.[12]

Charlotte Sweeney Martinson. Port Edwards, WI -
The girls were told to stay inside as the prisoners came to and from the nearby Biron Cranberry Company Marsh. Their father, Louie Sweeney, managed the marsh at the time and became concerned about the PW's whistling and hollering at his daughters as they rode by in the open trucks. The oldest girl, Charlotte, was in high school and remembered those days when the cranberries were raked by hand, all the men wading in hip boots. Just down the road from their house Native Americans pitched their tents each season as they annually prepared to help with the raking. For that one harvest, German PW's, Native Americans and her father were all in the marsh together.[13]

Elwell Shannon. Edgerton, WI -
Returned from the South Pacific, Edgerton native Sgt. Elwell Shannon was now assigned as a security guard at the camp. He admitted to discipline problems with two former SS men. They refused to work and generally attempted to disrupt camp order and discipline. "We put one troublemaker in a hot shed next to the hangar," he said. But with no change in attitudes or actions, the guards sent the two incorrigible Nazis back to Fort Sheridan.[14]

Glenn Prusynski. Wisconsin Rapids, WI -
Glenn Prusynski remembered riding on a truck taking a load of cranberries from the Hoffman, Nash and Dempsey Marsh to the railroad at Biron. Several prisoners rode along on the truck to help upload the berries at the rail stop. On the return back to the marsh, someone bought ice cream bars for everyone including the prisoners. The PW's must not have been familiar with the treat, because some tried to put the ice cream bars into their pockets.[15]

Ellsworth Oilschlager. Pittsville, WI -
After the war, former-prisoner Willi Straeler was sponsored by George Yetter of Pittsville and returned to the area in 1955. Straeler had spent time in both Camp Wisconsin Rapids and Camp Marsh-

field. The Walter Oilschlager family also helped, both in purchasing a small home for the Straelers in Port Edwards and in finding Willi a job in the Nekoosa Paper nursery in the summer.16

Afterword

Stalag Wisconsin was a fascinating and huge success story of WWII. The PW camps in Wisconsin and around the nation provided a WIN-WIN situation for all sides. The military found a useful and safe system to intern and utilize this onslaught of captured soldiers. The author's three years of research has not uncovered one incident where a civilian was intentionally injured or even directly threatened by a PW captive or escapee. Through the payment system established for the PW labor, the military not only collected more than enough to pay the maintenance of the prisoners but also millions more for the U.S. Treasury which saved taxpayers those millions of dollars. The availability of PW's greatly reduced the civilian labor shortages, especially in those seasonal jobs required in agriculture. PW labor literally saved thousands of tons of food that would have otherwise been unharvested and gone to waste.

The vast majority of PW's seemed content with their existence as prisoners of war in America. They found themselves fairly treated and better fed than in their own armies, with a warm dry place to sleep, good physical work to keep them strong and no one shooting at them. Furthermore, both the structured and incidental exposure of these prisoners to American geography, culture, democracy and capitalism provided them a new awareness of what a capitalistic democracy could achieve.

As hoped, some of these repatriates became leaders of reform movements in Europe and Asia. The compassion and kindness extended to many of these prisoners by individual commanders, enlisted men and civilians has never been forgotten. Some international friendships spawned between the civilians and PW's still remain intact today, extending to following generations.

The prisoners leaving Wisconsin for their homelands left one final legacy. They made a major contribution to local charity. The PW's assigned to the Sixth Service Command requested and received the privilege of contributing to the National Community Fund raising nearly nine thousand dollars by surrendering canteen coupons of that value.[1]

End Notes

Why POW's in Wisconsin

1. Lewis, George, and Mewha, John. *History of Prisoner of War Utilization by the United States Army: 1776-1945* (Pamphlet No. 20-213. Washington, D.C.: Department of the Army, 1955), 83.

2. Robin, Ron. *The Barbed Wire College: Reeducating German POW's in the United States During WW II* (Princeton, NJ: Princeton University Press, 1995), 91.

3. Krammer, Arnold. *Nazi Prisoners of War in America* (Briarcliff Manor NY: Stein and Day, 1979) 3.

4. "Japs Leave Camp McCoy." *Tomah Journal*, 4 October 1945, 1.

5. John Wasieleski. PW Guard at Camp McCoy & personal guard of Ensign Sakamaki, Interview by author, Glidden, 29 December, 1997.

6. Camp McCoy. "Fort McCoy Prisoner of War Camp," information pamphlet, 2.

7. "No Fraternizing with Prisoners," *Barron County News Shield* (Barron), 26 July 1946, 1. This article quotes Fort Sheridan numbers as 19,000 PW's working in Upper Michigan, Wisconsin and Illinois. In other press releases including numbers of PW's, sources consistently suggest that two-thirds of Fort Sheridan prisoners work in Wisconsin. Therefore, the author estimates about 13,000 under Fort Sheridan in Wisconsin at the time. These figures do not include PW's under the authority of Camp McCoy also working in the state.

8. Norris, Tim. "Prisoner in a Free Land." *Milwaukee Journal-Sentinel Sunday Magazine,* 1 October 1995, p. 14.

Camp McCoy

1. Robin, *The Barbed Wire College,* 91.

2. Keefer, Louis E. *Italian Prisoners of War in America, 1942-1946: Captives or Allies* (New York: Praeger Publishers, 1992), 3.

3. Camp McCoy. *Fort McCoy Prisoner of War Camp* (Camp McCoy, WI, 1999), 2.

4. Bath, David. *The Captive Samurai: Japanese Prisoners Detained in the U.S. during WW II* (University of North Dakota, Grand

Forks, ND, 1990), 68.

5. Gansberg, Judith, M. *Stalag: U.S.A.: The Remarkable Story of German POW's in America* (New York: Crowell, 1977), 2

6. "First Enemy Aliens Arrive Camp McCoy," *Sparta Herald* , 2 March 1942, 1.

7. Robin, *The Barbed Wire College,* 83.

8. "Japs Leave Camp McCoy," *Tomah Journal,* 4 October 1945, 1.

9. Wasieleski, interview.

10. Camp McCoy. *Fort McCoy Prisoner of War Camp,* 1999, 2.

11. "PW's Leave," *Antigo Daily Journal,* 14 June 1946, 1.

12. "Discharge and Receipt Center Converted to Accommodate 1,200," *Sparta Herald,* 15 January 1942, 1.

13. Fort McCoy Archaeological Resources Management Series, *Research Report No. 5,* Fort McCoy, Wisconsin Archaeology, Environmental and Natural Resources Division, Directorate of Public Works, Fort McCoy, WI: 1996, pp. 10-11.

14. DuWayne Scott. Sergeant in the Registrar's Office of the Camp McCoy Station Hospital. Correspondence and telephone interview with author, Fort Atkinson, August-November, 2000.

15. Wasieleski, interview.

16. Robert Gard. Camp McCoy PW guard, 1944. Interview by author, Appleton, November, 24, 2000.

17. Arthur Hotvedt. GI stationed at Camp McCoy, 1945-1946, Interview by author, Eau Claire, 6 November, 2000.

18. George Mueller. GI stationed at Camp McCoy. 1944-1945, Telephone interview with author, Milwaukee, 18 August, 2000.

19. Devore, Robert. "Our 'Pampered' War Prisoners," *Collier's,* 14 October 1944, 57.

20. Camp McCoy. *Fort McCoy Prisoner of War Camp* (Camp McCoy, WI, 1999), 4.

21. Gansberg, *Stalag: U.S.A.* 53-54.

22. Scott, interview.

23. "Hawaiian 100th Infantry Battalion," *The Real McCoy* (Camp McCoy), 25 August 1967, 17.

24. "Jap Prisoners of War Moved from McCoy," *Monroe County Democrat* (Sparta), 4 October 1945, 1.

25. "PW's Leave," *Antigo Daily Journal,* 14 June 1946, 3.

Work and Contract Labor

1. Lewis and Mewha, *History of Prisoner of War Utilization,* 112-

113.

2. Wasieleski, interview.

3. Lewis, and Mewha, *History of Prisoner of War Utilization*, 77-78.

4. Krammer, Arnold. *Nazi Prisoners of War in America*, 47.

5. Kurt Pechmann. Former PW held in Wisconsin camps, 1943-1946, immigrated to Wisconsin in 1952. Interview by author, Hartford, 17 June, 1998.

6. "Janesville War Prison Home to 500," *Beloit Daily News,* 18 February, 1984, 3.

7. Lewis, and Mewha, *History of Prisoner of War Utilization,* 102.

8. Richard A. Hipke. Owner of A.T. Hipke & Sons Canning Factory in New Holstein, Correspondence and telephone interview with author, Manitowoc, 9 March, 1998.

9. Pechmann, interview

10. Phyllis Larsen Beaulieu. Encountered PW's working on father's farm. Telephone interview with author, Milltown, 29 June, 1998.

11. Lewis, and Mewha, *History of Prisoner of War Utilization*, 118.

12. Ibid., 171.

13. "Asylum chosen For Prison Camp," *The Sheboygan Press*, 2 July 1945, 1.

14. "High Hopes for the Future of Hartford's Landmark Ballroom," *The Daily News* (Hartford), 19 October 1997, 1.

15. "Prisoners Will Assist Local Canneries," *Waukesha Daily Freeman*, 12 June 1944, 1.

16. "Newsmen Taken on Tour of Prisoner of War Camp," *Arcadia News Leader,* 12 July 1945, 1.

17. "German Prisoner of War Picking Beans for Cannery at Bayfield," *Washburn Times,* 30 August 1945, 1.

18. Burnell Spuhler. Bus driver who transported and arranged meals for PW's in Hartford area. Interview by author, Hartford, 17 June, 1998.

19. Mary Lee. Lived in Camp Janesville (1944) with husband and commander Capt. Hugh Lee. Interview by author, Eau Claire, August 1998.

20. "Pickle Factory Denied Further Use of Germans," *Fond du Lac Commonwealth Reporter*, 31 August 1945, 1.

21. Allene Hatz Richgruber. Encountered PW hired by her father

and recalls escaped PW stopping at neighbor's door seeking food. Interview by author, Sparta, 23 & 29 December, 1997.

22. Hipke, interview.

23. George Lorenz. Took treats to PW's in West Salem. Telephone interview with author, Waupaca, 21 August, 2000.

24. Lucille Schultz Welter. Mother interpreted while PW was extricated from machinery in Lange Co. cannery. Interview by author, Eau Claire, March, 1998.

25. Pechmann, interview.

26. Leroy Vogelsang. Manager of canning factory trading punched cards for cigarettes as work incentive for PW's. Interview by author, Hartford, 17 June, 1998.

27. Thompson, William. F.. *The History of Wisconsin, Continuity and Change, 1940-1965* (Madison, WI: State Historical Society of Wisconsin, 1988), 65.

28. Lewis and Mewha. *History of Prisoner of War Utilization*, 151.

29. "Jap Prisoners of War Moved from McCoy," *Monroe County Democrat* (Sparta), 4 October 1945, 1.

30. "Japs Leave Camp McCoy," *The Tomah Journal,* 4 October 1945, 1.

Camp Life

1. Bath, David. *Captive Samurai,* 80-81.

2. Krammer, Arnold. *Nazi Prisoners of War in America,* 49.

3. Scott, interview.

4. Armond Lackas. MP at Camp Hartford. Interview by author, Hartford, 17 June, 1998.

5. "Prisoners' Menus Are Curtailed." *Hartford Times Press,* 11 May 1945, 7.

6. Ucker, Edward. MP in several Wisconsin POW camps 1944-1945. Telephone interview by author, Waupun, 18 July, 2000.

7. Lackas, interview.

8. Gansberg, *Stalag: U.S.A.,* 31.

9. Gard, interview

10. Bath, David. *Captive Samurai,* 93.

11. Lee, interview.

12. Kurt Pechmann. Former PW held in Wisconsin camps, 1943-1946, immigrated to Wisconsin in 1952. Interview by author, Madison, 17 June, 1998.

13. Wasieleski, interview.

14. Scott, interview.

15. Hong, Howard. *Reports on Visit to Prisoners of War Camp, Camp McCoy, Sparta Wisconsin, January 5-7 1944, Inspection Reports: Camp McCoy*. Records of the Provost Marshal General's Office, Prisoner of War Division, 1941-1946; Special Projects Division, 1943-1946. RG 389. (MMB-NA.)

16. Lee, interview.

17. Bath, David. *Captive Samurai*, 92.

18. Ibid., 93.

19. Hall, interview.

20. Wasieleski, interview.

21. Williams, Charles M.. *Captives & Soldiers, Camp McCoy and the War Years*. University of Wisconsin, La Crosse, WI, 1979, p. 9.

22. Gard, interview.

23. Lackas, interview.

24. Jack T. Jilek. Family hired PW's from Camp Antigo, provided correspondence between family and PW after war. Interview by author, Antigo, 16 July, 1998.

25. Gard, interview; Bath *Captive Samurai*, 92.

Resistance and Escape

1. Gansberg, *Stalag: U.S.A.*, 47.

2. Carlson, Lewis H. *We Were Each Other's Prisoners* (New York: Harper/Collins, 1997), 159.

3. Gansberg. *Stalag: U.S.A.*, 53.

4. Bath, *Captive Samurai*, 141.

5. Ibid., 106.

6. Ibid., 103.

7. "Jap Prisoner Hangs Himself," *Monroe County Democrat* (Sparta), 30 November, 1944, p. 1.

8. Harold Hoffman Jr.. Son of MP in charge of PW reeducation program at Camp McCoy. Interview by author, Sparta, 6 November, 1997.

9. Wasieleski, interview.

10. Williams, *Captives & Soldiers, Camp McCoy and the War Years*, p. 8.

11. "Jap PW Killed When Smuggled Bomb Explodes," *Monroe County Democrat* (Sparta), 19 October 1944, 1.

12. Gard, interview.

13. Ibid.

14. Bath, *Captive Samurai*, 109-111 & Gard. Robert & Wasieleski,

John & Camp McCoy. *Fort McCoy Prisoner of War Camp.* Camp Mc-Coy, WI, 1999 p. 6.

15. Lewis and Mewha, *History of Prisoner of War Utilization,* 151.

16. Gonzales, Señor. *Report on Visit to Prisoner of War Camp, Camp McCoy, Spanish Consul in Chicago, Illinois, September 30, 1944. Inspection Reports; Camp McCoy.* Records of the Provost Marshal General's Office, Prisoner of War Division, 1941-1946; Special Projects Division, 1943-1946. RG 389. (MMB-NA.)

17. Edward Kostuch. Reported seeing escaped PW's. Telephone interview by author, La Crosse, November, 2000.

18. Bath, *Captive Samurai,* 117.

19. "Jap Surrenders After Escaping," *Monroe County Democrat* (Sparta), 6 July 1944, 1.

20. "Two Escaped Jap PW's Are Apprehended," *The Tomah Journal,* 7 June 1945, 1.

21. "Capture One Escaped Jap Prisoner of War," *The Tomah Journal*, 31 May 1945, 1.

22. Bath, *Captive Samurai,* 119.

23. "Jap PW Caught by Biegel Near Norwalk," *Sparta Herald,* 9 July 1945, 1.

24. "One Jap Caught, One Jap Escapes, Third One Dies," *Monroe County Democrat* (Sparta), 19 July 1945, 1.

25. "Escaped Jap PW," *Sparta Herald*, 3 July 1945, 1.

26. "Geography Means Nothing to This Jap War Prisoner," *The Tomah Journal*, 6 September 1945, 1.

27. "Escaped PW Apprehended," *Monroe County Democrat* (Sparta), 14 March 1944, 1.

28. "Apprehension of Escapee Delbert Clark by 2 MPs in La Crosse," *Real McCoy* (Camp McCoy), 20 February 1943, 1.

29. Richgruber, interview.

30. "Prisoner Who Fled McCoy Is Captured," *The Eau Claire Daily Telegram,* 16 April 1945, 1.

31. Vera Schaller Olson. Witnessed father chasing after escaped PW. Telephone interview with author, Fort Atkinson, 26 July, 2000.

32. Darwin Wosepka. Civilian driver transporting PW's to work sights around state. Telephone interview by author, Haugen, 26 June, 1999.

Repatriation

1. "Prisoner in a Free Land," *Milwaukee Journal Sentinel Sunday Magazine,* 1 October 1995, 12.

2. Roger Young. Civilian driver transporting Japanese PW's to and from work sites. Japanese Prisoner died after falling from his truck. Interview by author, Sparta, 30 December, 1997.

3. Carlson, *We Were Each Other's Prisoners,* ix.

4. Lewis and Mewha, *History of Prisoner of War Utilization,* 173.

5. Ibid., 91.

6. Erwin Scheinast. Shared stories his father repeated about his PW years in Wisconsin. Correspondence with author, Heidenheim, Germany, October, 2000/February, 2001.

7. Pechmann, interview.

8. Willi Rau. Former PW held in Wisconsin. Correspondence with author, Echzell, Germany, October- December, 2000.

9. Carlson, *We Were Each Other's Prisoners,* 248.

10. Gansberg, *Stalag: U.S.A.,* 67.

11. "Yanks Pave Way for Repatriation of Captive Japanese," *Milwaukee Journal,* 19 September 1945, 1.

12. Carlson, *We Were Each Other's Prisoners,* 248.

Branch Camps

1. Stare, Fred A.. *The Story of Wisconsin's Great Canning Industry,* (Wisconsin Canners Association. Madison, WI: 1949), 157.

2. Ibid., 157.

3. "PW's Earned $41,000 Here," *Barron County News Shield* (Barron), 20 September 1945, 1.

4. "No Fraternizing with Prisoners," Barron County News Shield (Barron) 26 July, 1946, 1. This article quotes Fort Sheridan numbers as 19,000 PW's working in Upper Michigan, Wisconsin and Illinois. Other sources consistently refer to two-thirds of Fort Sheridan numbers as working in Wisconsin. Therefore, the author estimates about 13,000 under Fort Sheridan in Wisconsin at the time. These figures do not include those PW's under authority of Camp McCoy also working in the state.

5. "100 Prisoners For Late Harvest are Sought: Neitzke," *Manitowoc Herald Times,* 31 July 1945, 2.

Camp Antigo

1. "CONTRACTORS HERE PAID $31,730 FOR POW LABOR," *Antigo*

Daily Journal, 15 December 1945, 1.

2. "20 Farmers Using Prisoner Labor," Antigo *Daily Journal,* 21 September 1945, 1.

3. "Pea Pack Begun," *Antigo Daily Journal*, 16 July 1945, 3.

4. "Forty Additional Prisoners Arrive to Work Here," *Antigo Daily Journal,* 13 September 1945, 2.

5. Dean Antoniewicz. Neighbor to NYA Center whose family regularly had guests from the Camp Antigo for Sundays dinners. Telephone interview by author, Milwaukee 15 August, 2000.

6. "Officer in Charge POW Camp Here Rotary Speaker," *Antigo Daily Journal* 17 July 1945, 5.

7. "POW's at Antigo Perform $10,730 Worth Of Work," *Antigo Daily Journal*, 15 September 1945, 1.

8. "Former POW Here Thanks Local Club for Gift Parcels," *Antigo Daily Journal*, 12 May 1949, 1.

9. "Mom And Dad Sent Them Clothing. There Was Nothing In Germany," *Antigo Journal*, 11 September 1995, 1.

10. "Post War Prisoners Help Here," *Antigo Daily Journal,* 11 September 1995, 1.

11. Ibid., 1.

12. Ruth Johnson. Family hired PW's from Camp Antigo, donated photos of PW's on the farm. Correspondence and Telephone interview by author, Peshtigo, 20 March, 1998.

13. Jilek, interview.

Camp Appleton

1. "German Prisoners Worked," *Appleton Post-Crescent*, 29 May 1994, 1

2. "86 Placements in Farm Labor," *Appleton Post-Crescent*, 8 August 1945, 1.

3. "Prisoners Work 12 Hours Daily," *Appleton Post-Crescent*, 14 July 1945, 1.

4. "War Prisoners' Work Valued at $15,556 in Appleton During July," *Appleton Post Crescent*, 15 August 1945, 4.

5. Carpenter, Matthew. "Presenting the Fuhremann Canning Company." *History Today*, Second Quarter, 1995, 10.

6. "Visit by German Youth Traces Grandfather's Tracks," *Appleton Post-Crescent,* 8 July 1995, Lifestyles p. 8.

7. Theresa Otte. Visited Camp Appleton with best friend who was engaged to guard. Telephone interview with author, Neenah, 11 July, 2000.

8. "Prisoners Work 12 Hours Daily," *Appleton Post-Crescent*, 14 July 1945, 1.

9. "Beet Pack is Scheduled to Start Aug. 27," *Appleton Post-Crescent*, 17 August 1945, 1.

10. "Prisoners Help Pack 30,000 Cases of Peas," *Appleton Post-Crescent,* 22 August 1945, 1.

11. " PW's at Antigo Perform $10,730 Worth of Work," *Antigo Daily Journal*, 15 September 1945, 1.

12. Paul J. Wassenberg. Witnessed PW's being transported. Telephone interview by author, Appleton, 15 August, 2000.

13. Anthony La Loggia. Worked with PW's in Appleton. Telephone interview by author, Newburg, 15 August, 2000.

14. Helen Van Handel. Worked with PW's at Dundas Canning Factory. Correspondence and telephone interview with author, Appleton, 26 September, 2000.

15. Merlin Romenesko. Worked with PW's near Kaukauna. Telephone interview by author, Walworth, August, 2000.

16. Richard and Alice Van Handel. Father worked with PW's at viner, provided photos. Correspondence and Telephone interview with author, Appleton, September-October, 2000.

Camp Barron

1. "200 Germans in Camp at Barron," *Rice Lake Chronotype* , 5 July 1944, 1.

2. "Prison Camp is Activated," *Barron County News Shield* (Barron), 6 July 1944, 1.

3. "Prisoners Still think That Germany Will Win War," *Rice Lake Chronotype,* 2 August 1944, 1.

4. "Prison Camp Opens July 8," *Barron County News Shield* (Barron), 28 June 1945, 1.

5. "Prison Camp Opens July 8," *Barron County News Shield* (Barron), 28, June 1945, p. 1.

6. "Peace & Quiet Return to German Prison Camp," *Rice Lake Chronotype*, 9 August 1944; Pechmann, interview.

7. Ronald E Greener. Farm manager hiring PW's near Barron. Telephone interview by author, Rice Lake, 19 July, 1999.

8. "Prisoners earned $48,056.91 Here," *Barron County News Shield* (Barron), 18 October 1945, 1.

9. Chuck Rieck. MP guarding PW's at Barron, Wisconsin Rapids and Sheboygan. Telephone interview by author, Middleton, 17 October, 2000.

10. Ken McDonald. Witnessed PW's at Camp Barron. Telephone interview by author, Barron, 20 April, 2000.

11. Donald Neuenfeldt. Family hired PW's to work farm. Barron, Telephone interview by author, 15 July, 1999.

12. Name withheld. Interview by author, Eau Claire, 4 November, 2000.

13. Stuart Hegna. Family hired PW's to work farm. Telephone interview author, Cameron, 16 July, 1999.

14. Greener, interview.

15. Joseph Operpriller. Witnessed PW's at viner. Interview by author, Chippewa Falls, 15 July, 1999.

16. Floyd Thompson. Worked in canning factory with PW's. Telephone interview by author, Cumberland, 29 July, 1999.

17. Wilma Calloway. Worked with PW's in cannery. Pellston, MI, Telephone interview with author, 29 July, 1999; Carol Cormany. Worked with sister Wilma and PW's in cannery. Interview by author, Chippewa Falls, 30 July, 1999.

18. Wosepka, interview.

19. Harold Kringle. Worked with PW's harvesting. Telephone interview by author, Barron, 25 June, 1999.

20. Norman and Ruth Rydberg. Hired PW's to pick beans on their farm in 1944 and 1945. Telephone interview by author, Spooner, 11 August, 2000.

Camp Bayfield

1. "German Prisoners of War Picking Beans for Cannery at Bayfield," *Washburn Times,* 30 August 1945, 1.

2. "75 German Prisoners Arrive to Work in Bayfield," *Ashland Daily Press,* 27 August 1945, 1.

3. "German Prisoners of War Picking Beans for Cannery at Bayfield, " *Washburn Times,* 30 August 1945, 1.

4. "War Prisoners on Move, Bean Fields to Orchards," *Bayfield County Press,* 27 September 1945, 1.

5. "Nazi Prisoners Aid Harvesting of Beans in Bayfield Area," *Ashland Daily Press*, 29 August 1945, 1.

6. "German Prisoners of War Picking Beans for Cannery at Bayfield," *Washburn Times,* 30 August 1945, 1.

7. "Nazi Prisoners Aid Harvesting of Beans in Bayfield Area," *Ashland Daily Press*, 29 August 1945, 1.

8. Edward Erickson. Worked with PW's on family farm picking raspberries, beans and apples. Telephone interview by author,

Bayfield, August, 1999.

9. "Nazi Prisoners Aid Harvesting of Beans in Bayfield Area," *Ashland Daily Press*, 29 August 1945, 1.

10. "German Prisoners May Possibly Stay for Herring Season," *Ashland Daily Press,* 17 October 1945, 1.

11. James Erickson. Orchard family hired PW's on farm. Telephone interview by author, Bayfield, 17 July, 1999.

12. Jack Erickson. Witnessed PW's working family farm. Interview by author, Bayfield, 1 November, 2000.

13. John Hauser. Encountered PW's in family orchards. Interview by author, Bayfield, 1 November, 2000.

14. Wojak, Tony B. President of Washburn Historical Society, author, *B Book II.* Telephone interview by author, Bayfield, 18 July, 1999.

15. Harriet Haugen Johnson. Witnessed PW's at Camp Bayfield. Interview by author, Ashland, 1 November, 2000.

16. Merton Bruce Benton. Personal experiences with PW's in Bayfield area. Interview by author, Correspondence with and interview by author, Ashland, 2 October - 1 November, 2000.

17. J.A Krueger. Witnessed PW's working in family orchard. Correspondence and telephone interview with author, Minneapolis, Minnesota, November, 2000.

18. Mary Torbick McCarty. Encountered PW's working on family farm and orchard. Interview by author, Bayfield, 1 November, 2000.

19. Ruth Moon. Chief bookkeeper for Bayfield Fruit Growers Association while PW's worked there. Provided several photos of Camp Bayfield and PW's. Correspondence and interview by author, Ashland, 1 November, 2000.

Camp Beaver Dam

1. "German Prisoners to Help With Pea Crop," *Beaver Dam Argus, 1* June 1944, 1.

2. "1944 - When Nazi Troops Packed Peas in Beaver Dam," *Daily Citizen,* 9 April 1977, 1.

3. "Ban Curious from Prisoners Camp," *Beaver Dam Argus,* 19 June 1944, 1.

4. "179 Prisoners of War Arrive at Jefferson," *Watertown Daily Times*, 22 June 1944, 1.

5. "Harvesting of Pea Crop Underway," *Beaver Dam Argus*, 22 June 1944, 1.

6. "Nazi Prisoners Leave Beaver Dam," *Watertown Daily Times*, 5 August 1944, 1.

7. Robert Frankenstein. Witnessed PW's in area, and current member of Dodge County Historical Society, provided photos of Camp Beaver Dam. Correspondence and telephone interview with author, Beaver Dam, July, 2000.

8 James Hammitt. Witnessed PW's at Camp Beaver Dam. Telephone interview by author, Eau Claire, 6 November, 2000.

9. Gilbert Bleck. Witnessed PW's in Camp Beaver Dam and on area farms. Telephone interview with author, Greendale, November, 2000.

Camp Billy Mitchell

1. "When POW's Stayed Here," *Milwaukee Journal*, 12 October 1975, 1.

2. "It Looked Nicer on Outside, Nazis' Explanation for Escape," *Milwaukee Journal*, 15 January 1945, 1.

3. "Mitchell Field is Branch Base," *Fond du Lac Commonwealth Reporter*, 6 June 1945, 2.

4 "German POW's Make Batteries; Appear at Ease," *The Reminder* (Cudahy), 22 March 1945, 1.

5. "PW Exhibit," *Portage Register-Democrat*, 23 May 1945, 1.

6. "German POW's Make Batteries; Appear at Ease," *The Reminder* (Cudahy), 22 March 1945, 1.

7. "PW Camps Under New Head," *Racine Journal-Times*, 5 June 1945, 1.

8. "State to Get More PW Aid," *Racine Journal Times*, 27 June 1945, 1.

9. "POW's at Antigo Perform \$10,730 Worth of Work," *Antigo Daily Journal*, 15 September 1945, 1.

10. "When POW's Stayed Here," *Milwaukee Journal*, 12 October 1975, 1.

11. William Michaelis. He had personal encounters with PW's. Correspondence and telephone interview with author, Crivitz, 31 July, 2000.

12. Gerie Peter Sobocinski. Secretary to Post Surgeon, Station Hospital at Billy Mitchell Field and wife of Special Service officer. Telephone interview with author, Cudahy, 1 August, 2000.

13. Ibid.

14. Ibid.

15. Carolyn Anich. Witnessed PW's on break from Badger Mal-

leable. Correspondence and telephone interview by author, West Allis, August, 2000.

16. Harry Hetz, M.D. Former PW held in several camps in Wisconsin, later Captain in Medical Corps of the U.S. Army. Telephone interview with author, Kenilworth, IL, 22 August, 2000.

17. Jerry Zimmerman. Wisconsin State Fair Historian and witness to PW's in Wisconsin State Fair Grounds. Correspondence and telephone interview with author, West Allis, August, 2000.

18. Carol Wilinski Jungbluth. Joined PW's watching movie in Camp Billy Mitchell Field. Telephone interview with author, Hartland, August 2000.

19. Carl L Mueller Jr. Spent time in Billy Mitchell Field Hospital with PW's. Telephone interview with author, Milwaukee, August, 2000.

20. Richard R Figlesthaler. Personal experiences with PW's at Lake Keesus and Billy Mitchell Field. Correspondence and telephone interview with author, Greendale, August and November, 2000.

21. Mel Leonard. Witnessed PW's cutting cabbage north of Milwaukee. Telephone interview with author, River Hills,17 August, 2000.

22. Gene Haas. Visited PW cousin at Camp Mitchell Field. Telephone interview with author, Milwaukee, 5 September, 2000.

23. David Reimers. Witnessed escapees arrested by MPs near U.S. Disciplinary Barracks. Telephone interview with author, Brookfield, 9 November, 2000.

24. Robert T. Heldt. Guarded prisoners at Camps Billy Mitchell, Sturgeon Bay, Oakfield and Wisconsin Rapids. Correspondence and telephone interview with author, Chicago, IL, August-September, 2000.

25. Sobocinski, interview.

26. Donald Meyer. Member of Oak Creek VFW Post #434. Telephone interview with author, Oak Creek, 14 August, 2000.

27. John Flynn. Personal encounter with former PW in France. Telephone interview with author, Glendale, 14 August, 2000.

Camp Cambria
1. Hong, Howard. *Report of Visit to Prisoner of War Branch Camp, Cambria Wisconsin." Branch of Fort Sheridan IL, September 4, 1944, Inspection Reports: Fort Sheridan IL.* Records of the Provost Marshal General's Office, Prisoner of War Division, 1941-1946; Special

Projects Division, 1943-1946. RG 389. (MMB-NA.)

2. "Prisoners & Jamaicans to do Factory Work," *The Cambria News,* 16 June 1944, 1.

3. Stare, *Wisconsin's Great Canning Industry,* 158.

4. "P.W. Camp Moved," *The Cambria News,* 29 September 1944, 3.

5. "Soldiers Appreciate Courtesies of Townspeople," *The Cambria News,* 7 July 1944, 3.

6. "Let War Captives Alone," *The Cambria News,* 21 July 1944, 3.

7. "No Fraternization With German POWs," *The Cambria News,* 29 June 1945, 3.

8. "Report on the German Prisoners War Work," *Fox Lake Representative,* 16 August 1945, 1.

9. "POWs at Antigo Perform $10,730 Worth of Work," *Antigo Daily Journal,* 15 September 1945, 1.

10. Thomas Williams. Worked with PW's in Cambria, 1944. Telephone interview with author, Cambria, 12 July, 2000.

11. Margaret Williams. Worked with PW's in Cambria. Telephone interview with author, Cambria, 13 July, 2000.

12. Mona Lloyd Ferris. Dated and later married Cambria MP, James Ferris. Correspondence and telephone interview with author, Lansdowne, PA, July, 2000.

Camp Chilton

1. "Prisoners Only a Last Resort in Plants Here," *Manitowoc Herald-Times,* 20 June 1945, 1.

2. "War Prisoner Projects Pay Large Return," *Fond Du Lac Commonwealth Reporter,* 11 August 1945, 2.

3. "320 German War Prisoners to be Moved to Fair Grounds Next Week," *Chilton Times-Journal,* 21 June 1945, 1.

4. "An Inside Glimpse of the Fair Grounds Prisoner of War Camp," *Chilton Times-Journal,* 19 July 1945, 1.

5. "Former Nazi Soldiers Help in Harvesting County Pea Crop," *Manitowoc Herald Times,* 2 August 1945, 1.

6 . "320 German War Prisoners to be Moved to Fair Grounds Next Week," *Chilton Times-Journal,* 21 June 1945, 1.

7. "German Worker Fractures Skull," *Manitowoc Herald-Times,* 30 July 1945, 1.

8. "War Prisoner Camp Closed," *Two Rivers Reporter,* 11 August 1945, 1.

9. "Chilton Camp to Close Friday," *Chilton Times-Journal*, 9 August, 1945, 2.

10. "POWs Harvested The Region's Crops in '45," *Appleton Post-Crescent*, 29 May 1994, 1.

11. Hipke, interview.

12. Ronald Tordeur. Family hired PW's to harvest beets. Correspondence and telephone interview with author, Green Bay, February & October, 2000.

13. Elroy Kandler. Personal encounter with PW's. Telephone interview with author, Menomonie Falls, 15 August, 2000.

14. Jeannie Williams. Recalls father riding as a guard transporting PW's. Telephone interview with author, Green Bay, 14 August, 2000.

15. Mary Hipke Frisch. Worked in family canning factory with German PW's. Telephone interview with author, New Holstein, 9 March, 1998.

16. Laverne Hutterer. Personal experience with PW's in Rockwood. Correspondence and telephone interview with author, Manitowoc, August, 2000.

17. Mary Ann Gruber Ignera. Witnessed mother cooking for PW's at Rockwood. Telephone interview with author, Manitowoc, 21 August, 2000.

Camp Cobb

1. "War Prisoners Will Harvest the Pea Crop," *Dodgeville Chronicle,* 21 June 1945, 1.

2. "War Prisoners Doing Much Work," *Dodgeville Chronicle,* 27 September 1945, 1.

3. "Work by War Prisoners," *Democrat-Tribune (Mineral* Point), 18 October 1945, 1.

4. Elsie Masters. Encountered PW's on family farm. Telephone interviews with author, Dodgeville, 18 September & 3 October, 2000.

5. Everett Thomas. Encountered PW's on family farm. Telephone interview with author, Cobb, 13 October, 2000.

6 . June Billings Nagel. Encountered PW's on parents farm. Telephone interview with author, Cobb, 18 October, 2000.

7. Name withheld. Hired PW's on family farm near Telephone interview with author, Cobb. October, 2000.

8. Norman Nagel. Worked with PW's hired by father and uncle on their respective farms. Telephone interview with author, Cobb,

18 October, 2000.

9. Evelyn Mueller. Husband hired and worked with PW's on family farm and still corresponds with one former prisoner. Telephone interview with author, Cobb, 21 October, 2000.

10 Mulvey, Deb, Ed. *We Pulled Together...And Won!* (Greendale WI: Reminisce Books, 1993), 58.

Camp Columbus

1. Stare, *Wisconsin's Great Canning Industry*, 158

2. "Prisoners Arrive At Camp Friday; Canning Operations Are Started," *Columbus Journal-Republican*, 22 June 1944, 1.

3. "Two German Prisoners Escape; Caught After 16 Hours Freedom," *Columbus Journal-Republican,* 29 June, 1944, 1.

4. "Prisoners of War To Move In Week of June 25," *Columbus Journal-Republican,* 14 June 1945, 1.

5. "German Prisoners of War Move In Tuesday for Area Pea Pack," *Columbus Journal-Republican,* 28 June 1945, 1.

6. "Press Tour Through Columbus PW Camp Is Made Last Wednesday," *Columbus Journal-Republican,* 19 July, 1945, 1.

7. "Sensational Pea Crop Swamping Canneries," *The Milwaukee Journal,* 24 July 1945, 1.

8. Wilma Black. Community historian who witnessed PW's on family farm. Telephone interview by author, Columbus, 14 January, 2000.

9. "PW Labor Totals $1,827,586 in State," *Milwaukee Journal,* 16 September, 1945.

10. "Memories From The Summer War Prisoners Came To Town," *Wisconsin State Journal* (Madison), 30 January 1983, 1.

11. Hong, Howard. *Report on Visit To Prisoner of War Branch Camp Columbus, Wisconsin, September 4, 1944" Inspection Reports: Fort Sheridan, IL.* Records of the Provost Marshal General's Office, Prisoner of War Division, 1941-1946; Special Projects Division, 1943-1946. RG 389. (MMB-NA.)

12. Wilma Black. Witnessed PW's on family farm. Telephone interview by author, Columbus, January 14, 2000.

13. Thomas Mount. Witnessed PW's in Oconomowoc Canning Company at Sun Prairie. Telephone interview by author, Sun Prairie, 15 August, 2000.

Camp Eau Claire

1. "Pea Pack Started at Lange's; Some War Prisoners on Hand,

" *Eau Claire Leader,* 10 July 1945, 1.

2. June Knudtson. Still active with 4-H, she witnessed PW's at Camp Eau Claire. Telephone interview by author, Fall Creek, November 10, 2000.

3. "German Prisoners Housed in this City," *Altoona Tribune*, 12 July, 1945, 1.

4. "Balance of 175 German War Prisoners Arrive Here," *Eau Claire Leader,* 11 July 1945, 1.

5. "Many of 143 German Prisoners Here Helping Can Peas for Lange Canning Corp. from Rommel's Afrika Korps," *Eau Claire Leader,* 15 July 1945, 1.

6 . "Lange Company to Receive "A" Award Here Tonight," *Eau Claire Leader,* 1 August 1945, 1.

7 . "Work Performed by Prisoners of War totals $3,620,000," *Eau Claire Leader,* 12 August 1945, 5.

8 . "Lange Canning Corp. to Finish Pea Packing Today, "*Eau Claire Leader,* 26 July 1945, 6.

9. "German Prisoners of War Here for Sweet Corn Pack," *Eau Claire Leader,* 14 September 1945, 15.

10. Shirley Hoff. Visited with guards and observed Camp Eau Claire PW's daily. Interview by author, Eau Claire, April, 1998.

11. Knudtson, interview

12. Lucille Schultz Welter. Mother interpreted while injured PW removed from canning machinery. Telephone interview with author, Eau Claire, March, 1998.

13. Mary Wagner. Regularly observed PW's traveling past family Eau Claire home. Telephone interview with author, Eau Claire, April 1998.

14. Dave Foster. Worked with PW's in local cannery. Telephone interview with author, Eau Claire, July, 1999.

15. Lorraine Robillard McFarlane. Daughter of officer who arrested escaped PW in downtown Eau Claire. Telephone interview with author, Eau Claire, April 1998.

16. Rachel Kaeding. Witnessed PW's on family farm and at viner. Correspondence and telephone interview with author, Fall Creek, November, 2000.

17. Ida Ludwikoski. Widow of MP Edward Ludwikoski, guard at Camp Eau Claire. Telephone interview with author, Punta Gorda, Fla., May 14, 2000.

Camp Fond du Lac

1. "5 Fond du Lac Men Stationed in New Guinea File Protests on Privileges Given Germans," *Fond du Lac Commonwealth Reporter,* 28 August 1944, 3; Kenneth Blitzke, Interview with author, 6 April 2000.

2. "War Prisoners Arrive to Help Canning Plants," *Fond Du Lac Commonwealth Reporter,* 20 June 1944, 1.

3. "German Prisoners Stationed At Fairgrounds Camp Leave," *Fond Du Lac Commonwealth Reporter,* 5 August 1944, 1.

4. "Civilians Are Asked to Help Entertain Soldiers Assigned To Guard Prisoners At Camp," *Fond Du Lac Commonwealth Reporter,* 3 July 1944, 1.

5. "War Prisoner Discovered in Rural Tavern," *Fond Du Lac Commonwealth Reporter,* 22 July 1944, 1.

6. "Crews Are Busy At Fairgrounds," *Fond du Lac Commonwealth Reporter,* 15 August 1944, 1.

7. "Prisoners Must Be Well Fed, Says Custodian At City Dump," *Fond Du Lac Commonwealth Reporter,* 3 July 1944, 1.

8. Ucker, interview.

9. Lloyd Hatch. Shared stories his father repeated about PW's at Rosendale Canning Factory. Telephone interview by author, Rosendale, July, 2000.

10. James Megellas. Responded from the battle front about treatment of POWs in home town. Correspondence and telephone interview with author, Satellite Beach, FL., September, 2000.

11. Donald Marschall. Witnessed PW's in Rosendale cannery. Correspondence and telephone interview with author, Rosendale, July - November, 2000.

Camp Fox Lake

1. "Major General Aurand Inspects POW Camp," The *Beaver Dam Argus* , 31 August 1944, 1.

2. Tobler, Verner. (Ligation of Switzerland). *Report of Visit to Prisoner of War Camp Fox Lake, October 21, 1944. Inspection Reports: Fort Sheridan, IL.* Records of the Provost Marshal General's Office, Prisoner of War Division, 1941-1946; Special Projects Division, 1943-1946. RG 389. (MMB-NA.)

3. Hong, Howard. *"Report of Visit to Prisoner of War Branch Camp Fox Lake," September 4, 1944, Inspection Reports: Fort Sheridan, IL* . Records of the Provost Marshal General's Office, Prisoner of War Division, 1941-1946; Special Projects Division, 1943-1946. R.G.

389, (MMB-NA.)

4. "Prisoners of War Arrived Sunday," *Fox Lake Representative*, 5 July 1945, 1.

5. "Report on the German Prisoners War Work," *Fox Lake Representative,* 16 August 1945, 1.

6. "POWs at Antigo Perform $10,730 Worth of Work," *Antigo Daily Journal,* 15 September 1945, 1.

7. Scheinast, correspondence.

8. Robert Frank. Experienced PW's in Fox Lake area. Correspondence and telephone interview with author, Beaver Dam, 12 August, 1999.

9. Virginia Steinhorst Phelps. Encountered PW's working on family farm, provided thank you letter from PW. Correspondence and telephone interview with author, Fox Lake, March, 2001.

Camp Fredonia at Little Kohler

1. "Belgium Man in Charge of Little Kohler Prison Camp," *Ozaukee Press (Port Washington),* 21 June 1945, 1.

2. Ronald Schmit. PW's worked family farm at Little Kohler, he and brothers served as acolytes at special PW masses. Telephone interview by author, Little Kohler, 10 November, 2000.

3. "Belgium Man in Charge of Little Kohler Prison Camp," *Ozaukee Press (Port Washington),* 21 June 1945, 1.

4. Anthony Beres. Guard and staff member at Camp Fredonia and Camp Rhinelander. Correspondence and telephone interview with author, Dunedin FL, February-March, 2001.

5 . "POWs at Antigo perform $10,730 Worth of Work," *Antigo Daily Journal*, 15 September 1945, 1.

6. Leona Klemp. Worked with PW's in Fredonia Canning Factory, provided photo of repatriated Ludwig Mauder. Correspondence and telephone interview with author, Grafton, May 12, 2000

7. Arthur Schmitz. Night foreman at Krier Preserving Company, Belgium WI. Telephone interview by author, Port Washington, 7 April, 2000.

8. Schmit, interview.

9. Frank Deutsch, Frank. Witnessed three escapees from Fredonia cross river. Telephone interview by author, Cedarburg, 11 April, 2000.

10. Betty Allen Ewig. Worked at father's locker plant adjacent to the Knellsville Canning Company. Correspondence and telephone interview with author, Port Washington, 7 April, 2000.

11. Josephine Gantner. Widow of a foreman of Knellsville cannery. Telephone interview by author, Port Washington, 18 April, 2000.

12. Laverne Janeshek. Shared stories told by her uncle Captain Ray Thill, Commander of Camp Little Kohler. Telephone interview by author, Port Washington, 9 November, 2000.

13. Roger Mueller. Witnessed PW's pitching peas in father's fields. Telephone interview by author, Fort Atkinson, August 2000.

14. Harriet Scholz Knapp. Encountered PW's and shared recollections of mother's stories. Telephone interview by author, Sussex, September-October 2000.

15. Stella Thill. Widow of commander Ray Thill, provided photos of Captain Ray Thill at Camp Kohler. Correspondence and telephone interview with author, Oceanside, CA, November, 2000.

16. Andy T. Dieringer. Worked with PW's at Fredonia Canning Company. Telephone interview by author, Cedar Grove, October 2000.

17. William Parnitzke. Shared stories from brother-in-law working with PW's in Port Washington area. Telephone conversations with author, Fredonia, October, 2000.

18. Lawrence Slavik. Transported PW's to and from Camp Little Kohler to Knellsville daily. Telephone interview by author, Saukville, 2 November, 2000.

Camp Galesville

1. "Factory Operating With First of Pack," *Galesville Republican,* 22 June 1944, 1.

2. "Prisoners Help with Pea Pack," *Galesville Republican,* 29 June 1944, 1.

3. "Prisoners of War and Army Vacate," *Galesville Republican,* 20 July 1944, 1.

4 ."German Prisoners Here for Pea Pack," *Galesville Republican,* 28 June 1945, 1.

5 ."Newsmen Spend Day at POW Camp," *Galesville Republican,* 12 July 1945, 1.

6 ."Newsmen Visit POW Camp," *The Blair Press,* 19 July 1945, 1.

7. "The Prisoners are a Strange Lot," *The La Crosse Tribune,* 11 July 1945, 8.

8. "Prisoner Labor for Farmers Available," *Galesville Republican,* 2 August 1945, 1.

9. "POWs at Antigo Perform $10,730 Worth of Work," *Antigo Daily Journal*, 15 September 1945, 1.

10. Cram, James. Released from German POW camp to find German PW's in his home town. Clearwater, Fla. 20 February, 2001 & Zimmerman, Jerry, "Staff Sgt. James. V. Cram, German and US WW II Prisoner of War," *High Ground Magazine*, 1997.

11. Vava Norwood. Encountered PW's on family farm. Correspondence and telephone conversations with author, Hixton, 14 March, 1999.

12. Audrey C. Fillner. Camp Galesville fence adjoined her back yard. Telephone interview by author, Galesville, 5 April, 2000.

13. Boyd Relyea. Transported and hired PW's. Correspondence and telephone interview with author, Blair, 5 April, 2000.

14. Rod Van Vlect. Encountered PW's on family farm. Telephone interview by author, Hastings, MN, 23 June, 2000 .

15. Hetz, interview.

16. Lynn Rall Olson & Gerald Rall. Lynn relayed father's story through correspondence, Gerald drew replica of "toilet seat Hitler" he displayed during war. Correspondence and telephone interview with author, Rochester, MN, May-June, 2000.

17. Ruth Emmons. Hired PW's on family farm. Correspondence and telephone interview with author, Galesville, 19 September, 2000.

18. Name withheld. Worked with PW's on family farm out of Galesville. Telephone interview by author, Mondovi, 6 November, 2000.

Camp Genesee

1. "Genesee to Have Prisoner Camp," *Waukesha Daily Freeman*, 21 June 1945, 1.

2. "No Coddling POWs Here," *Waukesha Daily Freeman*, 23 June 1945, 1.

3. "Record Harvest of Peas Ended," *Waukesha Daily Freeman*, 6 August 1945, 1.

4. "Fire at Prison Camp Causes Light Damage," Waukesha *Daily Freeman*, 22 September 1945, 1.

5. "German POWs Canned Peas But Wouldn't Eat 'Em," *Waukesha Freeman*, 7 July 1973, 1.

6. "German POWs Canned Peas But Wouldn't Eat 'Em," *Waukesha Freeman*, 7 July 1973, 1.

7. "See Close Soon of Prison Camp," *Waukesha Daily Freeman*,

25 October 1945, 1.

8. "POWs at Antigo Perform $10,730 Worth of Work," *Antigo Daily Journal*, 15 September 1945, 1.

9. "German POWs Canned Peas But Wouldn't Eat 'Em," *Waukesha Freeman*, 7 July 1973, 1.

10. Richard Kraus. Supervised PW's on night crew at J. G. Cox Cannery. Correspondence and telephone interview with author, Whitewater, 27 July, 2000.

11. Gerald Herrmann. Worked with PW's in Genesee area. Correspondence and telephone interview with author, Genesee, 29 July, 2000.

12. Ibid.

13. John Tehan. Witnessed PW's working for his father. Correspondence and telephone interview with author, El Cajon, CA, 29 August, 2000.

14. Beverly Reinders. Witnessed PW's visiting family and working nearby. Correspondence and telephone interview with author, Waukesha. October, November, 2000.

15. Arthur Mayo. PW's worked on family farm. Telephone interview by author, Genesee, 31 July, 2000.

16. Arland Krummroy. PW's worked on family farm. Telephone interview by author, Oconomowoc, 2 August, 2000.

17. Dale Burnell. Family hired PW on their Waukesha farms. Correspondence and telephone interview with author, Waukesha, August, 2000.

18. John Rohrer. Family hired PW's on their farm. Telephone interview by author, Watertown, 16 August, 2000.

19. Ruben Herrmann. Encountered PW's in and around Genesee. Telephone interview by author, La Crosse, 30 August, 2000

20. Leslie Hendrickson. PW's stole his Christmas tips and gifts. Telephone interview by author, Waukesha, 2 August, 2000.

Camp Green Lake

1. Ucker, interview.

2. "Prison Camp to Be Filled Here," *Green Lake County Reporter,* 15 June 1944, 1.

3. "Prisoners of War Reach Camp Green Lake Mon.," *Green Lake County Reporter,* 22 June 1944, 1.

4. "Green Lake Prisoners of War Go on One Day Sympathy Strike," *The Ripon Commonwealth,* 14 July 1944, 1.

5. "Prisoner Camp Report Studied, "*Fond Du Lac Commonwealth*

Reporter, 15 July 1944, 1.

6. "Two Nazis Stray from Camp Here," *Green Lake County Reporter,* 27 July 1944, 1.

7. "Break-up German Prisoner Camp," *Green Lake County Reporter*, 27 July 1944, 1.

8. "German War Prisoners Leave Green Lake Area for Other Crop Harvests," *The Ripon Commonwealth,* 28 July 1944, 1.

9. "German PW's To Arrive Shortly," *Green Lake County Reporter,* 3 August 1944, 1.

10. "Prisoners Have Left Green Lake," *Green Lake County Reporter,* 5 October 1944, 1.

11. Ucker, interview.

12. Daniel Nitzke. Transported PW crews to/from work sites. Telephone interview by author, Ripon, April, 1998.

13. Ucker, interview.

14. Ibid.

15. Jeanette M. Weber. Camp Green Lake neighbor. Telephone interview by author, Fond du Lac, 17 April 2000.

16. Russell Clark. Family hired PW's to harvest their crops. Telephone interview by author, Princeton, 31 July 2000.

17. Ruth Smith Allison. Worked with PW's in Milwaukee. Telephone interview by author, Green Lake, 16 August 2000.

18. Earl Hoth. Worked with PW's in Ripon. Telephone interview by author, Ripon, 2 August 2000.

19. Tabbert, Robert. *Growing up in Rural Wisconsin During the 30's and 40's.* Lac du Flambeau, WI, revised, August, 2000.

20. Roger Tornow. Spent a day with PW's out of Pickett. Correspondence and telephone interview with author, Oshkosh, 3 February 2001.

21. Jack Thrall. Owner of Winneconne Canning Factory, hired PW's from Green Lake. Telephone interview by author, Fond du Lac, 4 February 2001.

22. Albrecht, Alvina. Oral history dictated 9 October 1998, provided by Brandon Historical Society, Brandon, August and September, 2000.

Camp Hartford
1. "High Hopes for the Future of Hartford's Landmark Ballroom," *The Daily News* (Hartford), 17 January 1998, 1.

2. "Prisoner Help for Canneries," *The Hartford Times Press*, 2 June 1944, 1.

3. "High Hopes for the Future of Hartford's Landmark Ballroom," *The Daily News* (Hartford), 17 January 1998, 1.

4. Hong, Howard. *Report on Visit to Prisoner of War Branch Camp, Hartford Wisconsin, November 22, 1944, Inspection Reports: Fort Sheridan, IL.* Records of the Provost Marshal General's Office, Prisoner of War Division, 1941-1946; Special Projects Division, 1943-1946. RG 389. (MMB-NA.)

5. Pechmann, interview; Hall, interview.

6. "Who Doesn't Have Fond Memories of the Swartz?" *Hartford Times Press,* 20 March 1997, 20.

7. Pechmann, interview; Hall, interview.

8. Ibid.

9. Armond Lackas. Provost Marshall/interpreter at Hartford. Interview by author, Hartford, 17 June 1998.

10. "Hartford PW Camp Compiled Excellent Record of Service," *The Hartford Times Press*, 26 October 1945, 1.

11. Amy Parent Fissel. Witnessed PW's in St. Killian's Catholic Church, Hartford. Correspondence and telephone conversations with author, Oshkosh, 11 April 2000.

12. Mary Von Rohr Whritenour. Daughter of Rev. Adolph Von Rohr who ministered at Camp Hartford. Telephone interview by author, Wauwatosa, 15 August 2000.

13. Lucile Selmikeit Lechner. Daughter to Rev. Selmikeit who ministered at Camp Hartford. Telephone interview by author, Brown Deer, September, 2000.

14. Ted Komp. Witnessed PW's at Hartford. Telephone interview by author, Hartford, 15 August 2000.

15. Gertrude Indermuehle. Co-worker of PW's in Hartford area plants. Interview by author, Hartford, 17 June 1998.

16. Pechmann, interview.

17. Wlasak, Rolf. *Jungend hinter Stacheldraht* (Youth behind barbed wire) (Dresden, Germany). Translated with permission by Herrn Werner Wolpert, Hartford WI, 1997.

18. Lackas, interview.

19. Hall, interview.

20. David Lau. Worked with PW's at Clyman Canning Company, 1944 & 1945. Telephone interview by author, Telephone interview by author, Watertown, 9 March 1998.

21 Dorothy Weise. Fed PW's lunch at Hartford. Telephone conversations with author, Hales Corners, August, 2000.

22. Rev. Herbert Stelter. Personal experiences with PW's. Tele-

phone interview by author, Sheboygan, 30 August 2000.

23. Name Withheld. Foreman of night shift including PW's at Borden Company, Columbus. Telephone interview by author, Columbus, 18 October 2000.

24. Stuart Grulke. Encountered PW's at local viner and his home. Telephone interview by author, Fairhaven, NY, 7 March 2001.

25. Ellen Place Schuette. Sold leather goods to former PW who had worked for family business in Hartford. Correspondence and telephone interview with author, Bradenton, FL, November, 2000.

Camp Hortonville

1. Arthur Kalchik. Guard at Camp Hortonville. Telephone interview by author, Hortonville, 17 January 2000.

2. Joanne Buchmann Schwarz. Camp Hortonville was on family property, she provided photos of camp and PW's. Correspondence and telephone conversations with author, Hortonville, 24 January 2001.

3. "Prisoners of War Arrive Monday for Work at Canning Factories," *The Appleton Post-Crescent,* 20 June 1945, p. 1.

4. "POW's Harvested The Region's Crops in '45," *Appleton Post-Crescent* 29 May 1994.

5 ."50 German PW's at Canning Company," *Clintonville's Tribune Gazette* 2 August 1945, 1.

6. "German Prisoners at Work," *Appleton Post Crescent,* 9 August 1945, 1.

7. "POWs at Antigo Perform $10,730 Worth of Work," *Antigo Daily Journal,* 15 September 1945, 1.

8. Kalchik, interview.

9 . Ibid.

10. William Ratzburg. Observer of Camp Hortonville. Telephone interview by author, Hortonville, 17 January 2000.

11. Nellie Krueger. Girlfriend and later wife of guard at Camp Hortonville. Correspondence and telephone interview by author, New London, 27 January 2000.

12. Donald Reinke. Drove bus transporting PW's from Camp Hortonville to Bear Creek. Telephone interview by author, Bonduel, 10 April 2000.

13. John Groat. Shared stories of father-in-law who hired PW's from Camp Hortonville to work on his farm. Telephone interview by author, New London, 19 January 2000.

14. Ralph Melchert. Parents hired PW's to help with farm work. Telephone interview by author, Seymour, 7 August 2000.

15. Marion Books. Neighbor to Camp Hortonville. Correspondence and telephone interview by author, Hortonville, 15 February 2000.

16. Bernita Rynders. Hired guards from Camp Hortonville for off-duty work. Telephone interview by author, Hortonville, 17 January 2000.

17. Peter Olke. Retold Aunt's stories of Hortonville PW's. Telephone interview by author, Land O' Lakes, 14 August 2000.

18. Name Withheld. Witnessed PW's in Hortonville area and provided correspondence from former PW. Black Creek, November, 2000 through January 2001.

19. Lois Melcher Coomer. PW was hired hand of family farm. Telephone interview by author, Fond du Lac, 4 August 2000.

Camp Janesville

1. "Camp Janesville Is Established," *Janesville Daily Gazette,* 21 June 1944, 1.

2. Mary Lee. Lived in Camp Janesville in 1944 with husband, Camp Commander Capt. Hugh Lee. Interviews by author, Eau Claire, August 1998.

3. "War Prisoners Coming to City," *Janesville Daily Gazette,* 2 June 1944, 1.

4. "Camp Janesville is Established," *Janesville Daily Gazette,* 21 June 1944, 1.

5. "War Prisoners Due This Week," *Janesville Daily Gazette,* 14 June 1944, 1.

6. Lee, interview.

7. "Camp Janesville Closes Monday," *Beloit Daily News,* 27 October 1945, 1.

8. "19 German War Prisoners Hurt," *Janesville Daily Gazette,* 11 August 1945, 1.

9. "Prisoners Created Curiosity," *Janesville Daily Gazette,* 14 August 1985, 6 E.

10. "Prisoners Glad the War is Over," *Janesville Daily Gazette,* 15 August 1945, 1.

11. "Janesville War Prisoners Camp Will Close Oct. 30" *Beloit Daily News,* 23 October 1945, 1.

12. "Canning Company Reports Quality and Quantity of Peas Excellent," *Elkhorn Independent,* 29 June 1944, 1.

13. "Prison Labor Now Employed at Factory," *The Whitewater Register*, 24 August 1944, 1.

14. Lee, interview.

15. "WW II Child Recalls POW Camp," *Janesville Daily Gazette*, 11 October 1977, 1.

16. "Janesville War Prison Was Home to 500," *Beloit Daily News*, 18 February 1984, 1.

17. "Janesville War Prison Was Home to 500," *Beloit Daily News*, 18 February 1984, 1.

18. Robert Voss. Witnessed PW's working in neighboring field. Walworth, 9 August 2000 & Nash, Myrl. Family hired PW's to bundle and load hemp. Telephone interview by author, Walworth, 9 August 2000.

19. Mary L. Jensen. Witnessed POWs in Elkhorn. Telephone interview by author, Darien, August, 2000.

20. Hildegard Hoefler. Fed PW's working on her Whitewater area farm. Telephone interview by author, Whitewater, 21 August 2000.

21. Edward Witcpalek. Witnessed PW's in Janesville and area farms. Telephone interview by author, Ashland, 17 October 2000.

22. Leigh Morris. Recalled discussion with father who shot PW. Correspondence and telephone conversations with author, Naperville, IL, August through September, 2000.

23. Arthur Pratt. Worked with PW's at Johnstown Creek viner, provided photo of crew there. Correspondence and telephone conversations with author, Beloit, 24 October 2000.

Camp Jefferson

1. "Nazi Prisoners Looking Not At all Like Supermen," *Jefferson Union*, 23 June 1944, 1.

2. "Canner's Lease Expires August 5," *Jefferson Banner*, 22 June 1944, 1.

3. "179 Prisoners of War Arrive at Jefferson," *Watertown Daily Times*, 22 June 1944, 1.

4. "179 Prisoners of War Arrive at Jefferson," Watertown *Daily Times*, 22 June 1944, 1.

5. "Parents Responsible for Camp Annoyance," Jefferson *Banner*, 29 June 1944, 2.

6. "Nazi Prisoners To Work At Local Canning Factory," *Watertown Daily Times,* 31 May 1944, 1.

7. "Prisoners and Guards Leave Tuesday, July 25th," *Jefferson*

Banner , 27 July 1944, 1.

8. Name Withheld. Jefferson, 26 June 2000.

9. Thomas Tiller. Witnessed PW's responding to the dog call. Telephone interview by author, Greendale, 16 August 2000.

10. Faith Blaese Madzar. Encountered PW's at Watertown. Correspondence and telephone interview with author, Natick, MA August, 2000.

11. Alma Haubenschild. Witnessed PW's in Jefferson. Telephone conversations with author, Jefferson, August, 2000.

12. Betty Buelow. Encountered guards at Jefferson Telephone interview by author, Goddard, 20 August 2000.

13. Barbara Whally Suetzholz. Witnessed PW's on farms outside Watertown. Racine, 4 November 2000 & Fischer, Ellen. Witnessed PW's marching to Rock River in Jefferson for swim. Telephone conversations with author, Fort Atkinson July, 2000.

Camp Lake Keesus

1. "Prisoners Will Assist Local Canneries," *Waukesha Daily Freeman*, 12 June 1944, 1.

2. Robert Weber. Transported PW's from Camp Lake Keesus to canning factory and worked with them the second shift. Telephone interview by author, Merton, 19 June 2000.

3. William Fieldhack. Family leased the resort hotel to the military. Telephone interview by author, Merton, 2 August 2000.

4. Schmidt, Ruth. *North of the Bark*. (Merton, WI, 1987), p. 88.

5. "Nazi Escapees Are Returned," *Waukesha Daily Freeman,* 21 July 1944, 1.

6. Weber, interview.

7. Helen Schiek Johnson. Enjoyed music of PW's at Camp Keesus Telephone interview by author, Oconomowoc, 7 August 2000.

8. Betty Fieldhack Dost. Family leased resort to military. Correspondence and conversations with author, Ogema, September and October 2000.

9. Richard R. Figlesthaler. Experienced PW's at Lake Keesus and Billy Mitchell Field. Correspondence and conversations with author, Greendale, August and November, 2000.

10. Fieldhack, interview.

11. John Eimermann. Witnessed PW's at Camp Lake Keesus. Telephone interview by author, Merton, 10 November 2000.

12. Owen W. Van Pietersom. Visited with PW's at the Granville Canning Factory. Correspondence and telephone conversations

with author, Menomonee Falls, August through November, 2000.

13. Dost, interview.

14. Dr. Michael Wheeler. Current owner of Essential Industries, housed in old Merton Canning Factory. Correspondence and telephone conversation with author, Merton, 23 June 2000.

Camp Lodi

1. "100 German Prisoners to Arrive Friday," *The Lodi Enterprise,* 1 June 1944, 1.

2. "Prisoners Return to Lodi Monday," *The Lodi Enterprise*, 17 August 1944, 1.

3. "Prisoner of War Camp to Be Evacuated Soon," *The Lodi Enterprise*, 3 August 1944, 1.

4. "Fair Park Being Made Ready for Prison Help," *The Lodi Enterprise,* 14 June 1945, 1.

5. "No Coddling is Rule as War Prison Camp Opens Here," *The Lodi Enterprise,* 28 June 1945, 1.

6. "Recent Pea Pack One of Largest in Local History," *The Lodi Enterprise,* 9 August 1945, 1.

7. "Guard and Group of Prisoners in Truck Accident," *The Sheboygan Press,* Friday, 10 August 1945, 1.

8. "Prisoners, Guard Still Hospitalized," *The Lodi Enterprise,* 16 August 1945, 1.

9. "Exhibits, Rides, Programs, All Ready," *The Lodi Enterprise*, 4 October 1945, 1.

10. "POWs at Antigo Perform $10,730 Worth of Work," *Antigo Daily Journal,* 15 September 1945, 1.

11. Herbert Noltemeyer. Payroll timekeeper and later personnel manager of the Del Monte Food Corporation in Arlington, WI. Telephone interview by author, DeForest, September, 2000.

12. Hazel Buchannan. Home adjacent to Camp Lodi. Telephone interview by author, Lodi, 5 September 1999.

13. Ibid.

14. Violet "Chic" Godfrey. Home adjacent to Camp Lodi. Telephone interview by author, Lodi, 10 September 1999.

15. Ann Hanneman Munz. Witnessed PW's in Lodi. Telepohne interview by author, Baraboo, August 2000.

16. Al Haller. Field supervisor in charge of PW's in 1944 and 1945 for Waunakee Canning Company. Correspondence and telephone conversation with author, Fort Atkinson, October-November 2000.

Camp Markesan

1. La Verne Pomplun. Worked with PW's in Markesan. Correspondence and telephone conversation with author, Wautoma, November, 2000.

2. "Markesan Was The Site of a Prisoner Of War Camp," *The Markesan Herald,* 11 September 1986, 1.

3. Clarence Krause, "Camp Markesan Collection of Notes, Photos and Memorabilia." Courtesy William Slate.

4. "Markesan Was The Site of a Prisoner Of War Camp," *The Markesan Herald,* 11 September 1986, 1.

5. Clarence Krause, "Camp Markesan Collection of Notes, Photos and Memorabilia." Courtesy William Slate.

6. "Markesan Was The Site of a Prisoner Of War Camp," *The Markesan Herald,* 11 September 1986, 1.

7. "POWs at Antigo Perform $10,730 Worth of Work," *Antigo Journal*, 15 September 1945, 1.

8. "PW Guards Trim Monarch Range Team," *The Markesan Herald,* 23 August 1945.

9. Pomplun, interview.

10. Nancy Sexton. Recalled PW's in movie theater. Telephone interview by author, Appleton, 10 July, 2000.

11. "Markesan Was The Site of a Prisoner Of War Camp," *The Markesan* Herald, 11 September 1986, 1.

12. "Markesan Was The Site of a Prisoner Of War Camp," *The Markesan Herald,* 11 September 1986, 1.

13. Roger Burlingame. Encountered PW's on family farm. Telephone interview by author, Ripon, 10 November, 2000.

14. Leona Kelm & Kathy Scheir, Joy Waterbury, Ruth Plautz, Judy Bender. *Common Threads.* (Madison, WI: Grimm Book Bindery Inc., 1998), 182.

15. John Scharschmidt. Encountered PW's working on the family farm and nearby viner. Telephone interview by author, Markesan, 14 November, 2000.

16. Lorraine Menke Laybourn. PW's shelled family peas at area viner. Telephone interview by author, Markesan, 8 March, 2001.

Camp Marshfield

1. Marshfield History Project. *The Marshfield Story 1872-1999* (Amherst, WI: Palmer Publications, 1997), 69.

2. "German War Prisoners to Work For Central State Pea Can-

ners," *Marshfield News-Herald*, 26 May 1945, 1.

3. "German War Prisoners to Arrive Here About July 7," *Marshfield News-Herald*, 20 June 1945, 1.

4. "Prisoners of War Arrive to Assist With Pea Pack," *Marshfield News Herald*, 10 July 1945, 1.

5. "4 POW'S Hurt in Car Crash," *Marshfield News-Herald,* 11 July 1945, 1.

6. "Marshfield POW Camp Disbanded," *Wisconsin Rapids Daily Tribune,* 2 October 1945, 1.

7. "POWs to Leave Canning Company Here Thursday," *Marshfield News-Herald*, 11 September 1945, 1.

8. "POWs at Antigo Perform $10,730 Worth of Work," *Antigo Daily Journal,* 15 September 1945, 1.

9. John Smrecek. Worked with PW's on father's farm. Telephone interview by author, Marshfield, 21 March, 2000.

10. Florence Smrecek. Worked in Marshfield cannery with PW's. Telephone interview by author, Marshfield, 21 March, 2000.

11. Vern Volrath. Personal encounters with PW's in Loyal Canning Factory. Telephone interview by author, Janesville, 15 September, 2000.

12. Barbara See. Witnessed PW's on father's rural Marshfield farm. Correspondence and telephone conversations with author, Spencer, 3 March, 2000.

13. Leatrice Seefluth Meier. Served PW's noon meals at Loyal Cafe. Telephone interview by author, Wisconsin Rapids, August, 2000.

14. Delmer Capelle. Father hired PW's to harvest peas on family farm. Telephone interview by author, Loyal, 18 July, 2000.

15. Herman Albrecht. PW's worked on family farm. Telephone conversations with author, Arpin, July, 2000.

16. Roger Liebzeit. Family hired PW's for farm work. Telephone interview by author, Greenwood, 29 July, 20000.

Camp Milltown

1. Stare, *Wisconsin's Great Canning Industry,* 158.

2. Hong, Howard. *Report of Visit to Prisoner of War Branch Camp, Sidnaw, Mich., September 1, 1944, Inspection Reports: Fort Sheridan, Ill..* Records of the Provost Marshal General's Office, Prisoner of War Division, 1941-1946; Special Projects Division, 1943-1946. RG 389. (MMB-NA.)

3. Ervin Christianson. Worked with father and hired PW's from

Stokely cannery in Milltown. Interview by author, Milltown, 20 July, 2000.

4. Stare, *Wisconsin's Great Canning Industry,* 160.

5. Lloyd Valrath. Witnessed PW's in Camp Barron and worked with PW's at canning factory. Interview by author, Frederic, 26 October, 2000.

6. "POW's At Milltown Did $88,970 in Labor," *Polk County Ledger (Balsam Lake),* 25 October 1945, 1.

7. Harriet Sund Anderson. Encountered PW's working on family farm. Interview by author, Eau Claire, 17 June, 1998.

8. Phyllis Larsen Beaulieu. Encountered PW's working on family farm. Telephone interview by author, Milltown, 29 June,. 1998.

9. Darwin Wosepka. Civilian hired to transport PW's to work sites. Interview by author, Haugen, 19 July, 1998.

10. Stuart Olson. Encountered PW's from Camp Milltown. Telephone interview by author, Taylors Falls, Minn, 16 May, 2000.

11. James Route. Encountered PW's at family store. St. Croix Falls, 16 May, 2000 & Route, Neal. Encountered Milltown PW's. Correspondence and telephone conversations with author, Osceola, September 2000.

12. Esther Anderson. Worked with PW's while husband, Alvin, supervised them at Milltown canning factory. Telephone interview by author, Milltown, 3 November, 2000.

13. Philip Enerson. Witnessed PW's in Milltown area. Interview by author, Siren, 26 October, 2000.

Camp Oakfield

1. Robert T. Heldt. Guarded prisoners at Camps Billy Mitchell, Sturgeon Bay, Oakfield, and Wisconsin Rapids. He provided photos of Oakfield. Correspondence and telephone conversations with author, Chicago, Ill. August-September, 2000.

2. "Oakfield Camp is Erected For War Prisoners," *Fond du Lac Commonwealth Reporter,* 19 June 1945, 2.

3. "German Prisoners of War Bring in Revenue Returns to Uncle Sam," *The Independent,* 27 September 1945, 1.

4. "War Prisoner Projects Pay Large Return," *Fond du Lac Commonwealth Reporter,* 11 August 1945, 2.

5. "German Prisoners of War Bring in Revenue Returns to Uncle Sam," *The Independent* (Juneau), 27 September 1945, 1.

6. Clifford Gelhar. As manager of Mammoth Spring Canning

Company hired PW's. Telephone interview by author, Oshkosh, 10 August, 2000.

7. "POW Staff, Men Entertain at Dancing Party," *Fond du Lac Commonwealth Reporter,* 4, September 1945, 12.

8. Maynard Chadwick, Jr. Witnessed PW's around town and recalled father's stories. Telephone interview by author, Oakfield, 7 August, 2000.

9. Gelhar, interview.

10. Heldt, interview.

11. Bonnie J. Gilbert. Witnessed PW's at Lomira plant. Telephone interview by author, Eau Claire, 5 November, 2000.

Camp Plymouth

1. "Pea Canning Starts Fri.; War Prisoners Are Here," *Plymouth Review* , 22 June 1944, 1.

2. "Fairgrounds Chosen for War Prison Camp," *The Sheboygan Press*, 29 May 1944, 1.

3. "Nazis at Plymouth Fairgrounds Camp Not Supermen," *The Sheboygan Press,* 24 July 1944, 1.

4. "Prisoners Arrive at Fair Grounds for Canning Season," *Plymouth Review*, 5 July 1945, 1.

5. "Nazi Prisoners Left Plymouth Friday Evening," *Plymouth Review*, 10 August 1944, 1.

6. "Prisoners of War Coming To Plymouth," *Plymouth Review*, 19 June 1945, 1.

7. "Prisoners Arrive at Fair Grounds for Canning Season," *Plymouth Review*, 5 July 1945, 1.

8. "Visit to Fair Grounds Shows How Army Handles War Prisoners," *Plymouth Review*, 26 July 1945, 1.

9. "Stokely To Start Beet Caning On Aug. 20; Need Help," *Plymouth Review,* 9 August 1945, 1.

10. Muriel Neerhof Storm. Encountered PW's on family farm. Telephone interview by author, Waldo, 15 August, 1999.

11. Voleria Mauk. Widow of Camp Plymouth PW driver/supervisor. Telephone interview by author, Elkhart Lake, 2 May, 2000.

12. Robert Koepsel. Shared father's stories of Camp Plymouth PW's. Telephone interview by author, Chippewa Falls, 5 November, 2000.

Camp Reedsburg

1. "From our Readers," *Reedsburg Times-Press,* 12 July 1945.

2. "To Quarter 137 Prisoners Here," *Reedsburg Times-Press,* 28

June 1945, 1.

3. "To Quarter 137 Prisoners Here," *Reedsburg Times-Press,* 28 June 1945, 1.

4. "POW's at Antigo Perform $10,730 Worth of Work," *Antigo Daily Journal*, 15 September 1945, 1.

5. Dr. James Pawlisch. Witnessed PW's in Reedsburg. Telephone interview by author, Reedsburg, 30 August, 2000.

6. Eber Janzen. Delivered milk to Camp Reedsburg. Telephone interview by author, Reedsburg, 24 August, 2000.

7. Philipp Schweke. Fished with PW's at Reedsburg. Telephone interview by author, La Crosse, March, 1998.

8. Marty Koenecke. Worked with PW's on family farm. Telephone interview by author, Reedsburg, 17 October, 2000.

9. Shirley Mahr Burmester. Worked with PW's in Reedsburg cannery. Telephone interview by author, Reedsburg, 22 March, 2001.

Camp Rhinelander
1. Anthony E. Beres. MP and staff officer stationed at Camp Rhinelander and Camp Fedonia, married Rhinelander woman. Correspondence and telephone interview with author, Dunedin, Fla., February-March, 2001.

2. "75 German Prisoners Arrive to Work in Bayfield," *Ashland Daily Press* 27 August 1945, 1.

3. "Ninety German Prisoners Here," *New North* (Rhinelander), 30 August 1945, 1.

4. "Need Help for Potato Harvest," *New North* (Rhinelander), 11 October 1945, 1.

5. "Prison Camps Close," *New North* (Rhinelander), 1 November 1945, 1.

6. Lynn Bell. Played with PW's outside Rhinelander. Telephone interview by author, Milwaukee, August, 2000.

7. DeLore Deau. Witnessed PW's in Rhinelander. Telephone interview by author, Rhinelander, 14 February, 2001.

8. Deau, interview.

9. Beres, interview.

10. Ibid.

12. Ibid.

13. Ibid.

14. Juanita Spafford Kichefski. Witnessed PW's working in family potato fields. Telephone interview by author, Rhinelander, 20 November, 2000.

15. Betty Kuczmarski. Hired PW's to work on family potato farm. Telephone interview by author, Rhinelander, November, 2000.

16. Marvin Spafford. Witnessed PW's working on family potato farm. Telephone interview by author, Eagle River, 20 November, 2000.

Camp Ripon

1. "War Prisoners are Working Efficiently," *Fond du Lac Commonwealth Reporter,* 3 August 1945, 1.

2. "War Captive Assigned For Canner Jobs," *Fond du Lac Commonwealth Reporter,* 19 June 1945, 1.

3. "German War Prisoners Camp in Ripon Will Supply Cannery Help," *Ripon Commonwealth,* 15 June 1945, 1.

4. "A Different 'Big Top' Sets Up in Community," *Ripon Commonwealth,* 29 June 1945, 1.

5. "Prisoners of War Get No Fancy Meats or Food" *Ripon Commonwealth,* 29 June 1945, 1.

6. "War Prisoners are Working Efficiently," *Fond du Lac Commonwealth Reporter,* 3 August 1945, 1.

7. "600 German Prisoners to Arrive in Ripon About June 28 for Vital Work," *The Ripon Commonwealth,* 22 June 1945, 1.

8. "Commander of POW Camp Tells Kiwanis About Camp Problems," Ripon *Commonwealth,* 6 July 1945, 1.

9. "Pickle Factory Denied Further Use of Germans," *Fond Du Lac Commonwealth Reporter,* 31 August 1945, 1.

10. "German Prisoners To Leave For Work in Nearby States," *Fond Du Lac Commonwealth Reporter,* 6 August 1945, 1.

11. "War prisoners to Aid Canners," *Fond du Lac Commonwealth Reporter,* 1 September 1945, 1.

12. "German War Prisoner Camp Moves from City," *Ripon Commonwealth,* 12 October 1945, 1.

13. Leander Wagner. Civilian PW crew boss for Pickett Canning Company. Telephone interview by author, Pickett, 8 August, 2000.

14. Peter Amend. Son of then owner of Picket Canning Company. Telephone interview by author, Ripon, September 25, 2000.

15. Glen Sasada. Worked with PW's on family farm near Ripon. Telephone interview by author, Ripon, 20 November, 2000.

16. Dwain Werch. Witnessed PW's on family farm. Telephone interview by author, Ripon, July, November, 2000.

17. Dr. John Steinbring. Worked with PW's in Ripon. Telephone

interview by author, Ripon, 3 December, 2000.

Camp Rockfield
1. Helen Beuscher. Worked with PW's in Rockfield canning factory. Correspondence and telephone conversations with author, Germantown, September/October 200.

2. "German War Prisoners from Afrika Corps are Camped at Rockfield," *Cedarburg News*, 5 July 1944, 1.

3. "German War Prison Camp at Rockfield is Subject of Club Talk," *Cedarburg News,* 11 October, 1944, 1.

4. "Memories Of Two POW Camps," *Germantown Banner Press*, 20 June 1985, 1.

5. U.S. Department of the Army. *Prisoner of War Camp Labor Report, Fort Sheridan, Ill,, 4, January, 1945*. Records of the Provost Marshal General's Office, Prisoner of War Division, 1941-1946. RG 389. (MMB-NA).

6. "Prisoner of War Labor," *Menomonee Falls News,* 6 August 1945, 1.

7. "POW's at Antigo Perform $10,730 Worth of Work," *Antigo Daily Journal,* 15 September 1945, 1.

8. Walter Hauser. Encountered PW's at Rockfield canning factory. Telephone interview by author, Germantown, August 24, 2000.

9. John Fromm. Manager of Neimann Brothers Fox Farms hiring PW's. Correspondence and telephone interview with author, Mequon, June 1998.

10. Fromm, interview.

11. "WW II POW's have gone home," *Menomonee Falls News,* 23 June 1988, 1.

12. Jerome Rinzel. Witnessed father and POW's at Rockfield. Correspondence and telephone interview with author, Muskego, August, 2000.

13. Beuscher, interview.

14. Dan Sennott. Provided gas to the military trucks at Camp Rockfield. Telephone interview by author, Whitefish Bay, August 23, 2000.

15. Reisweber, Phill. *Germantown Wisconsin During the Second World War* (Booklet of Gifted & Talented U.S. History, Germantown High School, 1993), 15.

16. John S. Peters. Worked with PW's at Pick Mfg. Telephone interview by author, West Bend, December 18, 2000.

17. Jean Johnson. Provided photos of Camp Rockfield. Cor-

respondence and telephone interview by author, Germantown, August, 2000.

18. Donna Kruepke Spaeth. Provided photo of Camp Rockfield PW's. Correspondence and telephone conversations with author, Jackson, September, 2000.

Camp Sheboygan

1. "Veteran Remembers Prison Camp," *Sheboygan Press*, 24 December 1989, 23.

2 "PW Camp to Close," *Sheboygan Press*, 7 December 1945, 1.

3. "First Group of Prisoners of War Here," *Sheboygan Press*, 3 July 1945, 1.

4. "Asylum Chosen for Prison Camp," *Sheboygan Press*, 2 July 1945, 1.

5. Carl Birkholz. Son of camp commander, family lived in camp, donated photo of pencil sketch of father by PW. Correspondence and telephone conversations with author, Elkhart Lake, 3 May, 2000.

6. "Pay Government $1,827,586 For Prisoner Of War Labor," *Sheboygan Press*, 15 September 1945, 1.

7. "Veteran Remembers Prison Camp," *Sheboygan Press*, 24 December 1989, 23.

8. Birkholz, interview.

9. Wilfrid Turba. Worked with PW's from Camp Sheboygan. Correspondence and telephone conversation with author, Elkhart Lake, August, 2000.

10. Martin Bangert. Father accompanied pastor to Camp Sheboygan for services. Correspondence and telephone interview with author, Sheboygan, August, 2000.

11. Chuck Rieck. MP stationed at Barron, Wisconsin Rapids and Sheboygan. Telephone interview by author, Middleton, 17 October, 2000.

12. Sharon Prange Claerbaut. Received toy made by PW who worked with father in Oostburg. Correspondence and telephone conversations with author, Oostburg, October-November, 2000.

13. Mary Howard Hawkins. Witnessed PW's in Camp Sheboygan. Telephone interview by author, Eau Claire, 7 November, 2000.

14. Robert Lawrenz. His PW uncle visited family while held at Camp Sheboygan. Telephone interview by author, Sheboygan, 15 January, 2001.

Camp Sturgeon Bay

1. "No Prisoners Nor Guards Killed in Door Co. Orchards," *Green Bay Press-Gazette,* 25 July 1945, 2.

2. "No Work, No Eat Policy for POWs," *Record Herald* (Wausau), 3 August 1945, 1.

3. "War Prisoners Worked Here 30 Years Ago," *Door County Advocate* (Sturgeon Bay), 10 June 1945, 5.

4. "2,000 PW's Coming to Harvest Cherries," *Door County Advocate* (Sturgeon Bay), 13 July 1945, 1.

5. Martha Brauer. Lived at Martin Orchard 31 years. Correspondence and telephone interview with author, Sturgeon Bay, 8 March, 2000.

6. "German War Prisoners Arrive in Door Co. to Pick Cherries," *The Green Bay Press-Gazette* , 18 July 1945, 2.

7. "50 Years ago, August 31, 1945," *Door County Advocate* (Sturgeon Bay), 31 August 1995.

8. Joyce Johnson Janeshek. Personal experiences with PW's in orchards and Camp Sturgeon Bay. Correspondence and telephone interview with author, Kingsford, MI., 8 March, 2000.

9. "Prisoners of War Helped Harvest Wartime Crops," *Door County Advocate* (Sturgeon Bay), 2 August 1965, 6.

10. Gladys Anschutz Schultz. Owner of box handmade by PW. Correspondence and telephone interview with author, Sturgeon Bay, June 2000.

11. Connie Nebel Brick. Worked with PW's in uncle's Door County orchard. Telephone interview by author, Sturgeon Bay, 16 August, 2000.

12. Robert Bjorke. Witnessed PW's in orchards. Telephone interview by author, Sturgeon Bay, 16 August, 2000.

13. Lucille Eckert Stadler. Witnessed the PW's in Camp Witte and worked with them in area orchards. Telephone interview by author, Cottage Grove, 21 March, 2001.

14. "Cherry Harvest 45 Years Ago Proves Fruitful Experience," *The Door County Advocate* (Sturgeon Bay), 22 June 1990, 1 A.

Camp Sturtevant

1. "250 Prisoners will Work on Farms in State," The *Sheboygan Press,* 25 May 1944, 1.

2. "Nazi Prisoners of War Arrive," *Racine Journal-Times*, 14 June 1944, 1.

3. Ibid.

4. Ibid.

5. Ibid.

6. "Dance for War Prisoners?" *Racine Journal Times,* 18 July 1944, 1.

7. "Sturtevant Prisoner Camp Will Be Reopened May 26," *Racine Journal Times,* 23 May 1945, 1.

8. "Once Proud Nazi Soldiers Weed County Food Crops," *Racine Journal Times,* 20 June 1945, 1.

9. "Sturtevant Prisoner Camp Will Be Reopened May 26," *Janesville Daily Gazette*, 23 May 1945, 1.

10. "Citizens too Friendly With Prisoners, Claim," *Fond du Lac Commonwealth Reporter,* 14 September 1945, 1.

11. "General Visits Prisoner Camp," *Racine Journal Times*, 25 August 1945, 1.

12. Racine County Historical Museum. *Grassroots History of Racine County.* Racine, Wis., 1978, 115.

13. "POWs at Antigo Perform $10,730 Worth Of Work," *Antigo Daily Journal,* 15 September 1945, 1.

14. Batikis, John. Witnessed Camp Sturtevant. Racine, August, 1997.

15. "Nazi Prisoners of War Arrive," *Racine Journal Times,* 14 June 1944, 1.

16. Fred Zimbars. Recalled PW's on family farm. Telephone interview by author, Racine, 2 May, 2000.

17. Emery and Virginia Creuziger. Hired prisoners of family farm, donated photo of Virginia with PW's. Correspondence and telephone interview with author, Sturtevant, 5 July, 2000.

18. Jeremiah Dustin. Hired PW's as farm labor. Telephone interview by author, Crivitz, 14 August, 2000.

19. Pauline Mertz Hoye. Worked with PW's in Kenosha County. Telephone interview by author, Mentor, OH, August, 2000.

20. Charles Moelter. Encountered PW's in Sturtevant area. Telephone interview by author, Lake Geneva, 10 September, 2000.

21. Lee Wood. Worked with PW's picking potatoes and onions outside Racine. Telephone interview by author, Racine, 6 November, 2000.

22. Eric Riesselmann. Shared grandparents' stories of PW's on their farm outside Kenosha. Correspondence and telephone interview with author, Kenosha, October-November 2000.

Camp Waterloo

1. "Prisoner War Camp Has Opened Here to Harvest Peas," *Waterloo Courier,* 29 June 1945, 1.

2. "Sensational Pea Crop Swamping Canneries," *Milwaukee Journal,* 24 July, 1945, 1.

3. "German Prisoners Produce Many Man Hours Labor," *Waterloo Courier,* 21 September 1945, 1.

4. Oral history dictated by Earl Weichmann, Feb. 23, 1996, Sun Prairie Historical Society.

5. Ibid.

6. Ibid.

Camp Waupun

1. "350 Prisoners Due in Waupun," *Waupun Leader-News,* 21 June 1945, 1.

2. "Canning Companies Run Long Hours to Process Extra Large Pea Pack," *Waupun Leader-News,* 26 July 1945, 1.

3. "Corn Pact to be Finished Today," *Waupun Leader-News,* 4 October 1945, 1.

4. "POW's at Antigo Perform $10,730 Worth of Work," *Antigo Daily Journal,* 15 September 1945, 1.

5. " POW Involved in Adultery Charge," *Waupun Leader-News,* 20 September 1945, 1.

6. "Woman Tells Offense with War Prisoner," *Fond du Lac Commonwealth Reporter,* 21 September 1945, 2.

7. "Capt. Knowles to Remain at Prisoner of War Camp," *Waupun Leader-News,* 27 September 1945, 1.

8. Theresa Dreikosen. She hired PW's for farm work. Correspondence and telephone interview with author, Waupun, 10 April, & 23 June, 2000.

9. Ucker, interview.

10. Eugene Buchholz. President of Waupun Historical Society, worked with PW's. Telephone interview by author, Waupun, 21 February, 2001.

11. Chester Possin. Worked with PW's on family farm near Waupun. Telephone interview by author, Big Green Lake, 8 November, 2000.

Camp Wisconsin Rapids

1. *Nekoosa Edwards Paper Company correspondence, April 30,*

1945. Alexander House Center for Art & History, Port Edwards, Wis. Selected correspondence of Nekoosa - Edwards Paper Company on Prisoner of War Contract. 1945.

2. "Prisoners of War to Work as Field Hands in This Area," *Wisconsin Rapids Daily Tribune,* 7 May 1945, 1.

3. "Tour Shows Prisoners Earn Their Salt, Are Not Coddled," *Wisconsin Rapids Daily Tribune,* 16 May 1945, 3.

4. "Donations Furnish Day Room for PW Camp Army Personnel," *Wisconsin Rapids Daily Tribune,* 2 June 1945, 1.

5. "Tour Shows Prisoners Earn Their Salt, Are Not Coddled," *Wisconsin Rapids Daily Tribune,* 16 May 1945, 1.

6. "Prisoner of War Injures Leg at Work," *Wisconsin Rapids Daily Tribune,* 29 May 1945, 1.

7. "Prisoner of War is Injured at Marsh," *Wisconsin Rapids Daily Tribune,* 21 June 1945, 1.

8. "POWs at Antigo Perform $10,730 Worth of Work," *Antigo Daily Journal,* 15 September 1945, 1.

9. David Rucinski. Worked with PW's at Griffith State Nursery and spent time in and around Camp Wisconsin Rapids, Wisconsin Rapids, 6 March 2000.

10. Joan Staub Haasl. Witnessed PW's being transported and reported story of her friends caring for hospitalized PW. Interview by author, Wisconsin Rapids, 10 October, 1999.

11. Engel, Dave. *The Fat Memoirs* (Wisconsin Rapids, WI: South Wood Historical Corporation, 1988), 166.

12. Walter S. Schalla. Worked with PW's at Potter's Cranberry Marsh. Telephone interview by author, Bridger, MT., 4 August, 2000.

13. Charlotte Sweeney Martinson. Witnessed PW's her father hired to work on cranberry marsh he managed. Telephone interview by author, Port Edwards, 11 October, 2000.

14. Engle, *Fat Memoirs,* 166.

15. Marlys Steckler. POW collection of articles and interviews. Wisconsin Rapids, 2001.

16. Ellsworth Oilschlager. Family co-sponsored former PW Willie Strahler's return to America. Telephone interview by author, Pittsville, 14 January, 1998.

Afterword

1. "War Prisoners Have Gone," *Bayfield County Press,* 1 November 1945, 1.

9 781878 569837